Architectural Documentation

Built Environment, Modernization, and Turkish Nationalism

Serra Akboy-İlk

Series in Built Environment

www.vernonpress.com

In the Americas:
Vernon Press
1000 N West Street, Suite 1200
Wilmington, Delaware, 19801
United States

In the rest of the world:
Vernon Press
C/Sancti Espiritu 17,
Malaga, 29006
Spain

Series in Built Environment

Library of Congress Control Number: 2022939794

ISBN: 978-1-64889-565-4

Also available: 978-1-64889-177-9 [Hardback]; 978-1-64889-520-3 [PDF, E-Book]

Cover design by Vernon Press. Cover image: Field note for the Pertev Mehmed Pasa Camii, İzmit, Turkey, delineated by Ali Saim Ülgen, 1937. SALT Research, Ali Saim Ülgen Archive, TASUDOCM0297024.

Table of contents

List of figures *v*

Notes on names, pronunciation, and sources *xvii*

List of acronyms *xix*

Preface *xxi*
Prof. Dr. Lucienne Thys-Şenocak
Department of Archaeology and the History of Art
Koç University, Istanbul

Acknowledgements *xxv*

Chapter 1 **Introduction: Documentation culture in republican Turkey** 1

Constructing measured drawings

Documenting as an archival record

Structuring a book on architectural documentation

Chapter 2 **Modern construct of architectural documentation** 21

Rising nationalism to grant a collective past

Delineating Ottoman monuments

Surveying as the basis of physical interventions

Appraising the documentation work of Ottoman scholars

Recording an architectural legacy in the republican state

Institutionalizing documentation as a tenet of historic preservation

Compiling a scientific review of built works

Chapter 3 **National cultivation of the built environment** 77

Negotiating a binding architectural identity in the Late Ottoman Empire

Lending a voice for monuments in the Turkish History Thesis

Selecting monuments to be surveyed

Building Anatolian humanism in the aftermath of the Turkish History Thesis

Celebrating the quincentenary of the Ottoman conquest of Constantinople

Becoming the "other" monuments

Surveying Byzantine Istanbul

Turkifying Byzantine architecture

Reading the built works of the *Beyliks*

Compartmentalizing built heritage of the Late Ottoman Era

Chapter 4 **Formal delineation of Turkish architecture** 143

Turning to European institutions for methodical documentation

Projecting the formal order of descriptive drawings

Constructing images through drawing styles

Streamlining the processes of documentation and restoration

Illustrating the priorities of Turkish nationalism

Chapter 5 **Conclusion** 191

Bibliography *205*

Index *225*

List of figures

Figure 1.1. Creating fieldnotes in the documentation campaign of Erzurum Çifte Minareli Madrasa, undated. SALT Research, Harika and Kemali Söylemezoğlu Archive, TSOH485006. 4
Figure 1.2. Photograph of Istanbul's Zeyrek Mosque (Church of Christ Pantokrator), street view, undated. SALT Research, AHISTZEYR001. 6
Figure 1.3. Measured drawing of Zeyrek Mosque, delineated by Ali Saim Ülgen, undated. SALT Research, Ali Saim Ülgen Archive, TASUDOC0568010. 7
Figure 1.4. Field note of Sultan Murad II's mansion in Bursa (today, Ottoman House Museum), delineated by Ali Saim Ülgen, April 21 1946. SALT Research, Ali Saim Ülgen Archive, TASUDOC0568. 8
Figure 1.5. Gathering measurements from the courtyard wall of the Erzurum Çifte Minareli Madrasa, undated. SALT Research, Harika and Kemali Söylemezoğlu Archive, TSOH485015. 8
Figure 1.6. Drawing of a balustrade, drawn by Mehmet Nihat Nigizberk, 1909-1919. Koç University, Suna Kıraç Library Special Collections and Archives, Mehmet Nihat Nigizberk Collection of Architectural Drawings and Photographs, MNN_NB_01, 282. 9
Figure 1.7. Proposed repairs to Jerusalem's Mosque of Omar, 1909-1919. Koç University, Suna Kıraç Library Special Collections and Archives, Mehmet Nihat Nigizberk Collection of Architectural Drawings and Photographs, MNN_NB_01313. 11
Figure 1.8. An interpretive illustration of Erzurum depicting the city 200 years ago, drawn by Ali Saim Ülgen and Dündar Beyce, 1944. SALT Research, Ali Saim Ülgen Archive, TASUH5964. 12
Figure 1.9. A measured drawing sheet of Bakırköy's Siyavuş Pasha Pavilion, delineated by Ali Saim Ülgen, 1934. SALT Research, Ali Saim Ülgen Archive, TASUPA0914001. 13
Figure 1.10. Cover page of the *Fatih Devri Mimarisi,* by Ekrem Hakkı Ayverdi, İstanbul: İstanbul Fetih Cemiyeti Neşriyatı, 1953. 14
Figure 1.11. Site plan of the Fatih Mosque Complex in Istanbul, drawn by Ali Saim Ülgen. Halim Baki Kunter and Ali Saim Ülgen,

Fatih Camii, Ankara: Vakıflar Umum Müdürlüğü Neşriyatı, 1938. 15
Figure 2.1. Elevation drawing of the Green Mosque, Bursa. *Usūl-i Mi'mārī-i Osmānī,* İstanbul, 1873. SALT Research, AMN1100200203. 27
Figure 2.2. An architectural element with Ottoman order rendered on a regular grid. *Usūl-i Mi'mārī-i Osmānī,* İstanbul, 1873. SALT Research, AMN1100200116. 28
Figure 2.3. A drafting guide for the Ottoman order. *Usūl-i Mi'mārī-i Osmānī,* İstanbul, 1873. SALT Research, AMN1100200115. 29
Figure 2.4. A school project with two classrooms, drawn by Architect Şemseddin, April 12 1924. SALT Research, TMSSD179. 32
Figure 2.5. Analysis of a façade, delineated by Mehmet Nihat Nigizberk. Koç University, Suna Kıraç Library Special Collections and Archives, Mehmet Nihat Nigizberk Collection of Architectural Drawings and Photographs, MNN_NB_01, 51. 33
Figure 2.6. A school project at *Sanayi-i Nefise Mekteb-i Âlisi,* drawn by Architect Şemseddin. SALT Research, TMSSD108. 34
Figure 2.7. Drawings of Adapazarı's Orhaniye Mosque, 1865 (23-11-1281). Türkiye Cumhuriyeti Cumhurbaşkanlığı Devlet Arşivleri, Başkanlık Osmanlı Arşivi, HAT, 782. 36
Figure 2.8. The floor plan of the proposed inn in the premises of the hospital, 1824 (29-12-1239). Türkiye Cumhuriyeti Cumhurbaşkanlığı Devlet Arşivleri, Başkanlık Osmanlı Arşivi, HAT, 545-26941. 37
Figure 2.9. Measured drawing of the existing condition of the hospital at the Fatih Mosque Complex, 1824 (29-12-1239). Türkiye Cumhuriyeti Cumhurbaşkanlığı Devlet Arşivleri, Başkanlık Osmanlı Arşivi, HAT, 545-26941. 37
Figure 2.10. Measured drawing of Masjid Al-Aqsa, 1924. Koç University, Suna Kıraç Library Special Collections and Archives, Mehmet Nihat Nigizberk Collection of Architectural Drawings and Photographs, MNN_ALB14_phc_08. 38
Figure 2.11. Elevation drawing of Azapkapı Saliha Sultan Fountain, *Usūl-i Mi'mārī-i Osmānī,* Istanbul, 1873. SALT Research, Ali Saim Ülgen Archive, TASUDOC0310013. 40
Figure 2.12. Section drawing of Kadırga Sokollu Mehmet Paşa Mosque, delineated by Sedat Çetintaş. SALT Research, Ali Saim Ülgen Archive, TASUH0751. 41

Figure 2.13. Photograph of the Nizamiye Police Station located in Selâmsız in Üsküdar, 1880-1893, street view. Library of Congress, Abdul-Hamid II Collection, LOT 11909, no. 18. 43
Figure 2.14. Mustafa Kemal Atatürk and Ismet İnönü during the celebrations at the Ankara train station, 1931. Koç University, Ankara Studies Research Center (VEKAM), Ankara Photograph, Postcard and Engraving Collection, 2961_01. 45
Figure 2.15. Albert Louis Gabriel during his 1958-visit to Turkey, from the left, Ali Saim Ülgen, Ahmet Süheyl Ünver, and Gabriel. SALT Research, Ali Saim Ülgen Archive, TASUDOC0650031. 49
Figure 2.16. Measured drawing of Konya's Sırmalı Masjid, delineated by Mehmet Yusuf Akyurt. SALT Research, Ali Saim Ülgen Archive, TASUH2157. 50
Figure 2.17. Detail drawing from Mustafa Kemal Paşa-Lala Şahin Paşa Tomb, drawn by Ekrem Hakkı Ayverdi, undated. Ekrem Hakkı Ayverdi Institute Archive, Kubbealtı Waqf Collection, Istanbul. 51
Figure 2.18. Section drawing of Üsküdar's Rum Mehmed Pasha Mosque, delineated by Ekrem Hakkı Ayverdi, *Fatih Devri Mimarisi.* İstanbul: İstanbul Fetih Cemiyeti Neşriyatı, 1953. 52
Figure 2.19. A preliminary study of the Ivranya (Vrana) inn near the Adriatic shore, drawn by Ekrem Hakkı Ayverdi. Ekrem Hakkı Ayverdi, "Yugoslavya'da Türk Âbideleri ve Vakıfları," *Vakıflar Dergisi 3,* 1956. 54
Figure 2.20. Restitution analysis of the façade of Siyavuş Pasha Pavilion, delineated by Ali Saim Ülgen, then a student-architect at the Academy, ca. 1935. SALT Research, Ali Saim Ülgen Archive, TASUDOCM0314011. 55
Figure 2.21. The authentic sheet of drawing for the four-*eyvan* plan and section of Sivas' Gök Medrese that Suut Kemal Yetkin had published in *Türk Mimarisi,* delineated by Ali Saim Ülgen, undated. SALT Research, Ali Saim Ülgen Archive, TASUDOC1162011. 57
Figure 2.22. Photograph of the measured drawing sheet of the Tomb of Şehzade Mehmet, delineated by Sedat Çetintaş, May 5 1933. SALT Research, Ali Saim Ülgen Archive, TASUH0890. 62
Figure 2.23. Measured survey for Sivas' Güdük Minare, delineated by Ali Saim Ülgen, undated. SALT Research, Ali Saim Ülgen Archive, TASUDOC1073026. 69

Figure 2.24. Floor plan of the Orhan Gazi Mosque, delineated by Ekrem Hakkı Ayverdi, 1962. Ekrem Hakkı Ayverdi, "Bursa Orhan Gazi Camii ve Osmanlı Mimarisinin Menşei Meselesi," *Vakıflar Dergisi* VI, 1965. 76

Figure 3.1. Pertevniyal Valide Sultan Mosque, Aksaray, Istanbul, ca. 1890, street view. Library of Congress, LOT 13428, no. 016 [item] [P&P]. 80

Figure 3.2. Drawing for the Ottoman revivalist styled Bezmialem Valide Sultan Hospital, drawn by Mehmet Nihat Nigizberk, undated. Koç University, Suna Kıraç Library Special Collections and Archives, Mehmet Nihat Nigizberk Collection of Architectural Drawings and Photographs, MNN_NB_01, 536. 83

Figure 3.3. "Formerly it was the servants who swept the ministries, but now it is the ministers who clean them up." *Kalem*, September 3, 1908, delineated by Esad Arseven, Celâl and Cimcoz, Selah, University of Texas Libraries, Kalem Cartoon Satire Collection. 84

Figure 3.4. Aerial photograph of Istanbul's Süleymaniye Mosque Complex, undated. SALT Research, AHISTEMIN035. 87

Figure 3.5. İstanbul's Fourth Vakıf Han, designed by Kemalettin Bey, street view, undated. SALT Research, Harika and Kemali Söylemezoğlu Archive, TSOH126002. 88

Figure 3.6. Measured drawing sheet for Konya's Sadrettin Konevi Mosque and Tomb, delineated by Mehmet Yusuf Akyurt, 1933. SALT Research, Ali Saim Ülgen Archive, TASUDOC1146. 95

Figure 3.7. Field note for the survey of İznik's Ayasofya Mosque, delineated by Ali Saim Ülgen, September 3, 1937. SALT Research, Ali Saim Ülgen Archive, TASUDOC171001. 97

Figure 3.8. Measured drawing of İznik's Ayasofya Mosque, delineated by Ali Saim Ülgen. Ali Saim Ülgen "İznik'te Türk Eserleri," *Vakıflar Dergisi* 1, Ankara, 1938. 98

Figure 3.9. Site plan of the monuments within the citadel of Iznik, delineated by Ali Saim Ülgen. Ali Saim Ülgen, "İznik'te Türk Eserleri," *Vakıflar Dergisi* 1, Ankara, 1938. 99

Figure 3.10. Photograph of the sixteenth-century mihrab of the dilapidated İznik's Ayasofya Mosque, captured by Ali Saim Ülgen. SALT Research, Ali Saim Ülgen Archive, TASUH7391002. 100

Figure 3.11. Image of the sixteenth-century minaret of the İznik's Ayasofya Mosque, taken by Ali Saim Ülgen. SALT Research, Ali Saim Ülgen Archive, TASUH7391. 101

Figure 3.12. Elevation and plan of the Nilüfer Hatun Bridge, delineated by Ekrem Hakkı Ayverdi, 1963. Ekrem Hakkı Ayverdi Institute Archive, Kubbealtı Waqf Collection, Istanbul. 105

Figure 3.13. Section drawing of Bursa's Hamza Bey Mosque, delineated by Ekrem Hakkı Ayverdi, 1968. Ekrem Hakkı Ayverdi Institute Archive, Kubbealtı Waqf Collection, Istanbul. 106

Figure 3.14. Tiled Kiosk in the Late Ottoman Empire, when the building was used as the imperial museum, view from the courtyard. Koç University, Suna Kıraç Library Special Collections and Archives, Mehmet Nihat Nigizberk Collection of Architectural Drawings and Photographs, MNN_ALB18_phg_060. 113

Figure 3.15. Façade of the Tiled Kiosk, delineated by Ekrem Hakkı Ayverdi, 1948. Ekrem Hakkı Ayverdi Institute Archive, Kubbealtı Waqf Collection, Istanbul. 115

Figure 3.16. Drawing of the Tiled Kiosk, exhibiting the floor-plan when used as an imperial museum, delineated by Kemal Altan. Ekrem Hakkı Ayverdi, *Fatih Devri Mimarisi*, İstanbul: Istanbul Fetih Cemiyeti Neşriyatı, 1953. 116

Figure 3.17. Measured drawing of the Tiled Kiosk, 1948, delineated by Reşid Bey. Ekrem Hakkı Ayverdi, *Fatih Devri Mimarisi*, İstanbul: İstanbul Fetih Cemiyeti Neşriyatı, 1953. 117

Figure 3.18. Field drawing of the Kariye Mosque during the repairs of 1946, delineated by Cahide Tamer. Koç University, Suna Kıraç Library Special Collections and Archives, Cahide Tamer Historic Buildings Restoration Projects Collection, S102_D02_jpg, CTA_S102_D02_dra_03. 119

Figure 3.19. Map showing the armies of Byzantine and Seljuk in Battle of Manzikert. SALT Research, Ali Saim Ülgen Archive, TASUDOC0802003. 121

Figure 3.20. Photograph of the Fethiye Mosque (Church Pammakaristos Monastery) during the repairs of 1956, delineated by Cahide Tamer. Koç University, Suna Kıraç Library Special Collections and Archives, Cahide Tamer Historic Buildings Restoration Projects Collection, S098_D01, CTA_S098_D01_phg_01. 123

Figure 3.21. Field note showing the map of a Byzantine cistern under the Yayla Kambur Mustafa Pasha Mosque, Istanbul, delineated by Ali Saim Ülgen, undated. SALT Research Ali Saim Ülgen Archive, TASUDOC0437006. 126
Figure 3.22. Field note for the 1946-repairs of the Kariye Mosque (Church of the Chora Monastery), delineated by Cahide Tamer. Koç University, Suna Kıraç Library Special Collections and Archives, Cahide Tamer Historic Buildings Restoration Projects Collection, S102_D02_jpg, CTA_S102_D02_dra_12_02. 128
Figure 3.23. Measured drawing of Karaman's Nefise Hatun (Hatuniye) Madrasa, delineated by Yusuf Akyurt, 1932. SALT Research, Ali Saim Ülgen Archive, TASUDOC0246032. 135
Figure 3.24. Section drawing of the Divriği Great Mosque and Hospital, delineated by Ali Saim Ülgen. Ali Saim Ülgen, "Divriği Ulu Camii ve Darüşşifası," *Vakıflar Dergisi* V, (1962). 136
Figure 3.25. Şehzade Mosque, Istanbul, street view, undated. Koç University, Suna Kıraç Library Special Collections and Archives, Mehmet Nihat Nigizberk Collection of Architectural Drawings and Photographs, MNN_ALB18_phg_026. 140
Figure 3.26. Zeynep Sultan Mosque, Istanbul, street view, undated. SALT Research, Ali Saim Ülgen Archive, TASUH8099001. 141
Figure 3.27. Section drawing of the Yeni Mosque, 1941, delineated by Ali Saim Ülgen. Ali Saim Ülgen, *Yenicami*. Ankara: Vakıflar Umum Müdürlüğü Neşriyatı, 1942. 142
Figure 4.1. Example of a measured drawing drawn to 1:50 to guide the construction work for the Hindiler Dervish Lodge, July 7 1999, delineated by Willem van Winsen and Çağada Serdar. SALT Research, Cengiz Bektaş Archive, TCBPHTD001004. 144
Figure 4.2. A working drawing of 1:50 scale for the application of the restoration project for the Hindiler Dervish Lodge, July 27, 1999, delineated by Willem van Winsen and Çağada Serdar. SALT Research, Cengiz Bektaş Archive, TCBPHTD003003. 145
Figure 4.3. Perspective drawing of the Seljuk Sungurbey Mosque in Niğde, rendering its condition in the past, delineated by Albert Gabriel. Albert Gabriel, *Monuments Turcs D'Anatolie: Kayseri-Nigde*. Paris: Paris Libraire des écoles françaises d'Athènes et de Rome, 1931. Reprinted in idem, Istanbul: Arkeoloji ve Sanat Yayınları, 2014. 146

Figure 4.4. Photograph of the measured drawing folio of Bursa's Alaeddin Mosque, delineated by Sedat Çetintaş, January 1 1934. SALT Research, Ali Saim Ülgen Archive, TASUH0756002. 148
Figure 4.5. 1: 20 scaled plan drawing of the dome of the Darülhadis, June 29, 1961, delineated by Vakıflar Rölöve Bürosu (Surveying Office of General Directorate of Endowments). SALT Research, Ali Saim Ülgen Archive, TASUPAMS190. 151
Figure 4.6. 1: 20 scaled elevation and section drawing of the dome of the Darülhadis, June 29, 1961, delineated by Vakıflar Rölöve Bürosu (Surveying Office of General Directorate of Endowments). SALT Research, Ali Saim Ülgen Archive, TASUPAMS191. 151
Figure 4.7. The three-dimensional model of Bezmialem Valide Sultan Hospital, drawn by Mehmet Nihat Nigizberk, undated. Koç University, Suna Kıraç Library Special Collections and Archives, Mehmet Nihat Nigizberk Collection of Architectural Drawings and Photographs MNN_NB _01, 539. 164
Figure 4.8. The descriptive projection of two-dimensional plan, section, and elevation of a house,ca. early twentieth century, Ottoman Empire, delineated by Architect Şemsettin. SALT Research, TMSSD049. 165
Figure 4.9. Detail drawing of Bursa's Green Mosque. *Usūl-i Mi'mārî-i Osmānî,* Istanbul, 1873. SALT Research, AMN1100200211. 165
Figure 4.10. Façade of a library, watercolor on paper, school project, drawn by Şemsettin then a student at the Academy, ca. 1912, SALT Research, TMSSD121. 167
Figure 4.11. Detail drawing of a capital and its column, school project, drawn by Şemsettin then a student at the Academy, ca. 1912, SALT Research, TMSSD111. 168
Figure 4.12. A mosque façade designed in the Greek order delineated by Sedad Hakkı Eldem. SALT Research, Sedad Hakkı Eldem Archive, AEXSHE0010830. 169
Figure 4.13. Façade of a proposed mosque, school project, drawn by Ekrem Hakkı Ayverdi then a student at the *Mühendis Mekteb-i Âlîsi,* March 1920. Ekrem Hakkı Ayverdi Institute Archive, Kubbealtı Waqf Collection, Istanbul. 170
Figure 4.14. Section and plan drawing of the proposed mosque, school project, drawn by Ekrem Hakkı Ayverdi then a

student at the *Mühendis Mekteb-i Âlîsi*, March 1920. Ekrem Hakkı Ayverdi Institute Archive, Kubbealtı Waqf Collection, Istanbul. 171

Figure 4.15. Concept drawing of an expandable village house, school project, drawn by Ali Saim Ülgen then a student at the Academy. SALT Research, Ali Saim Ülgen Archive, TASUPA0043. 172

Figure 4.16. Elementary school of Süleymaniye Mosque Complex, delineated by Ali Saim Ülgen, 1940. SALT Research, Ali Saim Ülgen Archive, TASUPAMS213. 173

Figure 4.17. Drawing of a modernist *yalı* (waterfront mansion), drawn by Sedad Hakkı Eldem, 1927-1928. SALT Research, Sedad Hakkı Eldem Archive, AEXSHE0010292. 175

Figure 4.18. Section drawing of the Orhan Gazi Mosque, delineated by Ekrem Hakkı Ayverdi, 1962. Ekrem Hakkı Ayverdi, "Bursa Orhan Gazi Camii ve Osmanlı Mimarisinin Menşei Meselesi," *Vakıflar Dergisi* VI, 1965. 175

Figure 4.19. The measured drawing of the existing condition of the Seljuk Sungurbey Mosque in Niğde, delineated by Albert Gabriel. Albert Gabriel, *Monuments Turcs D'Anatolie: Kayseri-Nigde.* Paris: Paris Libraire des écoles françaises d'Athènes et de Rome, 1931. Reprinted in idem, İstanbul: Arkeoloji ve Sanat Yayınları, 2014. 178

Figure 4.20. The graphically restored depiction of the Seljuk Sungurbey Mosque in Niğde, delineated by Albert Gabriel. Albert Gabriel, *Monuments Turcs D'Anatolie: Kayseri-Nigde.* Paris: Paris Libraire des écoles françaises d'Athènes et de Rome, 1931. Reprinted in idem, İstanbul: Arkeoloji ve Sanat Yayınları, 2014. 179

Figure 4.21. Restitution drawing for Ilgın Lala Mustafa Paşa Mosque, delineated by Ali Saim Ülgen, 1952. SALT Research, Ali Saim Ülgen Archive, TASUPA0346. 180

Figure 4.22. Floor plan of the mosque and tomb of Cenabî Ahmed Pasha, drawn by Ali Saim Ülgen. Ali Saim Ülgen, *Ankara'da Cenabî Ahmed Paşa Camii ve Türbesi.* Ankara: Vakıflar Umum Müdürlüğü Neşriyatı, 1942. SALT Research, Ali Saim Ülgen Archive, TASUDOCA0101010. 182

Figure 4.23. Section of the mosque and tomb of Cenabî Ahmed Pasha, drawn by Ali Saim Ülgen. Ali Saim Ülgen, *Ankara'da Cenabî Ahmed Paşa Camii ve Türbesi.* Ankara: Vakıflar

Umum Müdürlüğü Neşriyatı, 1942. SALT Research, Ali Saim Ülgen Archive, TASUDOCA0101011. 183
Figure 4.24. Measured plan drawing of the Mosque of the Aghas, Topkapı Palace Museum, drawn by Ekrem Hakkı Ayverdi. Ekrem Hakkı Ayverdi, *Fatih Devri Mimarisi,* İstanbul: İstanbul Fetih Cemiyeti Neşriyatı, 1953. 185
Figure 4.25. Measured section drawing of the Mosque of the Aghas, Topkapı Palace Museum, drawn by Ekrem Hakkı Ayverdi. Ekrem Hakkı Ayverdi, *Fatih Devri Mimarisi,* İstanbul: İstanbul Fetih Cemiyeti Neşriyatı, 1953. 186
Figure 4.26. Restitution drawing for the Mosque of the Aghas, Topkapı Palace Museum, drawn by Ekrem Hakkı Ayverdi. Ekrem Hakkı Ayverdi, *Fatih Devri Mimarisi,* İstanbul: Istanbul Fetih Cemiyeti Neşriyatı, 1953. 187

To Mom and all the daughters of the Republic,

for their unconditional dedication to the ideals of Atatürk and for illuminating generations of young minds with art, culture, education, and science.

Notes on names, pronunciation, and sources

In this book, I have followed modern Turkish orthography for words of Turkish, Arabic, or Persian origin. Some of the letters of the 29 letter Turkish alphabet are different from English letters and these, with a guide to their pronunciation, are as follows,

c pronounced as a **j** in English

ç pronounced as **ch** in English

ğ not pronounced but silent and lengthens the preceding vowel

ı pronounced as the English **i** in cousin

ö pronounced as the English **u** in fur

ş pronounced as **sh** in English

ü pronounced as the English **u** in cute

I have used modern Turkish orthography for all words that appear in Turkish, with the exception of a few words that are commonly used in English, such as pasha or madrasa. "Istanbul" is spelled with an undotted capital I in the main text, but a dotted capital I is used in the footnotes and bibliography as this refers to a place of publication. For proper names, place names, and some terms, I have used a more Ottomanized version: *Usūl-i Mi'mārî-i Osmānî,* Âli, Celâl, or Cenabî.

List of acronyms

CUP	*İttihad ve Terakki Cemiyeti* (Committee of Union and Progress)
DP	*Demokrat Parti* (Democrat Party)
GEEAYK	*Gayrimenkul Eski Eserler ve Anıtlar Yüksek Kurulu* (Supreme Council of Immovable Antiquities and Monuments)
HABS	Historical American Buildings Survey
ICOMOS	The International Council on Monuments and Sites
RIBA	Royal Institute of British Architects
TDK	*Türk Dil Kurumu* (Turkish Language Society)
TTK	*Türk Tarih Kurumu* (Turkish Historical Society
VEKAM	*Koç Üniversitesi Vehbi Koç Ankara Araştırmaları Uygulama ve Araştırma Merkezi* (Koç University, Vehbi Koç Ankara Studies Research Center)
WWI	World War I
WWII	World War II

Preface

Prof. Dr. Lucienne Thys-Şenocak

Department of Archaeology and the History of Art

Koç University, Istanbul

Architectural Documentation: Built Environment, Modernization, and Turkish Nationalism is a timely and engaging study which focuses on the early years of the Turkish Republic, from 1923 to the1960s, the role that architects, both foreign and Turkish, played in shaping the discourse about the built heritage of the Turkic and Ottoman past; and their efforts to document and preserve this heritage. Creating architecture is a political act. What to document and preserve, and what to destroy, are also politically charged decisions. This is certainly the case in present-day Turkey, and *Architectural Documentation* convincingly argues that movements such as the National Architecture Renaissance of the late Ottoman era, and the Modern architecture projects in Turkey, or the "*Yeni Mimari*" (New Architecture) that emerged in Atatürk's newly established nation were equally contentious.

This book explores the entanglements of modernism, orientalism, state power, and architectural practice at this vibrant time of nation-building in Turkey, and illuminates the people and documentation processes involved in architectural preservation. Sibel Bozdoğan, who has written extensively about the architecture in the late Ottoman Empire and Republican era Turkey, has noted the "profound ambiguity of the modernist projects of the 1930s".[1] There are many reasons for this ambiguity, including the challenges that Turkish architects, in particular, faced as they negotiated their relationships with Europe, and the Ottoman, Turkic, and Islamic pasts. Equipped with an education rooted in the European traditions of the Ecole des Beaux-Arts, and ideologies of the Modern Movement, this first generation of Republican era architects, at times with their European mentors (e.g., Ernst A. Egli, Albert

---

[1] Sibel Bozdoğan, Modernism and Nation Building: Turkish Architectural Culture in the Early Republic (Seattle: University of Washington Press, 2001), 10-11.

Louis Gabriel, Cornelius Gurlitt), and other times without them, were passionate about documenting the architectural remains still standing in the lands they had inherited from Ottoman, and earlier ancestors in Anatolia and the Balkans. For many of these architects, producing measured drawings and surveys of this architectural legacy, and recording them for posterity went beyond a professional duty and became an act of faith and patriotic devotion to the nation-state.

In *Architectural Documentation,* with its extensive use of publications from early architectural journals such as *Arkitekt,* the Ottoman State Archives, and private archival collections belonging to the "hero-architects" of Turkey's modernist era (e.g., Cahide Aksel Tamer, Ekrem Hakkı Ayverdi, Sedat Çetintaş, Sedad Hakkı Eldem, Ali Saim Ülgen), we gain a richer sense of the diverse mindsets of many of these fascinating "nation-builders" of Turkey and the challenges they faced as they struggled with questions of identity, political and economic instability, and a burgeoning state bureaucracy. With its emphasis on the goals and processes of architectural documentation and historic preservation in the young Republic, this book sheds light on the history, and architectural historiography of Turkey, as well as the more pragmatic aspects of putting pen to paper to record its historical buildings.

Serra Akboy-İlk is among the last generation of architects in Turkey whose training centered on putting pen to paper to create measured drawings of buildings. By the time Serra started her graduate education, the possibilities of documenting architecture with 3D LASER scanning and photogrammetric technology had just begun in Turkey. Serra, never putting aside her pen, enthusiastically embraced these new digital technologies and the potential they have for efficiently and accurately documenting the built environment, and particularly the architecture that is designated as cultural heritage in Turkey. Among the very few Turkish students awarded a US ICOMOS (International Council on Monuments and Sites) internship grant, Serra was tasked in the summer of 2006 with assisting a team from the US National Park Service to conduct a 3D LASER scanning of the Statue of Liberty in New York City, and producing measured drawings of that iconic symbol of the United States. It would be the first of many surveys and architectural documentation projects she would undertake in the US, a country of which she is now a citizen, along with her native Turkey.

Serra's training in Turkey, and her passion for its architecture and architectural history, have instilled in her a deep respect for the "old masters" of Turkish architecture, those aforementioned "hero-architects" of the late Ottoman and modern eras. She has continued to ask how the methodologies and the aesthetics of traditional architectural surveys and their measured drawings, like those produced by the architects of the late Ottoman and early Turkish republic eras, could be integrated with the newly emerging digital technologies used in the architectural and preservation professions today. *Architectural Documentation: Built Environment, Modernization, and Turkish Nationalism* is part of a process to answer those questions. It is also testimony to the steadfast belief the author has in the power of architecture to change society for the better, and the essential role that documentation plays in helping us to remember the lives of buildings and their architects.

Acknowledgements

I always drew. Thanks to my mother's early recognition of my passion for drawing, my childhood years are full of memories of making drawings. Watercolors to paint orange skies, oil pastels to draw dancing children, and messy finger paints to make animal prints. I was never out of resources either: cheerful teepees made from construction paper right in our living room, pink dinosaurs converted from rocks to be dutifully used as doorstoppers, and paper tubes painted as pencil holders that my parents had to take to the office.

When I started architecture school in Istanbul, Mimar Sinan Fine Arts University, formerly the State Academy of Fine Arts, my parents were thrilled. I was able to pursue my only passion and make it a lifelong career. Then, being an architect was associated with the craft of making good drawings. I remember the joyful day when my father handed over the rapidograph pen set he used while in engineering school. Hovering over my drafting board and looking at the forms flourishing on the tracing paper, he would proudly declare, "My daughter will be an architect." Little did we know then, I belonged to the last generation of architects who would still tape a scroll of drafting paper, stretch it flat, and draw.

I always read. Thanks to the perks of living in a household of bookworms, most of the world's classics were at my fingertips, along with native treasures of Azra Erhat, Feridun Fazıl Tülbentçi, Halikarnas Balıkçısı, Reşad Ekrem Koçu, and many more. If I could not find an engaging volume, I would always run to my great aunt Ümitçi to browse her bookshelves. During my years as a student-architect, Ümitçi developed the habit of conveniently adding a newly published volume on the history of art and architecture in her collection for her budding designer.

Throughout my graduate studies, the symbiotic relationship between drawing and reading proved to be highly beneficial as I have tremendously enjoyed making measured drawings of historic architecture and conducting research about its history. What sparked my interest to rethink architectural histories and to ask difficult questions, was due to my profound conversations with the chair of my master's committee, Lucienne Thys-Şenocak at Koç University. Lucienne has always given me the greatest enthusiasm and motivation to search for the overlooked yet integral elements of architectural histories. Some of the ideas in this book, such as the cross-cultural histories of artistic creativity and Turkish nationalism, were developed during those years at Koç University. I am indebted to Lucienne, for challenging me in different points along my path and always guiding me to find the light.

When I started my doctoral degree at Texas A&M University, I was under the wings of Robert B. Warden, the chair of my doctoral committee. Then the architecture schools, both in the U.S and Turkey, were to fully embrace the visualization and simulation methodologies in the curriculum. I find myself very lucky to work with Bob, since I had the professional opportunity to work at diverse heritage recording and documentation projects around the globe and to experiment with different technologies. My deepest gratitude goes to Bob for cultivating my interest in a critical thinking of digital mediation. Making helpful suggestions on my work, and above all, encouraging me to explore the production of measured drawings through the terrain of phenomenology, Bob installed in me an interest in writing a book on drawing many years ago.

I gratefully thank David G. Woodcock, whom I had the privilege to work with at Texas A&M University. David has been an inspirational mentor for generations of architects whom have been among the most prominent professionals to conserve architectural heritage. The larger field within which I have positioned my work– a field that spans the history on architectural documentation outside North America, Turkey, and U.K. - has been our shared theoretical terrain. David has been an instrumental figure for the implementation of Historical American Buildings Survey (HABS), one of the oldest federal programs in the U. S. It is through our discussions on HABS, the École des Beaux-Arts system, and the conceptions of architectural history, I was able to crystalize the overlapping areas between the establishment of HABS in the U.S. and the documentation campaigns in early republican Turkey.

My special thanks go to Elizabeth I. Louden-Powell, who have crisscrossed the path of my book at different stages with her open-minded and delightful insight. Our friendship is rooted at the documentation project of the Statue of Liberty Project in New York City, when she was supervising the Texas Tech University team as I was an intern of the International Council on Monuments and Sites (ICOMOS). Over the years, Elizabeth has given me many opportunities to professionally contribute to her graduate seminar classes in the Dallas-Fort Worth metroplex. It is through these excursions to historical properties in the area, we tapped on unchartered discussions of documenting and preserving buildings with difficult pasts. In her immense generosity and patience, Elizabeth listened to my flourishing ideas on Turkish nationalism and curatorial management of historic architecture.

Among my colleagues and friends, who have been supportive on writing a book on architectural documentation, I thank Burcu Selcen Coşkun for her generosity providing me any material I needed from Turkey. I also wish to thank Selcen for sharing her own work on different but overlapping topics of early republican architectural culture. My deepest gratitude goes to Şebnem Eryavuz for kindly allowing me to use Ekrem Hakkı Ayverdi's drawings located at Kubbealtı Waqf Collection and to Edhem Eldem for the drawings of Sedad Hakkı Eldem. I would like to express my gratitude to Suha Ülgen, for his sincere encouragement and his wholehearted support for my work on the legacy of his dad, Ali Saim Ülgen. Between many emails and correspondence, Suha Ülgen provided a personal dimension of his dad, often overlooked in the monographs dedicated to one of the most prominent historical figures in Turkey. I would especially like to thank İlhan Hattatoğlu for responding to my endless questions on the identification of archival documents that I came across my research.

I would like express my gratitude to Nezih Başgelen for his kind permission to reproduce images from Albert Louis Gabriel's *Monuments Turcs D'Anatolie* published by Arkeoloji ve Sanat Yayınları, to İstanbul Fetih Cemiyeti for drawings from Ayverdi's *Fatih Devri Mimarisi,* and to *Vakıflar Genel Müdürlüğü* for images from Ayverdi and Ülgen's miscellaneous earlier published articles in *Vakıflar Dergisi.*

Above all, I am grateful to specialists of archives and libraries. Without their help, the materialization of this book would have been impossible. For their immense patience and support, Mustafa Ergül at Suna Kıraç Koç University Library and Nalan Aslıhan Tarakçı at Koç University, Vehbi Koç Ankara Studies Research Center (VEKAM) responded to my endless questions about the contents of archival materials. Sinem Gülmez and Masum Yıldız at SALT Research facilitated my access to their collections and my communication with the copyright holders. In this context, I would like to express my special thanks to Müjde Dila Gümüş for helping me with the Ottoman-Turkish transcription of the drawings at the Mehmet Nihat Nigizberk Collection of Architectural Drawings and Photographs, Koç University. In addition, I thank everyone at the State Archives of Turkey in Ankara and Istanbul, Digital Collections at Library of Congress, Washington D.C., and Kalem Cartoon Satire Collection at the University of Texas Libraries at Austin for their help.

Also, I would like to thank Argiris Legatos, the editorial manager of Vernon Press for making it possible for me to conceptualize my flourishing ideas in the format of a book. Likewise, I am grateful to Ellisa Anslow, Javier Rodriguez, and Victoria Echegaray at Vernon Press for streamlining the processes of communication, marketing, and production. Without the commitment and support of Vernon Press, this book would not have materialized and have remained as a pending project. I am also indebted to the anonymous reviewers who meticulously read the manuscript; and provided positive and constructive commands on my work.

As much as this book is indebted to the people with whom my path has crossed in a professional capacity over the years, the writing of the manuscript has been a lonely enterprise. I thank my brother Levent Sacit Akboy for his overseas calls and consistently checking on me, "How is the book going on, sis?" Words are insufficient to express how my mother Rengin Akboy Karaca, has been an inspirational, motivating, and supportive figure in my life. A recognized academic and an author herself, my mother believed in the significance of writing a book of this scope to guide new generations on the vitality of republican reforms.

Unfortunately, we lost my father (Ahmet Zafer Akboy) and Ümitçi (Ümit Tarakçı), who were always proud of their beloved Serra and would have loved to see the completion of this book. I cherish their memories.

Finally, I thank Deniz and Dilhan İlk, the loves of my life, who first-hand experienced the dramatic ups and downs of writing a book of this scale and did not complain once for all the time I dedicated to conducting research and writing. I always turned to their supportive care and sense of humor in my moments of writer's block. They kept me sane and smiling; they still do.

Dallas 2022

Chapter 1

Introduction: Documentation culture in republican Turkey

> The foundation of the Republic of Turkey is culture... Culture amounts to reading, understanding, seeing, interpreting, observing, thinking, and nurturing intelligence.
>
> Mustafa Kemal Atatürk[1]

Where does Mustafa Kemal Atatürk's (1881-1938) definition of culture leave us? Can we state culture as the intellectual ideals of a nation? Rather, can we address culture as the collective road to the ways in which what was said and written helped to build as a nation? To be fair, revealing Atatürk's legendary authority in the formation of a modern nation is itself naive just probing a descriptive phrase, but his words depict the perception of culture in early republican Turkey. Atatürk, a modernizing revolutionary, conditioned the sovereignty of the Republic of Turkey through the commitment of the state to the economic, political, and scientific infrastructure. In this progressive plot, art, culture, and education were integral to the national movement to allow the citizens to know and appreciate their own country, history, and language. Atatürk ensured the state protection of the cultural and artistic values and dedicated resources for cultivating the culture of Turks.[2] The educational and cultural policy, institutionalized by state agencies, promoted a realization for the creative works of the nation and cultivated people's belonging to the national culture.

With the proclamation of the republic in 1923, the 600-year-old Ottoman Empire was abolished, including the dynastic cultural, economic, educational, and

---

[1] Afet İnan, *Atatürk Hakkında Hatıralar ve Belgeler*, ed. Arı İnan, (İstanbul: Türkiye İş Bankası Kültür Yayınları, 2014), 374.

[2] Kıymet Giray, *1920'li Yıllarda Sanat Politikası ve Yurtdışına Gönderilen Sanatçılar: 80. Yılında Cumhuriyet'in Türkiye Kültürü* (Ankara: TMMOB Mimarlar Odası ve Sanat Estetik ve Görsel Kültür Derneği ortak yayını, 2003), 12-13.

governmental institutions. The modern industrial civilization of the West became the model of progress for the newly found nation-state. Hence, the Western scientific knowledge, methods, and worldviews constituted the substance of the institutional reformation. The replacement of the Arabic script with the Latin alphabet, centralization of schools, adoption of the metric system of measurement, declaration of Sunday as the official holiday instead of "Holy Friday," establishment of a banking system and institutionalization of state-owned factories are just few examples to portray the extent of republican reforms to bring a rational and scientific era to the country.

Led by Atatürk, the reformers projected a structured, well-articulated, unbroken path of modernization through which the entire nation was going to proceed simultaneously and with uniform experience. The cultural, educational, and institutional reforms were instrumental in molding the Turkish nation into a monolithic force. Upon the rise of the nation-state, the Turkish society and mentality would overcome the cultural gap notoriously separating the nation from the West. With the civilizing mission of the republican reforms, the Turkish nation would be free from traditional obligations and the liberated Turks would move forward. At the end, a militantly secular and ethnically homogenous nation would join the civilized nations of the West.[3]

To engage with the republican present and to instill a proud sense of shared history, historical events and architectural heritage became central for the new order's durability in the long term. Atatürk and the founding leaders focused on the *Türk Tarih Tezi* (Turkish History Thesis) to advance the state agenda. The thesis was published in the book of *Türk Tarihinin Anahatları* in 1930 and introduced to a wider audience at the First History Congress in 1932. To revive the history of the nation on its own terms, the thesis proposed the existence of a pre-Ottoman ethnic group called the "Turks" who migrated from Central Asia to India, China, Mesopotamia, Anatolia, Balkans, and further onto Europe, populating almost the entire known world. The exodus from Central Asian steps sustained Anatolia, the modern borders of Turkey, as being the homeland of Turks. To authenticate this concept, the ancient Hittites and Sumerians were integrated into the ethnohistorical framework as the ancestors of Turks. In this regard, the trans-historical unity of Turkish

---

[3] Reşat Kasaba, "Kemalist Certainties and Modern Ambiguities," *Rethinking Modernity and National Identity in Turkey*, ed. Sibel Bozdoğan and Reşat Kasaba (Seattle: University of Washington Press, 1997), 16-17.

people denoted a national spirit among Turks in all periods of history. During centuries-long migrations, although some communities lost their fluency in Turkish or even their national identity, the race of the Turks prevailed.[4] Hence, republican Turkey constituted the latest of many Turkish states in world history. This modern state was distinguished with its zealous dedication to preserving the national identity and essence of Turks.

In this historicist reading, the faith of Islam, which was seen as detrimental to modernization,[5] became irrelevant to defining the culture of the Turks.[6] Although the Muslim dynasties of Seljuks, *Beyliks*, or Ottomans represented the larger Islamic community, which Turks belonged to by religion, it was specifically an individual Turkish culture, distinct from other cultures of nations in that Islamic community.[7] The built environment within the modern borders of Turkey, then served as a material embodiment of Turkish culture. Accordingly, in the mid-1930s, *Milli Eğitim Bakanlığı* (Ministry of Education) sent a memorandum to schools, addressing the teaching methods in order to integrate antiquities and historic monuments in their respective curricula. The memorandum insisted that all the historical works in Turkey exhibit the building traditions of the Turkish race and culture, although they had been named Hittite, Phrygian, Lydian, Roman, Byzantine, or Ottoman. These names only attested to certain periods in the history of the country. The protection of

---

[4] Ekrem Hakkı Ayverdi, "Târihimizde Anadolu ve Rumeli Devirleri," *Makaleler* (İstanbul: İstanbul Fetih Cemiyeti, 1985), 278.

[5] Perhaps one of the most conspicuous banishments of the Islamic culture in early republican Turkey is the architects' conception for a model village. These idealist plans included a uniform grid of houses arranged around a school, museum, and a village hall. The absence of a mosque in the plans, an unmistakable landmark of villages across Turkey, symbolized the secularizing agenda of the state. See, Sibel Bozdoğan and Esra Akcan, *Turkey: Modern Architectures in History* (London: Reaktion Books, 2012), 38.

[6] For Şerif Mardin, denying the place of Islam as the essence of the society increased the distance between the educated and the uneducated in republican Turkey. See, Mardin, "Some Thoughts on Modern Turkish Social Science," *Rethinking Modernity and National Identity in Turkey*, 71.

[7] Bozdoğan, *Modernism and Nation Building: Turkish Architectural Culture in the Early Republic* (Seattle: University of Washington Press, 2001), 35. In her seminal book, Bozdoğan probes how nationalist tendencies and institutional changes of modernization shaped the architectural forms in the "long" 1930s. In this matrix, historical forms devised by Turkish architects became a badge of inherent modernity of the built heritage; Niyazi Berkes, *Turkish Nationalism and Western Civilization: Selected Essays of Ziya Gökalp* (New York: Columbia University, 1959), 97.

this rich heritage was the national duty of every Turk, therefore, a cultural awareness, appreciation, and protection should be cultivated at schools. Clearly, this memorandum conceptualized cultivating a historic preservation culture by instilling an appreciation of art history and archaeology at a very early age.[8]

Inspired by the ideals of the Turkish History Thesis and significantly supported by state-agencies, architectural documentation (with other sciences of archeology, architecture, ethnography, history, museum studies, philology, and the like) became an agent in a much larger discursive project to generate and to disseminate a foundation myth, and common destiny as the unified nation of Turks. Architects and scholars, with supreme patriotic zeal and diligence, travelled across the remotest corners of the country and studied the historic architecture of the nation (Figure 1.1). Compiled in measured drawings, photographs, and textual materials, they catalogued the architectural landscape of the young country. The resulting records significantly mediated historic preservation work and facility management of buildings. Furthermore, these visual materials played a prominent part in the circulation of state-sponsored brochures, books, exhibitions, journals, and monographs.

Figure 1.1. Creating fieldnotes in the documentation campaign of Erzurum Çifte Minareli Madrasa, undated. SALT Research, Harika and Kemali Söylemezoğlu Archive, TSOH485006.

---

[8] Emre Madran, "Cumhuriyet'in ilk Otuz Yılında (1920–1950) Koruma Alanının Örgütlenmesi-I," *ODTU MFD* 16, no. 1-2 (1996):74; Nurettin Can Gülekli, *Eski Eserler ve Müzelerle ilgili Kanun Nizamname ve Emirler* (Ankara: Milli Eğitim Bakanlığı, 1948), 85-88.

Following Atatürk, the secular appraisal of the Turkish History Thesis was substituted for a religious-ethnic reading of the built heritage, which subsequent governments have extensively exploited. The imperial monuments associated with an Islamic past came to be the locus of Turkish identity, and constituted the basis for a new collective memory for the citizens of modern Turkey. Accordingly, the defining historical moments entailed the defeat of the Byzantines in the Battle of *Malazgirt* (Manzikert) [9] of 1071, which prompted Seljuk-Turks to pour into Anatolia to make their homeland; along with the Ottoman conquest of Constantinople in 1453, which sealed the end of the Byzantine Empire. Ideologically stressed as "Turkish," the Ottoman roots became a major source of pride for the nation. In 1953, the 500th anniversary of the Ottoman conquest of Constantinople marked an ideological change when a sophisticated public image of building tradition infused with a sacred history of Muslim-Turks came to the foreground. Significantly, the commemoration of the quincentenary accentuated the documentation and study of the built environment associated with the conquest and the Ottoman building traditions.

In the conflicting camps of the secular-ethnic identity politics reflected in the Turkish History Thesis, and the religious-ethnic phenomenon of Islamification, a thread remained: Turkish architecture. Given this, the genealogy of Turkish architecture essentialized a national spirit of architectural forms, distinguishing it from Byzantine as well as other "Islamic" schools of architecture (for example, Arab, Egyptian, or Persian). In effect, in the continuous historical experience from the early civilizations of Central Asia to the frontiers of Seljuk Anatolia and Ottoman Istanbul, "Turkish" elements had been embodied in diverse places, such as the tents of Turkic nomads, monumental portals of medieval monuments, or Architect Sinan's sixteenth-century domed-mosques. To probe these formal comparisons, republican scholars heavily depended on the typological and morphological classification of historic properties, illustrated with measured drawings.

Constructing measured drawings

Architectural recording and documentation, also interchangeably described as *rölöve* or a measured building survey, includes the systematic collection of building information of a historic property. In terms of architecture, a building, structure, district, site, or an object with historical or archaeological significance is considered a historic property. The purpose of the documentation

---

[9] Present day Malazgirt is located in the eastern part of Turkey.

activity is to collect, organize, explain, and illustrate building information that is relevant to the current understanding of the past and present the current configuration of the entity in question. For instance, a historic photograph of the changing cultural landscape of Istanbul documents the different time phases of the city (Figure 1.2). Likewise, a measured drawing with annotated fieldnotes and dimensions displays the existing condition of the building surface at the time of a survey (Figure 1.3). A thorough documentation project, in this context, is based on in-depth archival research and surveying fieldwork to provide the past and present qualities of the heritage environment. Ideally, a documentation dossier includes photographs, measured drawings, three-dimensional models, and written histories.

Figure 1.2. Photograph of Istanbul's Zeyrek Mosque (Church of Christ Pantokrator), street view, undated. SALT Research, AHISTZEYR001.

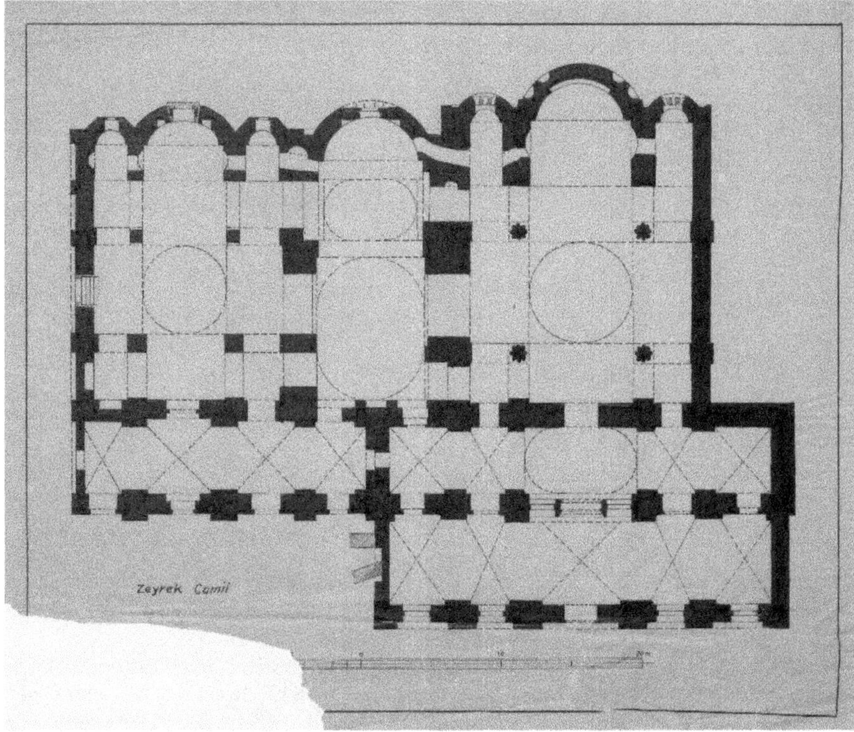

Figure 1.3. Measured drawing of Zeyrek Mosque, delineated by Ali Saim Ülgen, undated. SALT Research, Ali Saim Ülgen Archive, TASUDOC0568010.

In architectural culture, measured drawings, termed also as architectural survey drawings or measured survey drawings, entail a certain representational system to portray a three-dimensional property in two dimensions. These specialized drawings resemble the as-built architectural drawings in context as the latter are modified construction drawings that are produced immediately after construction. Measured drawings, however, are made years after a property is constructed (Figure 1.4). To document, architects carefully observe the material condition of the building, meticulously interpret the qualities that make up the architectural heritage, gather measurements from the surface using tape measures, cameras, or laser scanners, and then translate these field notes to measured drawings (Figure 1.1 and 1.5). Each drafted line in a drawing, consequently, corresponds to a cluster of measured points on a structural element (of an arch or a window), or refers to an intangible quality (of a circulation pattern, industrial process, or chronological development of the property), which are then translated to a horizontal or a vertical plane of two-dimensional plans, sections, and elevations (Figure 1.6).

Figure 1.4. Field note of Sultan Murad II's mansion in Bursa (today, Ottoman House Museum), delineated by Ali Saim Ülgen, April 21 1946. SALT Research, Ali Saim Ülgen Archive, TASUDOC0568.

Figure 1.5. Gathering measurements from the courtyard wall of the Erzurum Çifte Minareli Madrasa, undated. SALT Research, Harika and Kemali Söylemezoğlu Archive, TSOH485015.

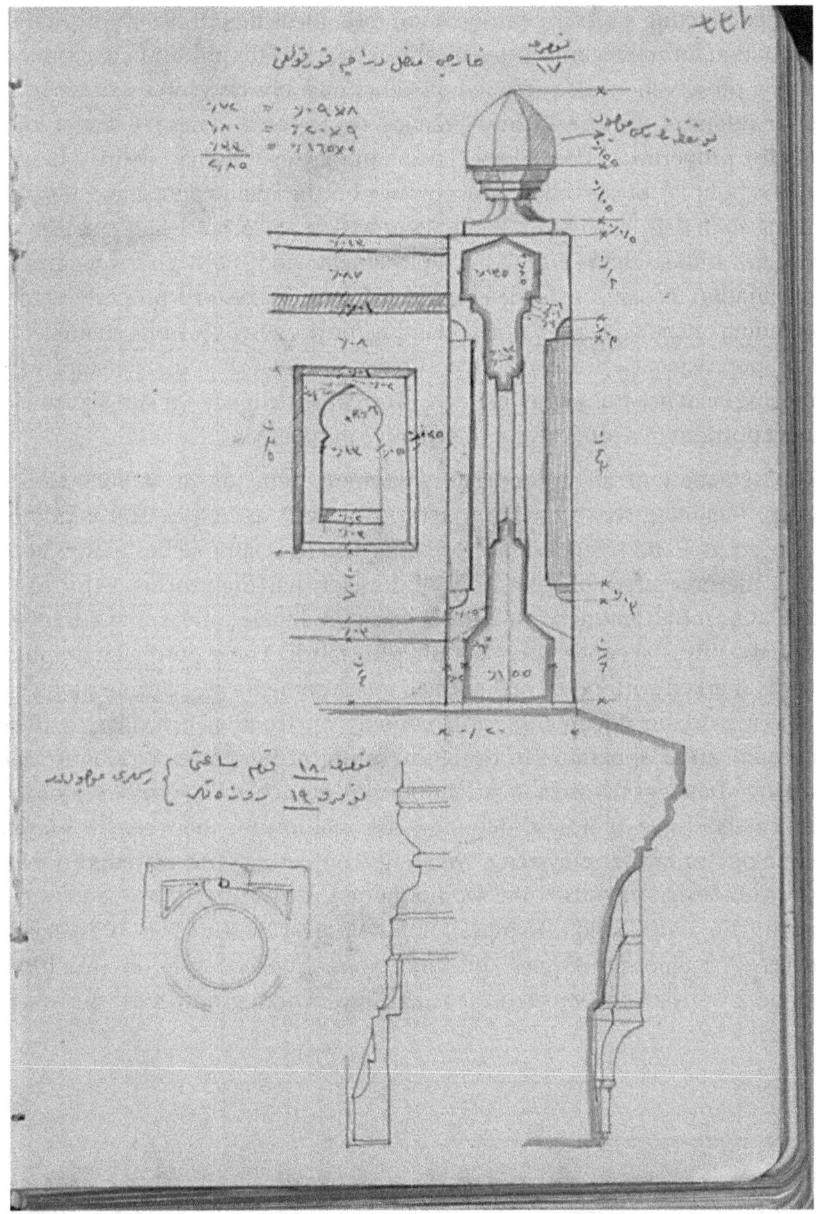

Figure 1.6. Drawing of a balustrade, drawn by Mehmet Nihat Nigizberk, 1909-1919. Koç University, Suna Kıraç Library Special Collections and Archives, Mehmet Nihat Nigizberk Collection of Architectural Drawings and Photographs, MNN_NB_01, 282.

When conducting a historic preservation task, measured drawings provide the information for the technical specifications required for physical interventions. Historic preservation, also referred to as heritage preservation or architectural conservation, is the theory and practice to preserve, conserve and protect historic properties. There are four approaches which define historic preservation: (a) preservation concentrates on the maintenance and repair of existing materials; such work includes provisions to protect and stabilize the property, rather than extensive replacement and new construction. (b) rehabilitation recognizes the need to alter or add to a historic property to meet continuing or changing uses while retaining the property's historic character, (c) restoration depicts a property at a particular period of time in its history, while removing evidence from other periods, (d) reconstruction re-creates vanished or extinct portions of a property for interpretive purposes.[10]

The selection of an appropriate treatment depends on a collection of factors, including the property's historical significance, physical condition, proposed use, and intended interpretation. All four approaches merge in the use of the measured drawings for the decision-making process. Prior to the application of a treatment, architects compile detailed measured surveys to probe the physical condition of the building fabric. These particular graphical records marked with notes and surface measurements allow professionals to produce working documents, also coined construction drawings, a major communication apparatus in designing physical interventions (Figure 1.7). Working drawings constitute an important source of information on the performance of a building, detailing the relationship between its design, technology or working systems (heating, ventilating, and air conditioning; electrical design or structural components). Therefore, these documents present the construction, material, and technical information to associated parties of builders, patrons, and colleagues. Consequently, in this highly technical transaction between measured and working drawings, the weight

[10] Technical Preservation Services, *The Secretary of the Interior's Standards for the Treatment of Historic Properties, with Guidelines for Preserving, Rehabilitating, Restoring & Reconstructing Historic Buildings*, ed. National Park Service, revised Anne E. Grimmer, (Washington D.C., U.S., 2017), 2-3. In the re-use of buildings, the priority is to retain the historic character of the property. The proposed four provisions should sustain the existing form, integrity, and materials of the property.

lies in providing an accurate, measurable replica of the physical building surface to be used in construction.[11]

Figure 1.7. Proposed repairs to Jerusalem's Mosque of Omar, 1909-1919. Koç University, Suna Kıraç Library Special Collections and Archives, Mehmet Nihat Nigizberk Collection of Architectural Drawings and Photographs, MNN_NB_01, 313.

[11] To provide the seamless transition between fieldnotes and working drawings and to deliver highly accurate data, digital technologies (for example, laser scanners, photogrammetric tools, and building information modeling software) heavily dominate the documentation fieldwork and the architectural production in today's practice.

Measured drawings serve as a lasting record of a historic property. These graphical prescriptions are integral methods of analysis to put the historic property in context, to acquire an understanding about peer-built heritage, and to determine how architectural resources relate to each other. Besides, these descriptive records provide insurance against the tragic loss of the architectural heritage due to ill-conducted physical interventions, inappropriate urban development, natural disasters, negligence, and wars.

Documenting as an archival record

Figure 1.8. An interpretive illustration of Erzurum depicting the city 200 years ago, drawn by Ali Saim Ülgen and Dündar Beyce, 1944. SALT Research, Ali Saim Ülgen Archive, TASUH5964.

Along with the act of documentation, the contents of measured drawings as the basis of working documents and of acquiring a historical understanding differ considerably. As the template for working documents, measured drawings technically include specific information gathered from the building surface, with construction in mind. However, measured drawings to encourage a broader historical understanding of architecture attest to interpretive illustrations wherein draftsmen investigate the best ways to represent particular aspects of a historic property.[12] To capture the unique qualities of architectural heritage, perhaps a floor plan, an undulated building skin, or a moving machinery part, architects use different rendering mediums of a plan, a three-dimensional perspective, an axonometric model, or a compilation of all these vantages (Figure 1.8).

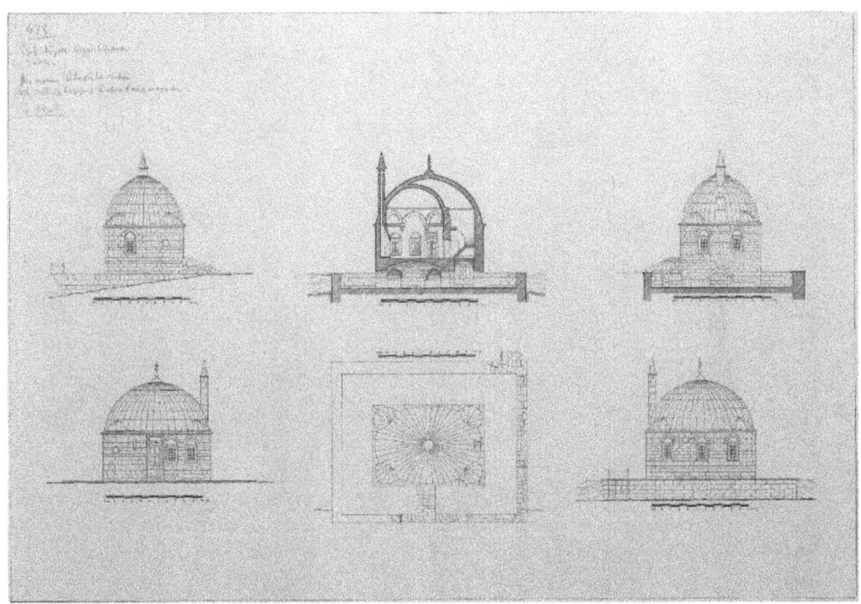

Figure 1.9. A measured drawing sheet of Bakırköy's Siyavuş Pasha Pavilion, delineated by Ali Saim Ülgen, 1934. SALT Research, Ali Saim Ülgen Archive, TASUPA0914001.

The published architectural surveys in the early Turkish republic, convincingly show that measured drawings became seen as self-referential scientific documents replicating the building on paper for archival building documentation, serving purposes of education and research. With annotated dimensions and to a lesser extent notes, these archival records served to intensify the epistemological grounds for Turkish architecture (Figure 1.9). Typically, restoration architects who had contributed to the preservation work published heavily illustrated books relying on measured drawings as the best means for communicating graphic design. Alternatively, state agencies directly

---

[12] For the use of interpretive measured drawings, see, Serra Akboy-İlk, "Architectural Documentation Through Thick Description," Enquiry, *The ARCC Journal* 12 no.1 (2016): 19-21.

commissioned scholars to conduct a measured survey on a certain topic, followed by the publication of its monograph. In terms of the scale and contents of folios, the published volumes of measured drawings were not directly allied with the line of preservation work. By contrast, most delineations were examples of archival documentation, usually set up as pattern books of architectural plans and selected individual building motifs (Figure 1.10).

Figure 1.10. Cover page of the *Fatih Devri Mimarisi,* by Ekrem Hakkı Ayverdi, İstanbul: İstanbul Fetih Cemiyeti Neşriyatı, 1953.

Seen in this light, the endeavors of archival building documentation were intended for classification, exhibition, and methodical analysis of historic properties. The resulting publications allowed republican scholars to communicate the flow of information with an academic focus and to disseminate their concepts with a wider circle of readers. On the home front, investing the measured and drawn built environment with ideological inclinations, republican intelligentsia sought for the conceptual roots of Turkish architecture within the modern borders of Turkey. On the international front, interpreting the built heritage with national identities, scholars strove to find a niche for Turkish architecture in world history, in particular against the critical eyes of the Orientalist Europeans who often viewed architecture coming out of the Islamic context as irrational. Prioritized as scientific tools, catalogues of measured drawings (Figure 1.11), then, provided the material evidence for the existence and development of Turkish architecture.

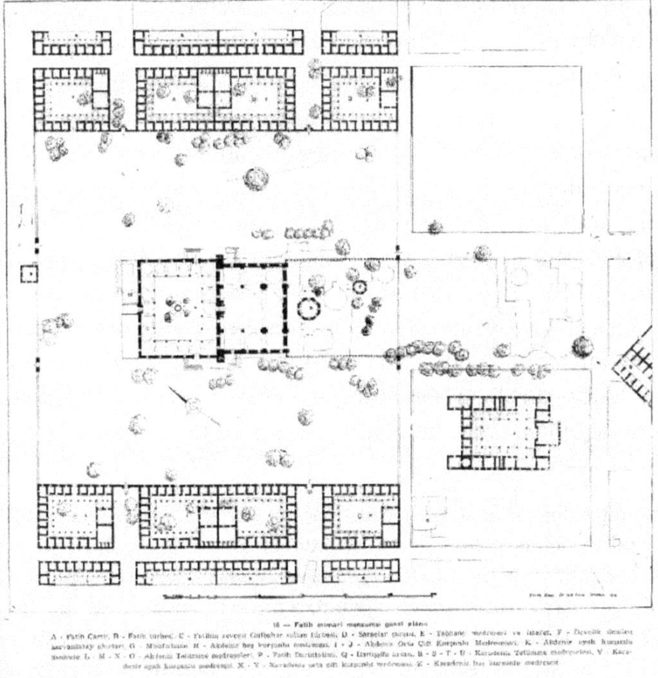

Figure 1.11. Site plan of the Fatih Mosque Complex in Istanbul, drawn by Ali Saim Ülgen. Halim Baki Kunter and Ali Saim Ülgen, *Fatih Camii,* Ankara: Vakıflar Umum Müdürlüğü Neşriyatı, 1938.

Synchronous with the changing visions of the republican state, the systematic documentation of the built environment significantly contributed to the national appropriation of the historic Turkish architecture. Resonating with the debates and involvement of different actors and institutions to reconcile the built environment, republican intelligentsia created a world of meanings as they selected memories of the past to perpetuate certain forms of understanding.

The Kemalist Republic of Turkey embraced a scientific perspective, which included a pragmatic understanding of positivism and materialism. The positivist assessment tried to theorize the distinction between historical process and historical knowledge. In other words, the more distant the socio-historical process from its knowledge, the easier to scientifically verify the claim. Monuments, in this context, became the material possessions of the country to manifest collective memory. When positivism and materialism was applied to architectural documentation, there was no room left for critical thinking. On paper, the measured and drawn monuments became architectural objects with an emphasis on their aesthetic qualities. In this linear representation, historical and socio-cultural conditions that brought the architectural works into being did not find a niche in the two-dimensional analysis of built heritage.

While built heritage found its value within the Turkish History Thesis, measured surveys of historic properties served to provide scientific proof of the Turkishness of architecture. Essentially, proof of the existence of Turks in Anatolia since prehistoric times became instrumental in affirming the territorial rights of the Turkish state against other ethnic groups who had collaborated with the Western powers against the aims of the Turkish War of Independence (1919-1923). Furthermore, the research was intended to prove the Turkish nation to be the equal of European nations by revealing the genealogical connection thought to reside in the racial and linguistic origins of Turks and Europeans.[13] Although implemented for a nationalist cause, the Kemalist era signified the first time a scientific discourse thoroughly

[13] In the early republic, archeology became the perfect discipline to certify Anatolia's Turkishness and to define the unified descendants of ancient civilizations under the umbrella of Turks. Yet, with the Islamic movement underway, conflicts between evidence and discourse turned archeology into a more political landscape. In the end, the Turkish-Islamic Synthesis discounted archaeological materials that predated the eleventh-century as it was seen to be non-Turkic, but the secularist discourse "objectively" read the same archaeological data to prove the Turkishness of the lands. Çiğdem Atakuman, "Value of Heritage in Turkey: History and Politics of Turkey's World Heritage Nominations," *Journal of Mediterranean Archaeology* 112, no. 23.1 (2010), 115.

permeated into the state propaganda of architectural heritage, where measured surveys as to be seen scientific apparatus in the ideological quest of the founding leaders. With the tremendous state support given to archaeology, architectural documentation, and historical research, the growing scholarship resulted in a fair degree of coordination with international developments in the academia at that time.

The changing ideological climate after the passing of Atatürk deprived the state agencies' patronage for academic quests at the highest level. While measured drawings remained as the scientific tool of historical analysis, without official support, the architectural scholarship of the early republic regressed. The quest for documentation was limited to signifying the architectural heritage created with the hands and minds of Muslim-Turks. Ultimately, the *Türk Islam Sentezi* (Turkish-Islamic Synthesis) of the 1970s completely disregarded historical evidence that preluded the eleventh century since the built heritage put forward prior to the Battle of Manzikert was seen to be non-Turkic.

Structuring a book on architectural documentation

This book, *Architectural Documentation: Built Environment, Modernization, and Turkish Nationalism,* is concerned with the efforts of archival building documentation from the Late Ottoman Empire (1798-1918) to the 1960s of republican Turkey. Rooted in the modernization schemes at the end of the empire, architectural documentation became an agent of ethnic nationalism. Albeit conducted on an intermittent schedule, antiquarians and scholars in the empire published monographs about the built environment, mainly focusing on Istanbul. Yet, this imperial construct of documentation often became the subject of the republican denigration of "unscientific" Ottomans. Interestingly, in a manner very similar to the compositional methods worked out by Ottoman architects and scholars, a constructive tradition of making measured drawings came full circle in the early republic. Within the operational mechanisms of modernization, the sporadic documentation efforts in the Late Ottoman Empire developed into a large-scale enterprise of surveying the national architecture of Turks. Supported by state agencies, many notable republican architects and scholars conducted systematic surveys of the historic works, and had academic access to publish their work.

In this study, the terminal date of the 1960s is due to the conspicuous deviation from the Kemalist ideologies following World War II (WWII), when Turkey entered a new phase of politics in pursuit of a closer union with Europe and the United States. Then, Turkey became a Cold-War security shield for the West, nurturing Islam and ethnic nationalism against the perceived threat of communism.[14] Subsequent to the 1950 general election, the secular ideals of the Kemalist establishment crumbled away as the populist *Demokrat Parti* (Democrat Party, DP) emerged victorious succeeding in a campaign that profitably exploited Islamic symbols. Followed by the five-hundredth anniversary celebrations of the Ottoman conquest of Constantinople in 1953, the Islamization of architectural heritage and an academic focus on its documentation had already been solidified. Although the revolutionary spirit of the early republic was still prevalent among numerous architects and scholars, the formal efforts of architectural building documentation could not meet the grand scale of state-supported academic work achieved in the early republic.

The thematic organization of this book follows an informal hierarchical structure, where each chapter stands on its own, examining one theme. "Modern construct of architectural documentation" maps the theory and practice of measured surveys from the Late Ottoman Era to the republican epoch. Reflecting on historical institutions and agents in the course of the movement of historic preservation, this chapter introduces historical personas and their documentation work. "National cultivation of built environment" includes the existential engagement with architectural heritage over the last two centuries. Despite the claim to a shared identity of the nation, each political priority intensified a different type of engagement with the material remains of the past and created new sites of conflict. Amid each ideological focus, the re-framed built environment found its way to publications of measured surveys. "Formal delineation of Turkish architecture" addresses the projective tool of descriptive geometry, a product grounded in the industrial progress of the Western world-view. In a judgement of efficient and neutral measured drawings, the simplistic objectification of plans, sections, and elevations blurred the compartmentalized tracks of documentation of the existing condition of buildings and the graphic idealization of historic architecture.

This book draws upon the resources and methodologies of three fields of interpretive-historical study: history of the Ottoman Empire and Republic of Turkey, historiography of art, and theory of architectural documentation. While there are questions and concerns shared by scholars involved in all of these areas, there are discourses, that are unique to each. The decline paradigm that once shaped the entire field of Ottoman history within the orbit of the rise of modern Turkey has now

[14] Ibid., 113.

lost its legitimacy. An evolutionary progression of architectural forms and subsequent manifestation of the centralizing economic and political policies of the sultan upon the creativity of a few select architects such as Architect Sinan, have become obsolete. Reading measured drawings, a term rooted in the eighteenth-century obsession with the mathematical description of space, has been superseded. With such a rich and varied array of archival evidence now available for scholars upon practicing history and architectural theory, the confining boundaries between respective fields of study have faded. Instead, formal doctrines have opened a wider field of interpretive-historical research that includes the study of architectural treatises, building plans, personal diaries, repair documents, and many other sources to enrich the process of the historical inquiry.

To date, the tendency of early republican professionals to materialize national and rational architecture has been well documented. How these agents operated within the idealized schemes of nationalism and the implementation of scientific architectural documentation methodologies has not been chartered. To find multiple perspectives on the act of drawing and surveying, this study explored primary sources of unpublished manuscripts, private letters, project memorandums, and reports written by the actors of historic preservation. Thus, this study contributes to the literature by exploring the backdrop behind the mindset of many early republican preservation professionals and the ideological roots for their documentation work.

The selection of case studies was shaped by the availability of primary sources. Owing to the physical constraints of a book, the text mainly includes sources from the archives of architecture and design of Koç University Libraries and SALT Research, Istanbul. Furthermore, the study includes documents from the Ekrem Hakkı Ayverdi Institute Archive at Kubbealtı Waqf Collection, Istanbul; Edhem Eldem Collection of documents of Sedad Hakkı Eldem; State Archives of Turkey at Ankara and Istanbul; Koç University, VEKAM at Ankara; Digital Collections at the Library of Congress, Washington D.C.; and Kalem Cartoon Satire Collection at the University of Texas Libraries at Austin. Rather than focusing on a sole case study, this book collects and provides insight from different projects in a chronological framework.

The academic roots of this book can be traced to my graduate studies at Koç University, Istanbul and Texas A&M University, College Station. In both institutions, I worked on diverse heritage recording and documentation projects, examining the often overlooked relationship between built heritage, the act of drawing, and digital surveying applications. My interest in the architectural historiography of early republican Turkey materialized years later, however, as I came across the archive at SALT Research of Ali Saim

Ülgen (1913-1963), the prominent restoration architect and historian. Examining Ülgen's rich portfolio of measured drawings and reading his handwritten manuscripts on Turkish architecture, I began to reflect on an unchartered territory of research pertaining to the integral role of archival building documentation formation of a modern nation-state. Since 2019, my publications have solely focused on analyzing Ülgen's monumental documentation work against the background of early republican scholarship. In the interim, I began to outline the concept of this book, bringing together many historical agents, institutions, and personas that had contributed to the field of architectural recording and documentation. Dedicated to acquire a better understanding of architectural voices, this resulting manuscript is the manifestation of years-long archival research, surveying fieldwork, and writing.

By evaluating the crossing boundaries between architectural documentation and built heritage modernization of Turkey, I hope that the complex layers of this fascinating intersection, the Ottoman thinking, the heroic feelings of nation-building, and the energy of the early republic can be better understood, and that, the scholarship created in the early days of the republic can be better understood. Because I came into the documentation field as an architect and a historian of architecture recording the built environment in Turkey, I have written this book as a way to see what was considered, inscribed, and recorded collectively in the culture of the Turkish nation-state. At each turn in my own journey documenting the architectural past and conducting research, Atatürk's wise words have made more sense to me: "Writing history is as important as making history. If the writers are not faithful to the makers, then the immutable truth will be altered in ways that confound mankind."[15]

---

[15] Hasan Cemil Çambel, "Atatürk ve Tarih," *T.T.K. Belleten Dergisi* 3, no. 10 (1939): 272.

Chapter 2

Modern construct of architectural documentation

> The only resolution to recover our architectural history from the ambiguity and deceitful end is to conduct a first-hand study of our monuments and to meticulously review them with a sincere interest, providing accurate measured drawings, revealing the artistic and technical qualities, and analysing [these characteristics] on paper. In this way, we will learn all the realities from the own expressions of our monuments.
>
> Sedat Çetintaş, 1946[1]

Sedat Çetintaş's words mark the weight of architectural documentation against the nationalist backdrop of the early republic. For Çetintaş and his many colleagues, measured drawings of historic properties were a sourcebook and a standard to understand the anatomy of architecture. Fueled with the nationalist and anti-colonialist spirit of the Kemalist regime, architect-scholars set to discover the architectural landscape of Turkey. Internalized as a national duty, they were racing to express the beauty of Turkish building forms. Driving to the furthest regions in the country, climbing into torrid attics, wet basements, and broken-down floors, and scaling unattainable heights with nothing but basic surveying equipment, they were searching for the soul of the monuments. With a great emphasis on draftsmanship, many of these renderings found their way into brochures, exhibitions, monographs, periodicals, and school books, in order to generate a voice for the architecture of Turks.

Çetintaş' statement also reveals the symbolic universe that the republicans assigned to the Ottoman past. When the Ottoman Empire, with its religious associations, was being dissolved and a new, secular ideal was being put forward under the leadership of Atatürk, an image of the incompetent

---

[1] Sedat Çetintaş, *Türk Mimari Anıtları: Osmanlı Devri,* (İstanbul: Milli Eğitim Basımevi, 1946), 4.

imperial intelligentsia was depicted. For many republicans, the statewide ignorance of unscientific Ottomans about the protection of architectural heritage led to the deterioration of national monuments symbolizing the spirit of the Turks. To Çetintaş, since "history began to be considered as science," no genuine book dedicated to studying "either the Turkish architecture or the architectural history [of the Turks]" had been produced. Due to the Ottoman historians' lack of interest in pursuit of "the technical and artistic traits of architecture" as well as the biographies of recognized Turkish personas, a scientific vision had not been achieved.[2]

Ironically, the drive to modernization and the implementation of scientific apparatus was deep-rooted in the late Ottoman Empire. When Ottoman authorities began to recognize the military superiority of Russian and European powers, they embarked on a series of reformations to regain authority and efficiency of the central state apparatus. In this multifaceted process of acculturation, imperial intelligentsia selectively adopted Western ideas, manners, and institutions to transform the Ottoman state, into a new kind of empire, more suited to the modern age. Aspiration for a modern country culminated in the *Tanzimat* (reorganization) period (1839-1876), which was distinguished by improving the status of non-Muslim citizens, reforming the educational system, and liberalizing the economy. The *Tanzimat* era ended with *Birinci Meşrutiyet Devri* (the First Constitutional Era) in 1876, demonstrating the general inclination toward a more secular conception of the state.

Sultan Abdülhamid II (r. 1876-1909), however, suspended the parliament and the constitution of the First Constitutional Era, after only two years. In 1878, Istanbul was almost occupied by the advancing Russian military force at the end of the Russo-Turkish War, which Sultan Abdülhamid II took as an excuse to abolish the parliament and to rule with absolute power for another thirty years. The 1908 Young Turk Revolution brought the European-educated "Young Turks" to power and marked the beginning of *İkinci Meşrutiyet Devri* (the Second Constitutional Era). The Young Turks forced Sultan Abdülhamid II to restore the constitutional monarchy by the revival of the Ottoman Parliament, the General Assembly of the Ottoman Empire and the restoration of the constitution of 1876. Until World War I (WWI), the *İttihad ve Terakki Cemiyeti* (Committee of Union and Progress, CUP) ruled the country while Sultan Mehmet Reşat V (1909-1918) remained on the throne as a front. CUP

[2] Ibid.

initiated urban modernization, sanitation, and transportation projects, in the hope of energizing the Ottoman state.[3]

By the same token, nationalist movements began to dominate the Christian European provinces of the Ottoman Empire. The weakness of central control, the severity of socio-economic problems, and the structural reality of an empire dominated by Muslims but encircled by Christian powers culminated in local uprisings.[4] The nationalist movement, soon began to pull the empire apart at its ethnoreligious layers, composing autonomous states (for example, Bulgarians, Greeks, Serbs). Following the Balkan Wars of 1912 and 1913; the Ottoman Empire lost the lands in the Balkan regions.[5] The retreat from the Balkan provinces, the very core of the empire for more than 500 years, largely materialized the focus of a new homeland for Turks in Anatolia and the establishment of a Turkish state.

During the last years of the Ottoman Empire, Turkish nationalists took over and stressed the centralization of a nation-state based on "Turkishness."[6] The plan of creating a homogenous Turkish state intensified with the establishment of the Republic of Turkey in the following years. The nascent

---

[3] Bozdoğan, *Modernism and Nation Building*, 18.

[4] M. Şükrü Hanioğlu, *A Brief History of the Late Ottoman Empire*, (Princeton: Princeton University Press, 2008), 51. Hanioğlu's reading on the late Ottoman Era distinguishes the interconnectedness of cultural, economic, and social trends in an empire. For Hanioğlu, the attempt to frame late Ottoman history and culture in a narrative of imperial collapse against the background of Westernization, nationalism, and secularization proved futile and hindered a clear understanding of the events, the people, and the intellectual ideas.

[5] The Balkans cannot be considered as a rigid geographical designation since the borders within the region heavily fluctuated since the late Ottoman era. At the turn of the twentieth century, the Balkans meant the Ottoman European territories of Eastern Rumeli, Macedonia, Kosovo, Bulgaria and Bosnia-Herzegovinia, Greece, Romania, Serbia and Montenegro. See, Ebru Boyar, *Ottomans, Turks and the Balkans: Empires Lost, Relations Altered*, (London, New York: Tauris Academic Studies, 2007), 34. Although Rumeli and the Balkans were used interchangeably, the two terms did not equate with each other. Halil Inalcık defined Rumeli as "the geographical name given to the Balkan peninsula by the Ottomans, also the name of the Ottoman province which included this region." See, İnalcık, "Rumeli," *The Encyclopedia of Islam*, second edition, vol. VIII, (Leiden, 1995), 608-9.

[6] Büşra Ersanlı, *İktidar ve Tarih: Türkiye'de "Resmî Tarih" Tezinin Oluşumu (1929–1937)*, (İstanbul: İletişim Yayınları, 2003).

republic underwent a purification process, amplifying the everlasting essence of the Turkish spirit as the substance of that national identity.

Rising nationalism to grant a collective past

In the Ottoman Empire, architectural heritage reflected the national roots of diverse communities living in an imperial polity with their different ethnoreligious backgrounds. When these communities began to focus on their origins to determine their collective cultural and artistic development, architectural documentation became a way to claim their artistic roots. One example includes the documentation efforts of the Greek Ottomans in nineteenth-century Istanbul. Investing the Byzantine built environment with the Greek national identity, the native intelligentsia compiled histories and illustrations of the existing remnants. The resulting studies strove to present the cultural landscape of the former Byzantine capital city, Constantinople, to a Greek-speaking audience. In this regard, the works of Patriarch Konstatinias' *Constantinople, Old and New* (1824)[7] and Skarlatos Byzantios' three-volume study, *Constantinople, A Topographical, Archaeological & Historical Description* (1851- 1869)[8] represented the modern Greek historiography compiled in the late Ottoman Era.[9] [10] Both authors delivered the exquisite image of Istanbul as an antiquarian's endless strolls through the city. Permeated with architectural appearances, historical chronicles, and folk stories, they portrayed the Byzantine culture peppered by famous personas, historical events, monuments, and neighborhoods.

In this corpus of publications, Alexander Paspates' work is distinguished with its dedication to archival building documentation. Born on the Island of Chios, then educated in the U.S. and Europe, Paspates worked in Istanbul both as a teacher and a physician. However, due to his passion for Byzantine

---

[7] Patriarch Konstatinias, *Constantinople, Old and New* (İstanbul: Dimitris Paspallis Publishers, 1824).

[8] Skarlatos Byzantios, *Constantinople, A Topographical, Archaeological & Historical Description,* three vols. (Athens: Andreo Koromila Publishers, 1851- 1869) [in Greek].

[9] Byzantios, *Constantinople,* 1851-1896; I., K. Konstantinias, *The Ancient and Modern Environment of Constantinople, from the Beginning until Today* (İstanbul: Dimitris Paspallis Publishers, 1844) [in Greek]; Byzantios, *Constantinople,* trans. Haris Theodorelis-Rigas (İstanbul: İstos Yayın, 2019).

[10] Stephanos Pesmazoglou, "Skarlatos Vyzantios's Konstantinoupolis: Difference and Fusion," in *Economy and Society on Both Shores of the Aegean,* ed. L. Tanatar-Baruh and V. Kechriotis (Athens: Alpha Bank Historical Archives, 2010), 23-78.

architecture, he also cultivated a career in scholarship and research.[11] Documented in his own words, the derelict condition of the Byzantine monuments and further threats due to destructions of earthquakes, fires, and vandalism, fueled his interest in studying the Byzantine architecture.[12] Not unlike a contemporary documenter engaging with the heritage fabric and analyzing its components, [13] Paspates conducted archival research of the historic properties and compiled fieldnotes in-situ. He published the resulting work in the periodical of the Greek Literary Society of Istanbul (*Sillogos*), followed by his book *Byzantine Studies* (1877). What Paspates took as architectural documentation however, suited context-independent and historically constructed interpretations of building forms and traditions. With a tribute to the Byzantine past, Paspates overlooked the present nineteenth-century configuration of the city and recast the monuments in a setting with references to their patrons, saints, and historical personas that would grant self-confirmation through the eyes of the Greek people.

Paspates' tenure as a member, then the president of the *Sillogos*, thus, facilitated the launching of the ambitious project of the documentation of the Land Walls of Istanbul. The defensive stonewalls were initially built during the fourth century, and were later restored and expanded until the Ottoman

---

[11] Firuzan Melike Sümertaş, "Bizans Uzmanı Doktor Paspatis'ten İstanbul'un öteki yüzü," *Atlas Tarih*, (Aralık 2016-Ocak 2017): 49, 46-53. Paspates was born on *Sakız Adası* (Island of Chios) in 1814. He lost his father at a very early age, when he was only four-years-old. During the Greek War of Independence, the Greek rebellions launched attacks to the Turks, which ended up with the Ottoman forces landing a large force on the island to seal the end of the events. To escape the turbulence in the island, coupled with the economic hardship due to his husband's passing, Paspates' mother moved the family to Malta. There, under the guardianship of American missionaries, Paspates left for Amherst College in Massachusetts. Upon his graduation, he returned to Istanbul to work as a teacher at the missionary schools.

[12] Alexander Paspates, *Byzantine Studies*, (Istanbul: Koromilas Publications, 1877), 6. [in Greek] Also, see, Sümertaş, "Dr. Aleksandros G. Paspatis'ten Dersaadet Rum Cemiyet-i Edebiyesi'ne İstanbul'un Kara Surları üzerine bir Çalışma," *Toplumsal Tarih* 272, (Ağustos 2016): 42-49.

[13] In fact, technologies alter documenters' engagement with the heritage setting, see, Akboy-İlk, "The Mediated Environment of Heritage Recording and Documentation," *Preservation Education & Research* 6 (2013): 7-23; architectural documentation resonates with the reciprocal process of drawing and engaging with the built environment, see, Akboy-İlk, "Drawing to read architectural heritage," *Drawing: Research, Theory, Practice* 2, no.1 (2017): 97-116.

conquest of the city in 1453. When Paspates began studying the walls, they were in grave danger of demolition.[14] The decree of 1864 had paved the way for the flattening of the structures and the sale of spolia materials. Espoused by the other members of the *Sillogos*, the documentation of the walls was rapidly put into action in 1870s. The resulting measured drawings consisting of a site map, elevation drawings of the walls and the gates were 30 meters in length when completed.[15]

Delineating Ottoman monuments

In the wake of the *Tanzimat* era, documentation of the architectural heritage also became an academical response to modernity. To put forward a historiography of Ottoman architecture and to find a niche for the empire in the modern age, successive sultans appointed antiquarians and scholars to produce monographs of the dynastic heritage. One widely recognized publication of modern art historical scholarship includes *Usūl-i Mi'mārī-i Osmānī (Fundamental Principles of Ottoman Architecture). Usūl*, commissioned by Sultan Abdülaziz (r. 1861-1876) for the 1873 Vienna International Exposition, was the earliest formal study of built heritage to provide a theoretical reading of Ottoman architecture. Supervised by İbrahim Edhem Pasha, the Minister of Trade and Public Works, the authors of the monograph included Victor Marie de Launay, a naturalized Frenchman, Pietro Montani, an Ottoman Levantine artist of Italian descent, French artist Eugène Maillard, and the Ottoman painter Bogos Şaşıyan.

---

[14] Paspates, "On the Land Walls of Istanbul," *Greek Literary Society of Constantinople Syngramma Periodikon (1863 – 1915)* vol. 2 (İstanbul: Bizantidos Publishers, 1865a): 171-189. [in Greek]
Paspates, "The Epigraphy of the Land Walls," *Greek Literary Society of Constantinople Syngramma Periodikon (1863 – 1915)* vol. 2 (İstanbul: Bizantidos Publishers, 1865b): 189-209. [in Greek]
Paspates, "The Gates of the Land Walls," *Greek Literary Society of Constantinople Syngramma Periodikon (1863 – 1915)* vol. 2 (İstanbul: Bizantidos Publishers, 1865c): 209—221. [in Greek]

[15] Syngramma Periodikon, "Land Walls of Istanbul," supplement vol. 14 (İstanbul: Bizantidos Publishers, 1884): 4-6. [in Greek]

The authors of *Usūl* described a national imperial building tradition, *Osmanlı* (Ottoman). Principled in the harmony between structural elements, proportional relations, and arrangement of patterns, they underscored that the style of "Ottoman" showcased the weight of "the science of architecture" embodied in Ottoman thinking.[16] The national character of the Ottoman order originated in the paragons of the fifteenth-century Bursa, *Yeşil Cami* (the Green Mosque) (Figure 2.1) and the tomb of its donor, Mehmed I; and internally evolved with the school of Sinan in the sixteenth-century. Exemplified in its own pattern of stylistic progression and its authentic principles of design, the Ottoman order was a rational, fluid, and universally applicable system of building that was subject to continuous change and innovation (Figure 2.2).[17]

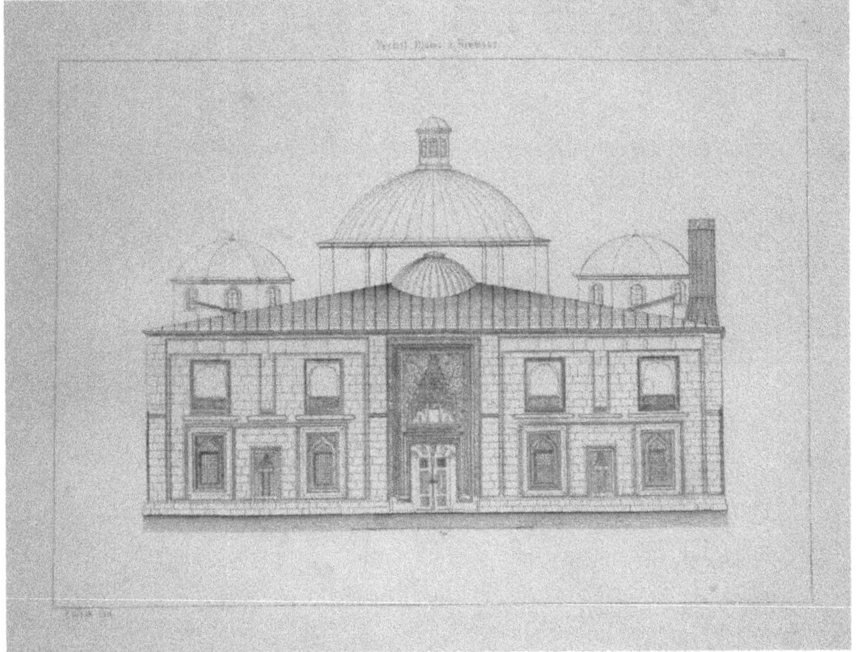

Figure 2.1. Elevation drawing of the Green Mosque, Bursa. *Usūl-i Mi'mārī-i Osmānī*, İstanbul, 1873. SALT Research, AMN1100200203.

---

[16] Pietro Montani et al., *Usūl-i Mi'mārī-i Osmānī* (İstanbul, 1873), reprinted in idem, *Osmanlı Mimarisi* (İstanbul: Çamlıca, 2015), 3.

[17] Ahmet A. Ersoy, "Architecture and The Search for Ottoman Origins in the Tanzimat Period," *Muqarnas* 24 (2007): 117.

Figure 2.2. An architectural element with Ottoman order rendered on a regular grid. *Usūl-i Mi'mārī-i Osmānī*, İstanbul, 1873. SALT Research, AMN1100200116.

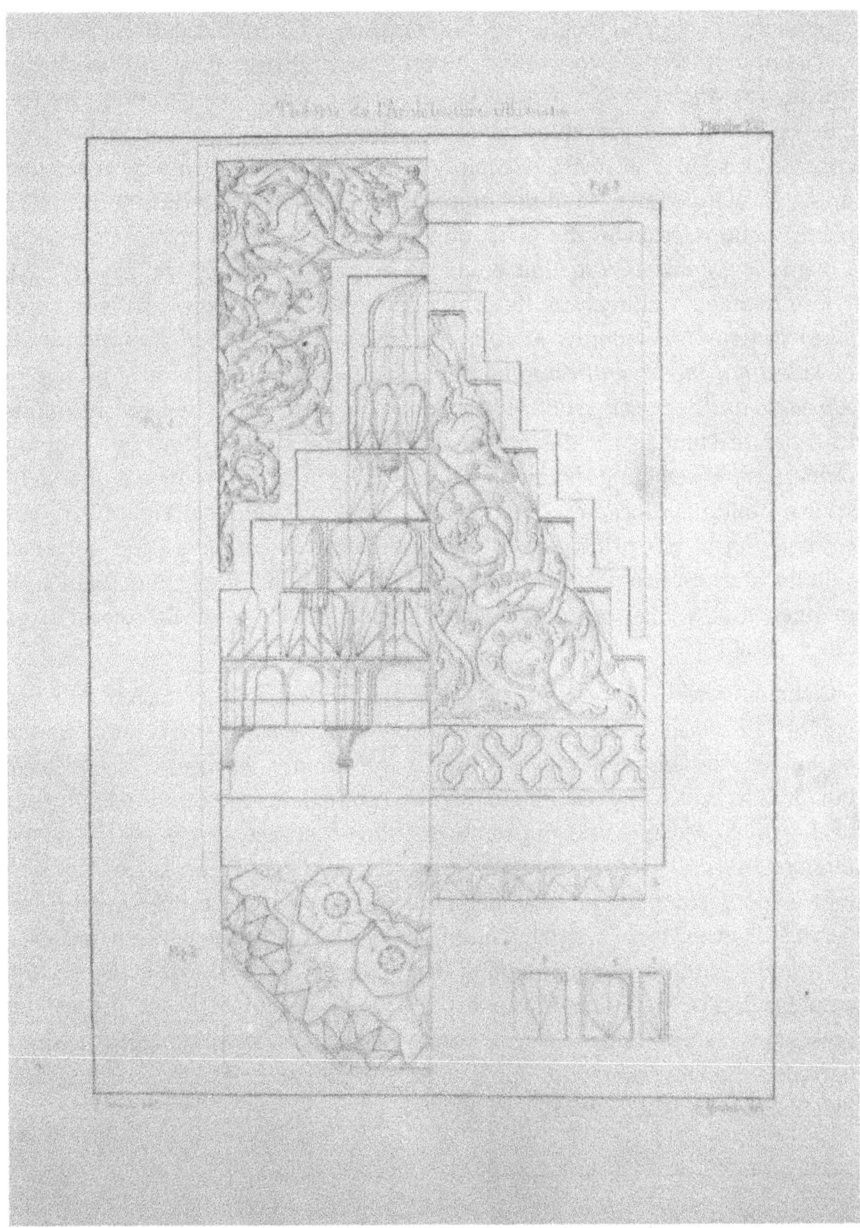

Figure 2.3. A drafting guide for the Ottoman order. *Usūl-i Mi'mārī-i Osmānī*, İstanbul, 1873. SALT Research, AMN1100200115.

The authors of *Usūl* described the purpose of compiling the theory of Ottoman architecture: to exhibit the artistic creativity of the nation and to provide references for architects to use in new construction.[18] The categorization and presentation of measured drawings in the monograph confirm this labor of division. Mainly delineated by Montani, the measured drawings of individual buildings presented a well-constructed composition of plans, sections, and elevations. Through sheets of drawings, historic buildings became a graphic record that could be accessed, viewed, and interpreted. These detailed architectural descriptions included the measured surveys of *Green Mosque, Süleymaniye Mosque, Selimiye Mosque and Yeni Mosque,* tombs of *Süleyman the Magnificent* and *Şehzade Mehmed,* along with fountains of *Ahmed III and Azapkapı Saliha Sultan.* Besides, Montani delineated specifications in order to standardize the old methods of construction for the Ottoman order. Simply selecting details (a capital, a door, or a window) from a well-known building, Montani crafted visual guides of reference (Figure 2.3). His clarification of the principles of the Ottoman order rendered the universal validity and applicability of the imperial forms, and presented them in a manner that would reproduce exceptionally well, either for research or design-build.

Coinciding with the release of *Usūl,* the French architect Léon Parvillée published *Architecture et Décoration Turques au XVE siècle* (1874).[19] Commissioned by Sultan Abdülaziz, Parvillée came to the empire to restore the historic buildings in Bursa. The resulting book was a compilation of measured drawings of the Green Mosque and the tomb of Sultan Mehmed I in Bursa, the same monuments that were thoroughly examined in *Usūl.* There is no apparent information linking the professional exchange between the authors of *Usūl* and Parvillée. Nevertheless, a striking resemblance prevails between these two texts, in regards to the analytical reading of buildings. The scale of drawings, the amplification of the points of interest, the selection of details, and the style of presentation are congruent. Considering both parties were working for the same patron in the late Ottoman Empire- Sultan Abdülaziz- it is likely that they had influenced each other's work.[20]

---

[18] Montani et al., *Usūl,* 4.

[19] Léon Parvillée, *Architecture at Décoration Turques au XVE siècle* (Paris: A. Morel, 1874).

[20] Ersoy, *Architecture and the Late Ottoman Historical Imaginary: Reconfiguring the Architectural Past in a Modernizing Empire* (New York: Routledge, 2016).

Following the publication of *Usūl,* intermittent efforts of architectural surveying were maintained in the late Empire. During the peak of the Ottoman-German alliance, Cornelius Gurlitt (1850-1938), an architectural historian from Dresden University, obtained permission from Sultan Abdülhamid II to study Istanbul's mosques. Gurlitt published two volumes of measured drawings and photographs, *Die Baukunst Konstantinopels* (*The Architectural Art of Istanbul,* 1907 and 1912).[21] Gurlitt's work was the earliest European monograph to acknowledge the originality of the Turkish school of architecture that emerged after the fall of Constantinople.[22] His survey included Byzantine and Ottoman built heritage, spanning from imperial complexes to smaller domed edifices.

As an inspirational source of new design, numerous Ottoman architects individually documented historic properties. Coinciding with the 1908 Young Turk Revolution, the new generation of architects searched for a new architectural style to symbolize the liberal reforms. Coined as *Birinci Ulusal Mimarlık Akımı* (First National Style or National Architecture Renaissance), a rather eclectic Ottoman revivalism dominated the theory and practice of architecture until the 1930s. Principled in the use of decorative elements from classical Ottoman architecture (for example, semispherical Ottoman domes, wide roof overhangs, and ornate tile decoration), the Beaux-Arts design principles (symmetry and axiality), and new construction methods (reinforced concrete, iron, and steel), symbolized the ideological aspirations of new designs (Figure 2.4).[23] Prominent architects of the era, Architect Kemalettin Bey (1870-1927), [24] Architect Vedat Bey (1873-1942),

---

[21] Cornelius Gurlitt, *Die Baukunst Konstantinopels,* two vols. (Berlin: Verlag Von Ernst Wasmuth:1907 and 1912); Gurlitt, *İstanbul'un Mimari Sanatı,* trans. Rezan Kızıltan (Ankara: Enformasyon ve Dokümantasyon Hizmetleri Vakfı, 1999).

[22] Gülru Necipoğlu, "Creation of a National Genius, Sinan and the Historiography of 'Classical' Ottoman Architecture," ed. Bozdoğan and Necipoğlu, *Muqarnas* 24 (2007): 151. For Necipoğlu, in the publication of *Die Baukunst Konstantinopels,* Gurlitt initiated the still-dominant categorization of Sinan's mosques pertaining to their domed baldachins resting on miscellaneous support systems, yet always dedicated to create centrally planned spaces for the ritual needs of Muslim congregations, 158.

[23] Bozdoğan, *Modernism and Nation Building,* 18; Aptullah Kuran, "Mimarlıkta 'Yeni-Türk' Üslubu ve Osman Hamdi Bey," in *Selçuklular'dan Cumhuriyet'e Türkiye'de Mimarlık/Architecture in Turkey from the Seljuks to the Republic,* ed. Çiğdem Kafescioğlu and Lucienne Thys-Şenocak (İstanbul: Türkiye İş Bankası Kültür Yayınları, 2018): 597-603.

[24] Prior to his appointment at the Ministry of Endowments, Kemalettin Bey, himself, traveled to Konya and Bursa to document the Seljuk monuments. Due to the restrictions

Mehmet Nihat Nigizberk (1878-1945), Architect Şemseddin (1889-1966), Vasfi Egeli (1890-1962), Macit Rüştü Kural (1899-1964), Arif Hikmet Koyunoğlu (1888-1982), and Süreyya Yücel (1903-1970) studied historic architecture as the academic foundation for the national forms of Turks (Figure 2.5). These architectural surveys, nevertheless, did not result in formulated publications.[25]

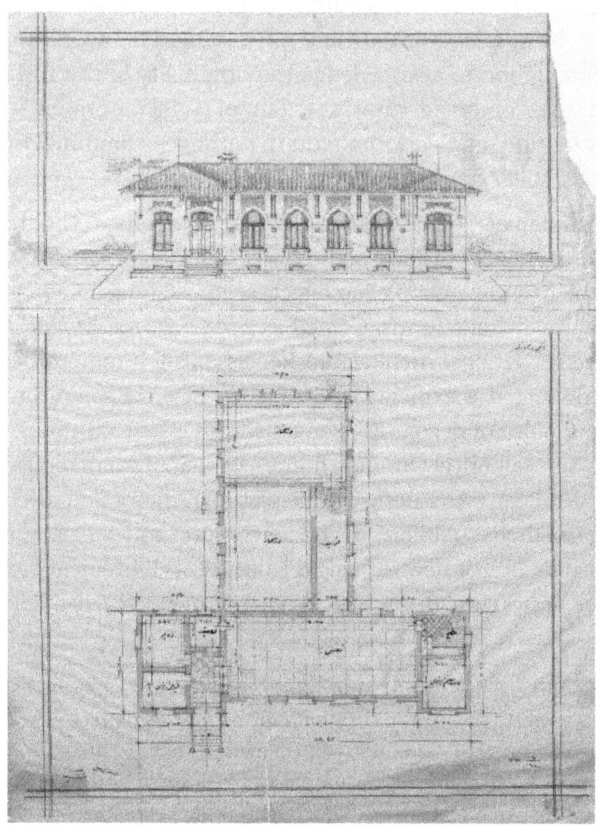

Figure 2.4. A school project with two classrooms, drawn by Architect Şemseddin, April 12 1924. SALT Research, TMSSD179.

under Abdülhamid II's rule, however, Kemalettin Bey obtained a pseudo-health excuse to travel. Unfortunately, we do not have Kemalettin bey's fieldnotes from these trips. Kemalettin Bey, "Bulgarların Ahval-i Medeniye-i Hazırası," in *Mimar Kemalettin'in Yazdıkları*, ed. İlhan Tekeli and Selim İlkin (Ankara: Şevki Vanlı Mimarlık Vakfı Yayınları, 1997), 79.

[25] M. Bülent Uluengin, *Rölöve*, (İstanbul: YEM Yayın, 2016), 11.

Figure 2.5. Analysis of a façade, delineated by Mehmet Nihat Nigizberk. Koç University, Suna Kıraç Library Special Collections and Archives, Mehmet Nihat Nigizberk Collection of Architectural Drawings and Photographs, MNN_NB_01, 51.

Figure 2.6. A school project at *Sanayi-i Nefise Mekteb-i Âlisi,* drawn by Architect Şemseddin. SALT Research, TMSSD108.

The roots of measuring and drawing as the intellectual source of the First National Style can also be explained with the design teaching at the *Sanayi-i Nefise Mekteb-i Âlisi* (Academy of Fine Arts, later named State Academy of Fine Arts, then Mimar Sinan Fine Arts University) at the time. The curriculum at the prestigious imperial school was based on the tenets of the French École des Beaux Arts System: classical composition, drawing, and rendering. There, students prepared projects with an emphasis on façade, axiality, and symmetry (Figure 2.6). Koyunoğlu who started the school in 1908 to pursue a degree in architecture, remembers that the first year included an emphasis on art education. The second year, however, included the study of Greek and Roman styles and the application of these forms in design projects. The third year expanded to the application of neo-classical and neo-Renaissance projects to large institutional buildings. The final year of the curriculum was distinguished by its emphasis on making measured drawings of classical Ottoman architecture and the use of these elements in a final project based on the First National Style.[26] The architectural courses in the *Mühendis Mekteb-i Âlîsi,* (Civil School of Engineering, later named Istanbul Technical University) followed a similar curriculum based on the study of classical orders.[27]

Surveying as the basis of physical interventions

As the modus-operandi of historic preservation projects, architectural documentation was seen as a scientific methodology in the Late Ottoman Empire. Measured drawings provided the information for the technical specifications required in the physical interventions. In regards to the protection of Istanbul's Land Walls, for example, two subsequent examples of correspondence (1892) between *Sadaret* (the Grand Vizierate) and *Dahiliye Nezareti* (the Ministry of Interior) indicate the official agenda of preservation. The agencies commissioned the compilation of a measured survey to exhibit the dilapidated parts of the historic structure. Once the existing condition of the walls would be documented, then the budget for the repairs could be determined. [28] Likewise, for the repairs of Adapazarı's Orhaniye Mosque, initially, the building was recorded with a floor-plan, façade elevation and a site plan (Figure 2.7). Another example of documentation concerns the fifteenth-century *darüşşifa* (hospital) building in the mosque complex of

---

[26] Arif Hikmet Koyunoğlu, "Anılar," in *Osmanlı'dan Cumhuriyet'e Bir Mimar Arif Hikmet Koyunoğlu: Anılar, Yazılar, Mektuplar, Belgeler,* ed. Hasan Kuruyazıcı, (İstanbul: Yapı Kredi Yayınları, 2008), 90.

[27] Bozdoğan, *Modernism and Nation Building,* 31.

[28] Sadaret (Letter, Türkiye Cumhuriyeti Cumhurbaşkanlığı Devlet Arşivleri, Başkanlık Osmanlı Arşivi, DH.MKT 1940/18, 12 Ramazan 1309 [April 10 1892]); Dahiliye Nezareti (Letter, Türkiye Cumhuriyeti Cumhurbaşkanlığı Devlet Arşivleri, Başkanlık Osmanlı Arşivi, BEO 126/9382, 30 Cemaziyülevvel 1310 [20 December 1892]).

Sultan Mehmed II (*Fatih Sultan Mehmet*, Mehmed the Conqueror, r. 1444-1446 and r.1451-1481). Due to the 1747 earthquake of Istanbul, the historic building was heavily damaged. In 1824, when the adaptive re-use of the hospital became a discussion, the process was followed by the study of the existing building and a proposed *han* (inn) project. The comparison between the measured drawing of the hospital and proposed the floor plan of the inn shows two major changes (Figure 2.8 and Figure 2.9). First, the dome structure of the hospital would be replaced by a hipped roof. Second, in the proposed inn, the gate of the perimeter wall and the entrance of the building would be merged to create a new wing with stores.[29]

Figure 2.7. Drawings of Adapazarı's Orhaniye Mosque, 1865 (23-11-1281). Türkiye Cumhuriyeti Cumhurbaşkanlığı Devlet Arşivleri, Başkanlık Osmanlı Arşivi, HAT, 782.

[29] Oya Şenyurt, *Osmanlı Mimarisinin Temel İlkeleri* (İstanbul: Doğu Kitabevi, 2015), 82-83. In this book, Şenyurt addresses a remarkably overlooked line of research pertaining to the Ottoman thinking: the reciprocal relationship between drawing and calligraphy in the representation of architecture.

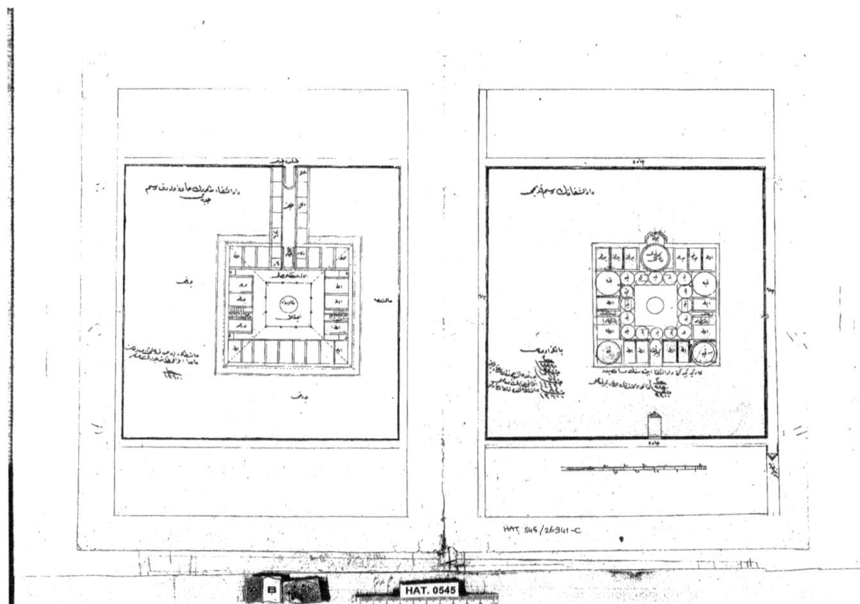

Figure 2.8. The floor plan of the proposed inn in the premises of the hospital, 1824 (29-12-1239). Türkiye Cumhuriyeti Cumhurbaşkanlığı Devlet Arşivleri, Başkanlık Osmanlı Arşivi, HAT, 545-26941.

Figure 2.9. Measured drawing of the existing condition of the hospital at the Fatih Mosque Complex, 1824 (29-12-1239). Türkiye Cumhuriyeti Cumhurbaşkanlığı Devlet Arşivleri, Başkanlık Osmanlı Arşivi, HAT, 545-26941.

Perhaps one of the most recognized projects was the documentation and restoration work of the Masjid Al-Aqsa in Jerusalem, the deeply distinguished monument of the faith of Islam. Between 1922-1926, invited by the Supreme Muslim Council of the Islamic State of Palestine under the British Mandate, Architect Kemalettin Bey conducted the restoration of the monuments in the Haram area. Prior, Kemalettin Bey worked as the director of constructions and restorations at *Evkaf Nezareti İnşaat ve Tamirat Heyet-i Fenniyesi* (the Ministry of Endowments' Scientific Commission for Repairs and Construction) between 1909 and 1919. Amid the fall of the empire and the Turkish War of Independence, Kemalettin Bey had a break from his office work when he accepted the invitation of Supreme Muslim Council of the Islamic State of Palestine to supervise the prestigious project in Jerusalem. Mehmet Nihat Nigizberk, his colleague from the Ministry of Endowments, accompanied

Kemalettin Bey during this work.[30] Of the three proposals Kemalettin Bey prepared, the council approved the consolidation work that addressed the preservation of Masjid Al-Aqsa and its dome.[31] The project included erecting scaffolding, reinforcing the foundations, rectifying the columns, replacing the tie beams, and conserving the elements of the dome. Later, Kemalettin Bey was awarded honorary membership in the Royal Institute of British Architects (RIBA) due to his methodological approach in documentation and restoration of the historic building.[32] A 1924-dated measured drawing remained a significant record from the prestigious project, which portrayed the layered configuration of the masjid with the rock cut-out vaults beneath. The folio was the first survey drawing depicting the totality of the historic building with its substructure (Figure 2.10).[33]

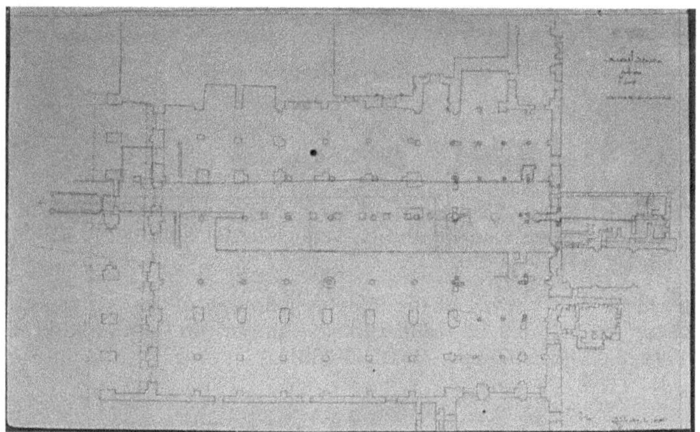

Figure 2.10. Measured drawing of Masjid Al-Aqsa, 1924. Koç University, Suna Kıraç Library Special Collections and Archives, Mehmet Nihat Nigizberk Collection of Architectural Drawings and Photographs, MNN_ALB14_phc_08.

---

[30] Haluk Zelef, "A Research on the Representation of Turkish National Identity: Buildings Abroad," (PhD diss., Middle East Technical University, 2003), 50.

[31] Ibid., 155. Of the three proposals that Kemalettin Bey prepared, one is particularly interesting to demonstrate his nationalist tendencies of architectural forms. The conceptual plan shows that Kemalettin Bey intended to insert a brand-new structure in the classical Ottoman style at the center of Masjid Al-Aqsa, replacing the three central aisles and twelve original columns.

[32] Alaettin Govsa, "Mimar Kemalettin," in *Türk Meşhurları Ansiklopedisi*, 1421-22, (İstanbul, 1946).

[33] Yıldırım Yavuz, "The Restoration Project of the Masjid Al-Aqsa by Mimar Kemalettin (1922-26)," *Muqarnas* 13 (1996): 153.

Under the leadership of Kemalettin Bey, the Ministry of Endowments operated as an educational institution for documenting, teaching, and reviving Ottoman architecture. Respectively, many architects, engineers, and craftsmen designed and constructed buildings of First National Style after their training at the Ministry. Kemalettin Bey also taught architectural classes at the Academy on the comparison of Ottoman monuments and their historic peers.[34] During his tenure at the Ministry of Endowments and his appointment at the Academy, Kemalettin Bey trained a generation of architect-restorers. In 1909, Kemalettin Bey recruited Nigizberk to the Ministry of Endowments to help with the repairs of the historic works.[35] Until his retirement from the Ministry of Endowments in 1943, Nigizberk got actively involved in devising the First National Style forms and restoring historical works of architecture.[36] Kemalettin Bey's other protégés included Çetintaş, Ali Saim Ülgen, and Ekrem Hakkı Ayverdi (1899-1984) who were among the first to restore and prepare measured drawings of Ottoman monuments and to write on national architecture.

Appraising the documentation work of Ottoman scholars

The early republican scholars' academic response to the documentation efforts in the late empire remained ambivalent, however. The proclamation of the republic signified an ultimate breakdown of the empire. Such existential commitment entailed a conspicuous de-emphasis of the activities and learning rooted in the empire. For example, when asked about the contents of the late imperial monograph, *Usūl*, Ülgen merely replied that the text did not entail academic merit and the contents of the measured drawings were not accurate, "[*Usūl*] is an absurd volume, which was written in different languages; today, experts identify [the work] as a book of errors and scientists

---

[34] Necipoğlu, "Creation of a National Genius," 286.

[35] Ali Cengizkan, "Mehmet Nihat Nigizberk Katkıları, Evkaf İdaresi ve Mimar Kemalettin," *Mimar Kemalettin ve Çağı*, ed. Ali Cengizkan (Ankara: TMMOB Mimarlar Odası, 2008), 179.

[36] Due to his active work at the Ministry of Endowments, Nigizberk collaborated with the new generation of restoration-architects. Nigizberk was very fond of the accomplishments of his younger colleague, Ülgen, and wished the protégé a flourishing career. See, Nigizberk, "Çok Muhterem Meslektaşım," (Letter, SALT Research, Ali Saim Ülgen Archive, TASUDOC0534043, April 5 1941). https://archives.saltresearch.org/handle/123456789/83487 (accessed September 20, 2021).

regard [these] measured drawings as an archaic corpus of documents."[37] Years later, nevertheless, Ülgen utilized the measured drawing of the eighteenth-century Azapkapı Saliha Sultan Fountain in *Usūl* as the foundation for the restoration of the historic structure. While the structure was built during the imperial degeneration of culture, the historic fountain was a "unique" example of Turkish architecture, Ülgen wrote. He posited that the measured drawing in *Usūl* was the most plausible record to represent the original form, its French Empire style reconfiguration (Figure 2.11). In the 1950s, Ülgen with Celâl Esad Arseven (1875-1971), historian and politician, guided the reconstruction of the-then-vanished roof of the fountain based on the late imperial drawing.[38]

Figure 2.11. Elevation drawing of Azapkapı Saliha Sultan Fountain, *Usūl-i Mi'mārī-i Osmānī*, Istanbul, 1873. SALT Research, Ali Saim Ülgen Archive, TASUDOC0310013.

[37] Ali Saim Ülgen, "[Ali Saim Ülgen to Refi Cevat Ulunay]" (Letter, SALT Research, Ali Saim Ülgen Archive, December 1961). https://archives.saltresearch.org (accessed September 20, 2021).

[38] Ülgen, "Rapor," (Paper, SALT Research, Ali Saim Ülgen Archive, TASUDOC0640021-2, undated). https://archives.saltresearch.org/handle/123456789/80622 (accessed September 20, 2021); Ülgen, "Restorasyon Projesinin İzahı" (Paper, SALT Research, Ali Saim Ülgen Archive, TASUDOC0640023-4, undated). https://archives.saltresearch.org/handle/123456789/80622 (accessed September 20, 2021).

From this perspective, Çetintaş also condemned imperial institutions for failing to elevate the scientific study of historic buildings, which would have created awareness of the national architecture of Turks. Instead, due to the cultural vacuum in the empire, foreign scholars occupied the field of documentation from the nineteenth century and onwards and created a corpus of documents with unwarrantable inaccuracies. Çetintaş, himself, began his career in architectural documentation to bridge the gap in the scholarship of Turkish architecture and to counter the domination of foreign scholars in the field. While a student-architect at the Academy in Istanbul, Çetintaş came across Gurlitt's published work on the monuments of Istanbul. Studying the measured drawings in awe, Çetintaş promptly realized the errors embodied in the illustrations. Coupled with the lack of publications on Turkish monuments, Çetintaş compiled measured drawings for the sixteenth-century Sokollu Mehmet Pasha Mosque in Kadırga (Figure 2.12), Istanbul for his graduation project in 1917. Ultimately, Çetintaş praised Gurlitt's enthusiasm and tenacity of making a record of historical monuments, which had inspired the young student's life-long passion of documentation.

Figure 2.12. Section drawing of Kadırga Sokollu Mehmet Paşa Mosque, delineated by Sedat Çetintaş. SALT Research, Ali Saim Ülgen Archive, TASUH0751.

With the same token, Çetintaş was highly critical of the Orientalist European scholarship, which alleged that Turks were a nomadic tribe without any building traditions or architectural styles. To Çetintaş, the

European scholars' Orientalist biases culminated in a flawed reading of the identity of Turkish architecture. The resulting monographs failed to materialize a truthful depiction of the Turkish monuments and categorized the Turkish art as a non-prominent collage of Arab, Byzantine, and Persian art. The ignorance of the native-grown scholars to the first-hand study of buildings had contributed to the methodological impasses of architectural scholarship, Çetintaş wrote. Rather than studying the architectural paragons and countering the Orientalist discourse, those Turkish scholars who had been trained in European schools chose to follow the biased Western texts.[39]

In this context, Tahsin Öz (1887-1973), historian and director of the Topkapı Palace Museum, concurred with Çetintaş in his concerns for foreign scholars' incompetent measured surveys of Turkish architecture. Öz stressed that foreigners were clearly unfamiliar with the Turkish culture, which in return hindered their understanding of the materials that they were studying. Coupled with the physical impossibility of recording monuments in cities like Sivas and Konya within a few days of fieldwork, the resulting publications included dramatic errors of accuracy. Öz warned that to expect foreign scholars to understand the soul of Turkish art and architecture would prove futile in a purely academic capacity. Therefore, Öz stressed that training native professionals "to be able to see our works of art with our own eyes" was the only remedy to overcome the congested state of architectural scholarship.[40]

To this end, Çetintaş suggested that the integration of surveying courses in the architectural curriculums would alleviate the stagnant air in the architectural scholarship. Yet, the state-propaganda had already created sites of conflict by perpetuating "otherness" on many scales. With an academic focus on pure and authentic national building forms of Turks, Çetintaş warned that teaching materials for the "corrupt" late Ottoman architecture had to be excluded from the curriculum. Concerning a student exhibition in 1942, organized at the Academy, Çetintaş repudiated the inclusion of a documentation study of the Nizamiye Police Station located in Selâmsız in Üsküdar, Istanbul. It was built in the French Empire style, in 1842, by a Greek master builder (Figure 2.13). Çetintaş fervently wrote, "...on the walls of the

---

[39] Çetintaş, *Türk Mimari Anıtları,* 15.

[40] Tahsin Öz, "Bir Münakaşa ve İki Konferans," in *Sivas Darüşşifası: 614-1217,* written by Çetintaş, 123-125 (İstanbul: İbrahim Horoz Basımevi, 1953), 125.

national architecture hall of the Academy, while I would like to see art treasures from Sinan and Hayreddin [a royal architect preceding Sinan], displaying structures of Christian builders assembled fifty-sixty years ago, that are impertinent to Turkishness and without a style, and then documenting these foolish buildings is dragging Turkish youth to a wrong path… This is a very tragic event for the children of Great Sinan who have matured to the republican era."[41]

Figure 2.13. Photograph of the Nizamiye Police Station located in Selâmsız in Üsküdar, 1880-1893, street view. Library of Congress, Abdul-Hamid II Collection, LOT 11909, no. 18.

Recording an architectural legacy in the republican state

To a large extent, the early years of the republic were stamped by the shattering changes brought by endless years of wars. The Late Ottoman Empire was a period of augmented unravelling with wars on several fronts,

---

[41] Çetintaş, "Milli Mimariden Ne Anlıyoruz?" in *İstanbul ve Mimari Yazıları*, ed. İsmail Dervişoğlu, 171-174 (Ankara: Türk Tarih Kurumu Basımevi, 2011), 171.

culminating in great loss of life, assets and territory. The defeat of the Empire in the WWI spelled the end of the imperial state, but also involved massive destruction of the built environment in the war fronts, such as Gallipoli, Levant and Mesopotamia. Subsequent to the 1918 Armistice, the Empire came under extensive occupation by the Allied Powers and lost its sovereignty. In this state of post-occupation, Atatürk, the emergent leader of the *Kuva-i Milliye* (nationalist liberation movement), pulled together a coalition opposing the foreign takeover of Anatolia. The resulting battles of the Turkish War of Independence were fought, most notably, on the western, eastern and southeastern fronts to liberate the regions from the occupation of the Allies.

When Atatürk and the military-bureaucratic cadre proclaimed a republic after defeating the Allies, the nationalists were challenged with the magnitude of the destruction of war upon built heritage. Coupled with years of neglect of repairs and maintenance, entire segments of architecture were lost in towns and cities at the war front. In the midst of institutionalizing reforms to craft a modern nation, the republican leaders began to formulate measures for the protection of the remaining historic properties across the country. As early as 1922, Atatürk instructed the protection and reuse of two dynastic symbols of architecture, Istanbul's imperial palaces of Dolmabahçe and Topkapı as museums. In the same year, during his visit to Konya, Atatürk famously instructed the repairs of the tiles of the thirteenth-century Karatay Madrasa, and the establishment of a museum on the premises.[42]

Atatürk articulated the official start of the historic preservation movement in a February 19 1931 telegraph sent to İsmet İnönü (1884 - 1973), Turkish general and statesman. In a trip that lasted more than three months, Atatürk visited numerous cities in the country and observed the systematic destruction of monuments due to neglect, poor planning of urban schemes, and ill-conducted preservation treatments (Figure 2.14). His resulting memorandum stated the dire conditions surrounding the monuments and the under-staffed museums. Without distinguishing between archaeological or architectural resources, Atatürk decided the protection of all "the unprecedented treasures of antiquities of civilization prevailing across the country."[43] The legendary leader signified the importance of methodical

---

[42] Fethiye Erbay and Mutlu Erbay, *Cumhuriyet Dönemi (1923-1938): Atatürk'ün Sanat Politikası* (İstanbul: Boğaziçi Üniversitesi Yayınevi, 2006), 165-166.
[43] Madran, "Koruma Alanının Örgütlenmesi-I," 69.

documentation and classification of historic properties as the scientific basis of maintenance and repairs. To achieve this overarching goal, Atatürk instructed to provide student fellowships for studying archaeology in Europe and to assign these native-grown specialists to the nationwide preservation campaign.[44]

Figure 2.14. Mustafa Kemal Atatürk and İsmet İnönü during the celebrations at the Ankara train station, 1931. Koç University, Ankara Studies Research Center (VEKAM), Ankara Photograph, Postcard and Engraving Collection, 2961_01.

Two subsequent circulars written by İnönü mark the priority of the state-level protection of historic properties. In a 1936-dated circular, İnönü proclaimed that regardless of its period, all the built heritage is "the treasured documents of the Turkish civilization... For any reason, there is no excuse for negligence or malevolence at these [monuments]. Even if a property is *dismissed from staff* [a.n. *tasnif harici*, discarded buildings slated to be demolished or sold], it cannot be unlawfully occupied without the written consent of the General Directorate of Endowments..."[45] In the following 1938-circular, İnönü confirmed the

[44] Ibid.

[45] İsmet İnönü, "10/8/1936," in *Anıtların Korunması ve Onarılması I*, written by Ülgen (Ankara: Maarif Matbaası, 1943), IX.

constitutional support of the preservation of historic properties. İnönü assured, "Let alone... the demolition of the treasured monuments that introduce our national existence and civilization to the present and future generations; preserving them with meticulous care against the destruction of the mankind and nature is not only a legal duty but a national debt." Subsequently, İnönü avowed that the perpetrators of the demolition of the hospice of the Mihrimah Mosque Complex in Üsküdar and the İkikapılı Han built by Sinan along with the vandalizing of a Seljuk monument, Sarıhan caravanserai, on the road between Ürgüp and Kayseri would be identified and persecuted.[46]

Seen as a scientific record, measured drawings became the core of the protection of historic architecture. Following Atatürk's telegraph, the cabinet of ministers devised the establishment of *Anıtları Koruma Kurulu* (Conservation Council of Monuments) in 1933 with members of archaeologists, architects and historians. The council became the first executive agency of architectural conservation in the young republic, taking measures to protect the monuments in the country.[47] By the end of 1933, the council registered more than 3500 historical monuments and initiated the systematic documentation of the built environment. Tasked by the government in 1933, Çetintaş began making drawings of the monuments in Bursa and Edirne. The resulting 49 plates of measured drawings were subsequently displayed in the Ankara Opera House, in 1935.[48] In 1936, the state efforts of documentation were institutionalized by the establishment of the *Rölöve Bürosu* (Surveying Bureau) under the umbrella of *Eski Eserler ve Müzeler Genel Müdürlüğü* (the General Directorate of the Antiquities and Museums). Çetintaş became the chief of the bureau operating from an office located at the premises of the tomb of the Sultan Mahmud II (r.1809-39), ironically, an Ottoman sultan who was a fervent supporter of the modernization reforms. The measured drawings compiled at the Surveying Bureau were displayed at numerous venues, such as the *Resim ve Heykel Müzesi* (State Art and Sculpture Museum), Istanbul Technical University, *Beyoğlu Olgunlaşma Enstitüsü* ("Technical Institute for Girls") along with the 1953 Paris exhibition.[49]

---

[46] İnönü, "31/1/1938," in *Anıtların Korunması ve Onarılması I*, written by Ülgen (Ankara: Maarif Matbaası, 1943), X.

[47] Ibid., 70.

[48] Uluengin, *Rölöve*, 15.

[49] Ayla Ödekan, "Sedat Çetintaş," *Restorasyon Yıllığı Dergisi* 11 (2015): 91-92.

Atatürk formulated the state efforts of studying the Turkish history and culture by instituting *Türk Tarihi Tetkik Cemiyeti* (Society for Turkish History Research) and *Türk Dili Tetkik Cemiyeti* (Society for Turkish Language Research) in 1931. These institutions were integral to maintain scientific research on the linguistic and historical origins of Turks. The first Turkish History Congress in 1932, organized by the Turkish History Research, fueled the intensification of studies, excavations, and reviews to generate and disseminate a synthetized story of the nation, while instilling a proud sense of shared history and common interests as a unified nation in a population that had been so profoundly traumatized and displaced by endless years of war. Subsequently, the names of the institutions were changed to *Türk Tarih Kurumu* (Turkish Historical Society, TTK), in 1935, and *Türk Dil Kurumu* (Turkish Language Society, TDK), in 1936. Concurrent with Atatürk's emphasis on the cultural progress of the nation, TTK and TDK promoted the protection, appreciation, and cultivation of works of language, literature, and fine arts integral to unite the citizens of the nation. In retrospect, the founding agenda of TTK included seeking, collecting, protecting, and restoring the historical vestiges of records, materials, and monuments, along with providing the scientific documentation and analysis of these remnants to formulate the Turkish History Thesis.[50]

In 1935 TTK appointed architect-scholar Ülgen to document the works of Architect Sinan, the Ottoman royal master builder and engineer of the sixteenth century.[51] Then a student-architect at the Academy, Ülgen began to make measured drawings of the built environment created by the royal architect. Until his untimely passing in 1963 at the age of fifty-years-of-age, Ülgen unceasingly travelled across Turkey to compile measured drawings of Sinan's architectural legacy. [52] After graduating from the Academy with a degree in architecture, Ülgen was awarded the state fellowship to study architecture-archaeology in Europe. Initiated by Atatürk, this fellowship was designed to cultivate young

---

50 Ersanlı, *İktidar ve Tarih: Türkiye'de "Resmî Tarih" Tezinin Oluşumu (1929–1937)* (İstanbul: İletişim Yayınları, 2018), 98 and 203.

51 İnan, "Büyük Türk Mimarı Sinan'ın 367. Yıldönümü Münasebetiyle Türk Tarih Kurumu'nun Sinan hakkındaki Çalışmaları: Atatürk ve Mimar Koca Sinan I ve II," *Yeni İstanbul*, April 9, 1955, 5.

52 Unfortunately, the monograph could not be completed during Ülgen's life. TTK published the measured drawings compiled by Ülgen in 1989. Ülgen, Filiz Yenişehirlioğlu, and Madran, *The Buildings of Mimar Sinan (Mimar Sinan Yapıları)*, (Ankara: Türk Tarih Kurumu, 1989).

Turkish students with a formal education in archaeology, who would contribute to the protection of cultural heritage in Turkey. Ülgen set off to Germany and France in 1939, yet with the outbreak of WWII he returned to Turkey within the same year. In 1944, Ülgen became the director of the newly founded *Anıtlar Şubesi* (Office of Monuments) under the direction of Hasan Âli Yücel (1897-1961), the legendary Turkish education reformer and philosophy teacher who served as minister of national education between 1938-1946.[53] With this role, Ülgen coordinated documentation, registration, and provisions for the preservation of historical works in Turkey.[54]

Besides the native-grown researchers, the French scholar Albert Louis Gabriel (1883-1972) extensively contributed to the documentation of historic architecture. Trained as an architect-archaeologist, Gabriel taught in the Faculty of Letters of Istanbul University between 1926 and 1930 and subsequently served as the first director of the French Institute of Archaeology until 1956 (Figure 2.15). Supported by the Turkish Ministry of Education and Culture, Gabriel then surveyed the built environment across the country and published monographs of written histories and measured drawings, including the *Monuments Turcs d'Anatolie*, 1931-1934, which was translated to Turkish years later. In 1936, when Gabriel requested for an assistant to aid with research on Turkish architecture, the then student-architect Ülgen was recommended.[55] Consequently, Ülgen helped Gabriel with the third volume of *Monuments Turcs d'Anatolia*, pertaining to the architecture of Bursa.[56] [57] During their time spent

[53] Ülgen, "Sayın Vekilim," (Letter, SALT Research, Ali Saim Ülgen Archive, TASUDOC0534040-41, April 18 1944). https://archives.saltresearch.org/handle/123456789/83487 (accessed September 20, 2021).

[54] For more information on Ülgen's contribution to the field of architectural documentation, see, Serra Akboy-İlk, "Ali Saim Ülgen: Building a Historiography of Turkish Architecture," *Turkish Historical Review* 10, no. 1 (2019): 71-97; also, Akboy-İlk, "Ali Saim Ülgen: A Dialectical Frame of the Republican Mind," *Tasarım Kuram* 15, no. 28 (2019) :96-110.

[55] To Reşit Saffet Atabinen, Ülgen was tasked with assisting Gabriel for his upcoming book, *Voyages Archéologiques Dans La Turquie Orientale,* which was then organized in two surveying campaigns in1932 covering the south-east region of Turkey. Atabinen, "Kaybedilen eski Anıtlar Aşığı Y. Mimar A. S. Ülgen," *Dünya Gazetesi*, February 15, 1963. Yet, in the Ali Saim Archive at SALT Research, there is no record to indicate if Ülgen was actually involved in this surveying work. See, Hilal Aktur, "Ali Saim Ülgen Arşivi üzerinden Erken Cumhuriyet Dönemi'nin Türk Mimarisi'ne Bakışı: Malatya Ulu Camisi Örneği," (Master's thesis, Istanbul Technical University, 2010), 30.

[56] Aktur, "Ali Saim Ülgen Arşivi," 31.

in the historic city for documenting the historical works, the duo also helped with the ongoing restoration work including the fifteenth-century *Green Mosque.*

Figure 2.15. Albert Louis Gabriel during his 1958-visit to Turkey, from the left, Ali Saim Ülgen, Ahmet Süheyl Ünver, and Gabriel. SALT Research, Ali Saim Ülgen Archive, TASUDOC0650031.

---

[57] The professional collaboration between Ülgen and Gabriel is self-evident in various official correspondence. For example, in 1939, Fahri Kiper, the general director of the General Directorate of Endowments, congratulated the duo's documentation work and requested information about their progress in Bursa. Kiper, "T.C. Vakıflar Genel Müdürlüğü Hususi," (Letter, SALT Research, Ali Saim Ülgen Archive, TASUDOC0534009, November 28 1939). https://archives.saltresearch.org/handle/123456789/83487 (accessed September 20, 2021). In another instance in 1939, Hamit Zübeyir Koşay, the Director of the Directorate of Antiquities and Museums requested Ülgen and Gabriel to provide their professional input on the restoration of the tiles of Green Tomb in Bursa. Koşay, "Yüksek Mimar Saim Ülgen, Bursa Müzesi Müdürlüğü Vasıtasıyla, Bursa," (Letter, SALT Research, Ali Saim Ülgen Archive, TASUDOC0534063, October 21 1939). https://archives.saltresearch.org/handle/123456789/83487 (accessed September 20, 2021).

In the preface of *Monuments Turcs d'Anatolie*, Gabriel noted that until this volume, there had been no scientific study on the Islamic antiquities of Turkey. Gabriel specified the autonomous Turkish architectural forms that had been uncontaminated from foreign influences and emphasized the primacy of Turkish architects as the creative minds responsible for their production. He celebrated Turkish building traditions (by which he meant the Seljuk and Ottoman heritage environment) as sources of inspiration for the young nation. Gabriel fervently chastised European art historians' ignorance and their introverted account of the Turkish artistic development in Anatolia and Trakya. He passionately advised that only young Turkish intellectuals could abolish these prejudiced assessments by documenting and studying their own monuments, and mobilizing public spaces to exchange scientific dialogs among every citizen.[58]

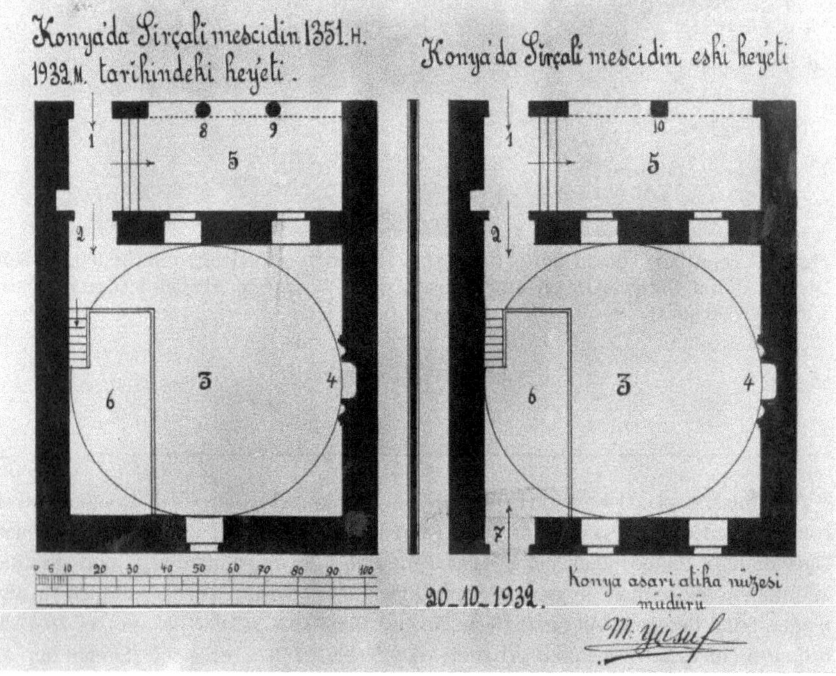

Figure 2.16. Measured drawing of Konya's Sırmalı Masjid, delineated by Mehmet Yusuf Akyurt. SALT Research, Ali Saim Ülgen Archive, TASUH2157.

---

[58] Albert Gabriel, "Türk San'ati ve Sa'nat Tarihindeki Yeri," *Hayat* 40 (1927): 36-37.

Along with the centralized efforts of surveying, provincial administrations began making measured drawings. Yusuf Akyurt, the renowned director of Konya Museum, compiled *Türk Asar-ı Atikası Binalarına ait Tarihi Mecmua* ("Historical Review of Buildings of Turkish Antiquities"), between 1930 and 1946. The volumes included the textual materials, photographs and measured surveys of the Islamic architectural heritage in Konya and its environs (Figure 2.16). In 1953, the General Directorate of Antiquities and Museums purchased the volumes to utilize the measured drawings in the registration of historical properties.[59] Akyurt prepared only one hand-written manuscript of eleven volumes, which is archived in the General Directorate of Museums today, still waiting to be published.

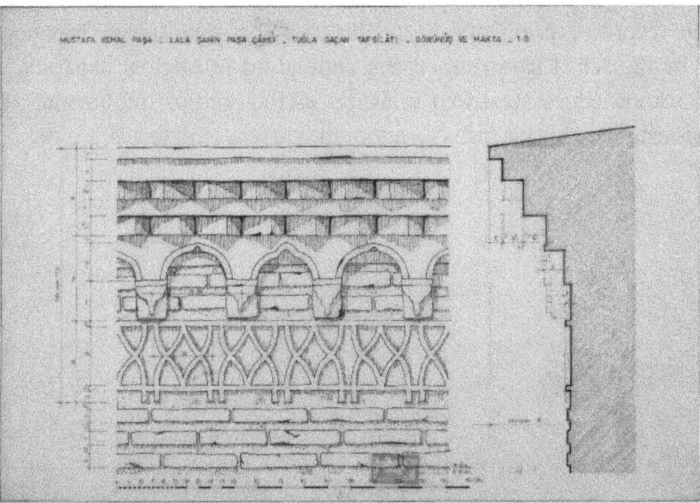

Figure 2.17. Detail drawing from Mustafa Kemal Paşa-Lala Şahin Paşa Tomb, drawn by Ekrem Hakkı Ayverdi, undated. Ekrem Hakkı Ayverdi Institute Archive, Kubbealtı Waqf Collection, Istanbul.

---

[59] T.C. Milli Eğitim Vekaleti, Eski Eserler ve Müzeler Genel Müdürlüğü, "Yusuf Akyurt'un Dairemize Alınmasında Fayda Umulan Eserlerinin Tetkiki için bir Komisyon Kurulması Hakkında," (Letter, SALT Research, Ali Saim Ülgen Archive, TASUDOC0438, July 24 1953). https://archives.saltresearch.org/handle/123456789/78739 (accessed September 20, 2021); T.C. Milli Eğitim Vekaleti, Eski Eserler ve Müzeler Genel Müdürlüğü, "Yusuf Akyurt'un Eserlerinin Tetkiki ve Kıymetlendirilmesi Hakkında," (Letter, SALT Research, Ali Saim Ülgen Archive, TASUDOC0438001, August 1 1953). https://archives.saltresearch.org/handle/123456789/78739 (accessed September 20, 2021).

Ayverdi, a graduate from the Civil School of Engineering and an honorary degree in architecture with a lifelong passion for Ottoman visual culture, extensively contributed to the corpus of architectural documentation (Figure 2.17). Ayverdi published versatile surveys on Istanbul, early Ottoman built environment, calligraphy, and imperial cadastral record books, which still serve as a cornerstone in the historiography of Turkish culture. Ayverdi's *Fatih Devri Mimarisi* (*The Architecture during the era of the Conqueror*, 1953), a catalogue of the architectural patronage of Mehmed II built across the empire, characterizes with his keen interest in capturing qualities of built environment through drafted lines (Figure 2.18). For its book review, Ülgen celebrated the published work as the first achievement of a Turkish scholar addressing such a grand scale survey of historic architecture.[60] Ülgen noted Ayverdi's efforts to embrace measured drawings as a scientific record of historical analysis. For buildings that Ayverdi was not able to survey by himself, Ülgen praised the addendum of original illustrations, "The author acknowledges measured drawings as the core of architectural research, [which is exhibited by] his focus on authentic surveys and details."[61]

Figure 2.18. Section drawing of Üsküdar's Rum Mehmed Pasha Mosque, delineated by Ekrem Hakkı Ayverdi, *Fatih Devri Mimarisi*. İstanbul: İstanbul Fetih Cemiyeti Neşriyatı, 1953.

---

[60] Ülgen, "Ekrem Hakkı Ayverdi Bibliografya Taslağı" (Manuscript, SALT Research, Ali Saim Ülgen Archive, TASUDOCA0113, 1953). https://archives.saltresearch.org/handle/123456789/69129 (accessed September 20, 2021).

[61] Ülgen, "Fatih Devri Mimarisi," (Manuscript, SALT Research, Ali Saim Ülgen Archive, TASUDOCA0155003, 1953). https://archives.saltresearch.org/handle/123456789/89737 (accessed September 20, 2021).

Ayverdi acutely advocated recording monuments in an unbroken narrative along the footprints of the Turkish civilization. He set out to canvass a sizeable region in the Balkan region with the national duty to identify the Turkish architecture in the former provinces of the Ottoman Empire. Due to logistical constraints, Ayverdi was not able to conduct a thorough measured survey at all times. Yet, his field notes culminated in a lasting record for a vanishing architectural legacy (Figure 2.19). In "*Yugoslavya'da Türk Âbideleri ve Vakıfları*" (The Turkish Monuments and Endowments in Yugoslavia, [62] 1956), a compilation of inscriptions, measured drawings, photographs, and written histories, [63] Ayverdi criticized the lack of native and international interest in the preservation of Turkish monuments abroad,

> For now, in Albania, Bulgaria, and Romania, the Turkish monuments are buried in the unknown; nothing much left in Hungary; the systematical destruction of Ottoman traces from the map of Greece equals to scraping. The Turkish architectural heritage in Yugoslavia, nevertheless, has been quite preserved.[64]

Sedad Hakkı Eldem (1908-1988), the renowned architect and scholar, is distinguished in this corpus of documentation work with his investigation of the Turkish house. A proponent of the Central Asian roots of Turkish architecture, Eldem's interest in the codification of building documentation was rooted in his early years at the Academy (1924-1928). There, Eldem had a classical design education reinforced with the Beaux-Arts model, focusing on the drawing methods of the Ottoman and Greco-Roman orders. [65] In these years as a student architect, Eldem embarked on a documentation campaign as a personal pursuit, strolling through the traditional neighborhoods of Istanbul and documenting the human scale embodied in the elements of design.[66] After graduation, between 1928 and 1930, Eldem went to Europe

---

[62] After the dissolution of the Socialist Federal Republic of Yugoslavia in 1992, these countries emerged: Slovenia, Croatia, Bosnia and Herzegovina, Montenegro, Serbia, North Macedonia, and Kosovo.

[63] Ayverdi also published "Dimetoka'da Çelebi Sultan Mehmed Cami'i," *Vakıflar Dergisi* 3 (1956): 13-16. This piece includes the survey of the historic mosque in the border town, Didymoteicho of Greece.

[64] Ayverdi, "Yugoslavya'da Türk Âbideleri ve Vakıfları," *Vakıflar Dergisi* 3 (1956): 151.

[65] Ödekan, *Yazıları ve Rölöveleriyle Sedat Çetintaş* (Istanbul: İTÜ Yayınları, 2004), 55-56.

[66] Engin Yenal and Süha Özkan, *Sedad Eldem ile Söyleşiler*, (İstanbul: Literatür Yayınları, 2014), 38-39.

with a fellowship and worked at diverse architectural offices. Eldem's growing interest in Turkish vernacular architecture was evident in his 1928 exhibition in Paris, where he unveiled his drawings of detached Anatolian houses in countryside settings.[67]

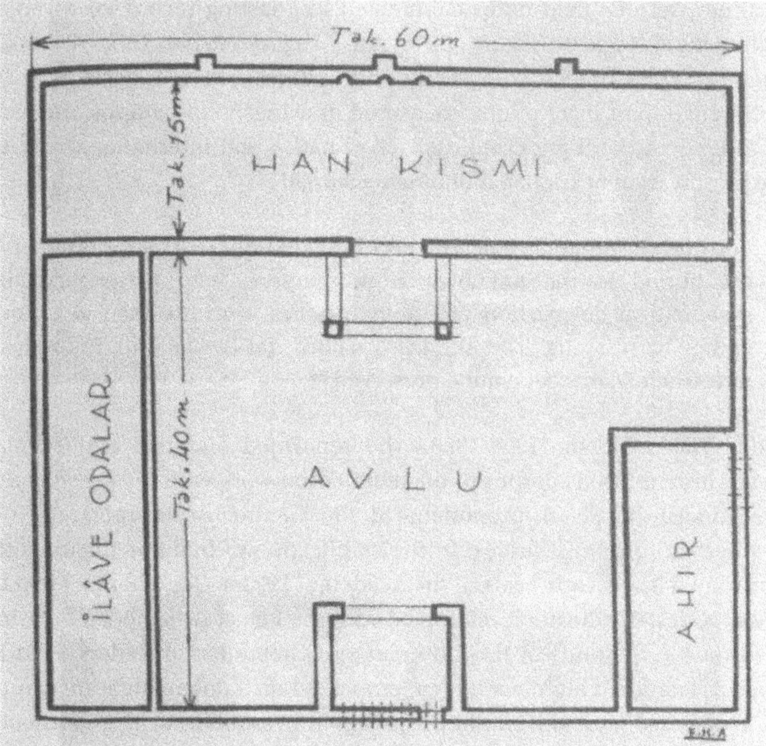

Figure 2.19. A preliminary study of the Ivranya (Vrana) inn near the Adriatic shore, drawn by Ekrem Hakkı Ayverdi. Ekrem Hakkı Ayverdi, "Yugoslavya'da Türk Âbideleri ve Vakıfları," *Vakıflar Dergisi 3*, 1956.

---

[67] Gülsüm Baydar Nalbantoğlu, "Between Civilization and Culture: Appropriation of Traditional Dwelling Forms in Early Republican Turkey," *Journal of Architectural Education* 47, no. 2 (1993): 68. For Nalbantoğlu the interest in framing a rationalist vision of national architecture was manifested in the analysis of vernacular building traditions in the early years of the republic. To envision the Turkish house as compatible with tenets of European modernism, architect-scholars established a narrative of an ahistorical rationalist vision of regional traditions.

Upon his return to Turkey, Eldem's concentration in the documentation of the Turkish house intensified during his appointment at the Academy; where he instilled a culture of measuring and drawing historical works to rationalize the rudiments of design. For his *Millî Mimari Semineri* (National Architecture Seminar), his students prepared measured drawings of houses and mansions across Anatolia (Figure 1.9 and 2.20). Eldem utilized the drawings to define the characteristics of the Turkish house and its geographical diffusion in the former provinces of the Ottoman Empire. Although a major portion of this drawing archive was destroyed during a fire in the Academy in 1948, Eldem's sustained efforts resulted in several volumes of publications including *Bursa Evleri* (Bursa Houses, 1948), *Türk Evi Plan Tipleri* (The Plan Types of the Turkish House, 1954), *Köşkler ve Kasırlar* (A Survey of Kiosks and Pavilions, 1969) and *Türk Mimari Eserleri* (Works of Turkish Architecture, 1975).[68]

Figure 2.20. Restitution analysis of the façade of Siyavuş Pasha Pavilion, delineated by Ali Saim Ülgen, then a student-architect at the Academy, ca. 1935. SALT Research, Ali Saim Ülgen Archive, TASUDOCM0314011.

Suut Kemal Yetkin (1903–1980), a scholar of aesthetics and literature, and a poet, compiled one of the earliest studies of Turkish architecture, in which the

[68] Nur Altınyıldız, "The Architectural Heritage of Istanbul and the Ideology of Preservation," ed. Bozdoğan and Necipoğlu, *Muqarnas* 24 (2007): 294.

tripartite periodization Seljuk–*Beylik*–Ottoman in Anatolia was naturalized in a linear chronological terrain.[69] For Yetkin, the advances of subsequent authoritative Turkish governments utterly correlated to the caliber of architectural forms and structural innovations. Therefore, a morphological analysis of the *Beylik* architecture was integral to defining the inspirational roots of the classical Ottoman architecture.[70] To achieve this rigorous task, Yetkin initiated measured drawings of various mosques built between the fourteenth and sixteenth centuries. For the design innovations cultivated during the *Beylik* period, Yetkin characterized the centralized prayer hall, perimeter walls with windows, transparency between the exterior and interior appearances, integration of an interior courtyard and narthex gallery, purification of monumental portals, and use of marble paneling.[71] These structural elements were carried to the classical architecture of Sinan. For Yetkin, the crowning example of Turkish architecture included Sinan's sixteenth-century Selimiye Mosque in Edirne, for which the imperial architect achieved perfection by advancing the structural innovations devised by the *Beylik* architects, and creating a building type with a centralized domed system.[72]

In *Türk Mimarisi* (Turkish Architecture), Yetkin's taxonomical gaze of Anatolian Turkish architecture coincided with the rise of the disciplinary study of Islamic Art, and a subsequent shift away from speculating about generic Islamic archetypes and analogues. Yetkin noted that to meet certain functions in the faith of Islam, comparable architectural solutions had emerged in the predominantly Muslim geographies. Despite these similarities, each nation had distinct architectural styles due to their national characteristics, customs, and traditions.[73] To locate evidence for the architectural styles of Turks on the migration routes from Central Asia to Anatolia, Yetkin emphasized the Lashkari Bazaar (also named the South Palace or the Grand Palace) built during the Ghaznavid dynasty (977–1186) in present-day Afghanistan. For Yetkin, the Lashkari Bazaar was the archetype of four-*eyvan* plans of Seljuk caravanserais

---

[69] Necipoğlu, "Creation of a National Genius," 174.

[70] Suut Kemal Yetkin, "The Evolution of Architectural Form in Turkish Mosques (1300-1700)," *Studia Islamica* 11 (1959): 73.

[71] Ibid., 73-74.

[72] Ibid., 90.

[73] Yetkin, *Türk Mimarisi* (Ankara: Bilgi Basımevi, 1970), 10-11.

and madrasas, which would then become a trademark of the architecture of Islam (Figure 2.21).[74]

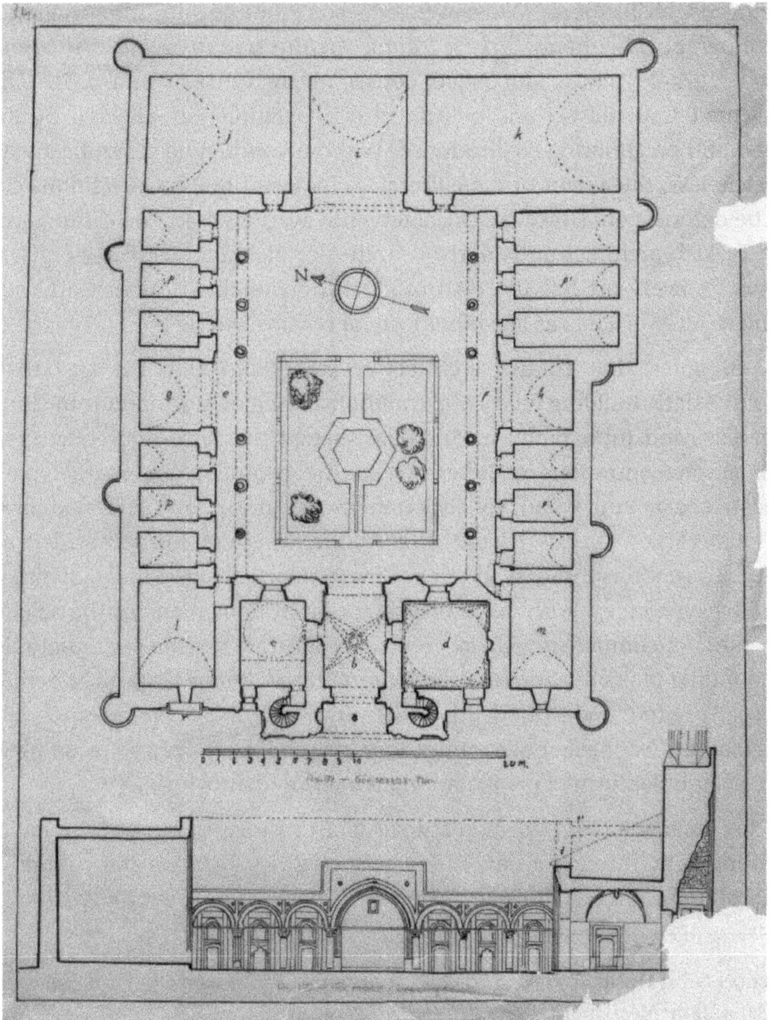

Figure 2.21. The authentic sheet of drawing for the four-*eyvan* plan and section of Sivas' Gök Medrese that Suut Kemal Yetkin had published in *Türk Mimarisi*, delineated by Ali Saim Ülgen, undated. SALT Research, Ali Saim Ülgen Archive, TASUDOC1162011.

[74] Ibid., 19-20.

Behçet Sabri Ünsal (1909-2006), an architect by training was another scholar, who extensively wrote on pre-Ottoman and Ottoman architecture and celebrated the essence of Turkish identity as the basis of an ancient and advanced civilization. A significant contribution to the nationalist historiography, his book *Turkish Islamic Architecture in Seljuk and Ottoman Times, 1071-1923* was published consecutively in 1959 and 1970. Ünsal confirmed that the art and culture of every nation was affected by those earlier and neighboring civilizations.[75] Without conducting scientific analysis, nevertheless, the extent of the cultural exchange of building traditions could not be determined. However, Ünsal fervently warned that, "we cannot accept that Turkish architecture is derived from that of India, Persia, Georgia, and Arabia."[76] Every art has its "own original individuality," Turkish art will be found to be as original as any other form of creative work.[77]

Ünsal noted that Turkish architecture was allied with Far Eastern and Central Asiatic building forms and traditions.[78] Regional variations of climate, materials, and topography in Anatolia, shaped the form and construction, such as concentrations of limestone in the central plain, marble on the Aegean coast, and wood construction in the north.[79] [80] His taxonomical analysis marked *Turkish Islamic Architecture*, where he located evidence for regional variations through an intense morphological comparison of different building typologies. With an academic focus on floor-plans as the scientific apparatus of comparison, Ünsal created an abstract and inspirational role of the building plans to showcase the materiality of the national architecture of Turks. To better understand the authenticity of Turkish architecture, Ünsal concluded, "we have been obliged to confine ourselves to a somewhat artificial tabular form of presentation [of measured drawings]."[81]

Oktay Aslanapa (1914-2013), a scholar of art history, sharpened the national historiography through a pan-Turkic gaze, with its focus on the cultural and political unification of all Turkic peoples. His book, *Turkish Art and Architecture*

---

[75] Behçet Sabri Ünsal, *Turkish Islamic Architecture in Seljuk and Ottoman Times, 1071-1923* (London: Alec Tiranti, 1970), 10.

[76] Ibid., 89.

[77] Ibid., 91.

[78] Ibid.

[79] Bozdoğan, "Reading Ottoman Architecture Through Modernist Lenses," 210; Also, see, Ünsal, *Turkish Islamic Architecture*, 8-9, 36.

[80] Ünsal, *Turkish Islamic Architecture*, 78.

[81] Ibid., 91.

(1971), included a broader Islamic geography incorporating other "Turkish" dynasties in Central Asia.[82] Aslanapa explained his aim, "to examine, from various points of view, the links connecting monuments of arts and architecture created in widely separated areas, and to reveal by means of plans and diagrams the unity and continuity of Turkish art."[83] His narrative expanded to include the art and architecture of all manner of Turkic societies, from India to Egypt, as a link in a long chain of national artistic expression.[84] Aslanapa's, *Turkish Art and Architecture,* constituted a reference book enriched with photographs from his own collection, while incorporating measured drawings from previously published volumes by Ayverdi, Çetintaş, Gabriel, and Ülgen.[85]

The ideological focus on Anatolia as the homeland of Turks marked these surveys of Ottoman architecture. The exodus to Anatolia cultivated an academic focus on the Central Asian roots of national architecture, for which authors brought forward slightly nuanced appraisals for the migrated building forms from the east to the west. The same authors, to a large extent, left out the architecture located to the west of Edirne, the former Balkan provinces that had been under the Ottoman domination since the medieval ages. The absence of Ottoman architecture in the Balkans is evident in Ünsal's standard *Turkish Islamic Architecture in Seljuk and Ottoman Times,* where the author did not include the architectural production in the Balkan provinces. Likewise, Balkan architecture did not find an academic niche in Aslanapa's *Turkish Art and Architecture* or Yetkin's *Türk Mimarisi.* Together, the authors put aside the centuries-long building traditions of Ottoman architecture in the Balkan lands, in favor of a morphological and typological analysis between Central Asian and Anatolian forms.

Ayverdi's efforts to document the Ottoman architecture in the Balkans was significantly different among these architectural surveys. On par with the theories of peer authors, Ayverdi supported the Central Asian roots of the Turkish nation and Anatolia as the homeland of Turks. Ayverdi, nevertheless, diverged with his emphasis on Turkish civilization, which had geographically spanned to Europe

---

[82] To Ünsal, those dynasties were Ghaznavid, Great Seljuk, Karakhanid, Mamluk, Tulunid, and Zengid.

[83] Oktay Aslanapa, *Turkish Art and Architecture,* (London: Praeger, 1971), 29.

[84] Scott Redford, "'What Have You Done for Anatolia Today?': Islamic Archaeology in the Early Years of the Turkish Republic," ed. Bozdoğan and Necipoğlu, *Muqarnas* 24 (2007):249.

[85] Aslanapa, *Turkish Art and Architecture,* 21-23 and 29.

with the domination of the Ottoman Empire. Therefore, for Ayverdi, the building forms created under the Ottoman reign in the Balkans exhibited the creativity of the Turkish nation. In retrospect, Ayverdi's four-volume monograph, *Avrupa'da Osmanlı Mimari Eserleri* (The Ottoman Architectural Works of Art in Europe),[86] published between 1979-1983, exhibits his zealous dedication to document and analyze the architectural works in the Balkans within the historiography of Ottoman architecture.

In this light, Eldem's archival documentation on the Turkish house had a dual nature when it came to his assessment of the building, both as a local and a global architectural type. Eldem concentrated on a formal analysis of the vernacular heritage within the modern borders of Turkey. A closer look at his publications, however, reveals a duality when assigning the universal values to the local Turkish house. For Eldem, the form of the Turkish house was a result of a centuries-long interaction between the territories of Asia and Europe under the Ottoman rule. The form of the house had crossed frontiers and had expanded to further geographical regions. After the dissolution of the Ottoman Empire, nevertheless, the former Balkan provinces manifested their cultural link to the empire through accepting, absorbing, or identifying themselves with their Ottoman heritage.[87] To locate the place of the Turkish house in the former Ottoman provinces, especially in the Balkans, and to probe its evolution, Eldem continuously consulted a network of scholars from Pakistan to Serbia, Tunis, and Leningrad to exchange information on vernacular architecture in their respective countries. These letters reveal that Eldem did not limit his quest to the search for a national identity of architecture, but also aimed to redefine the geographical boundaries of the Turkish house, and its possible variations in different climates.[88]

---

[86] Ayverdi and Aydın Yüksel, *Avrupa'da Osmanlı Mîmârî Eserleri, Romanya, Macaristan,* vol. I (İstanbul: İstanbul Fetih Cemiyeti, 1977); Ayverdi, Yüksel, Gürbüz Ertürk, and İbrahim Numan, *Avrupa'da Osmanlı Mîmârî Eserleri, Yugoslavya,* vol. II, (İstanbul: İstanbul Fetih Cemiyeti, 1981); Ayverdi, Yüksel, Ertürk, and Numan, *Avrupa'da Osmanlı Mîmârî Eserleri, Yugoslavya,* vol. III, (İstanbul: İstanbul Fetih Cemiyeti, 1981); Ayverdi, Yüksel, Ertürk, and Numan, *Avrupa'da Osmanlı Mîmârî Eserleri, Bulgaristan, Yunanistan, Arnavutluk,* vol. IV, (İstanbul: İstanbul Fetih Cemiyeti, 1982).

[87] Sedad Hakkı Eldem, *Türk Evi: Osmanlı Dönemi = Turkish Houses: Ottoman Period,* vol. 1 (İstanbul: Türkiye Anıt Çevre Turizm Değerlerini Koruma Vakfı, 1984), 21.

[88] Serena Acciai, "The Ottoman-Turkish House According to Architect Sedad Hakkı Eldem: A Refined Domestic Culture Suspended Between Europe and Asia," *ABE Journal* 11 (2017): 14-16.

Similarly, Eldem's emphasis on the totality of anonymous residential buildings, the Turkish house, was characterized by the appropriation of the multi-cultural Ottoman built environment with the nationalist sentiments of the Republic of Turkey. These houses, ranging from mansions of wealthy families to rudimentary dwellings of modest villagers, belonged to a wide circle of ethnic and religious groups including Alevis, Arabs, Armenians, Greeks, Jews, Kurds, and the like. While Eldem's formal interest in the vernacular heritage raised awareness of the recognition and protection of houses, his assimilation of the cultural diversity under the name "Turkish" removed the more cosmopolitan character of the imperial past.[89]

Institutionalizing documentation as a tenet of historic preservation

Çetintaş noted that, to a large extent, the commitment of the republican leaders' shifted the practice of architectural documentation in the early days, since making drawings of the monuments became to be seen as a national duty. Çetintaş, himself, driven by the scientific and national concerns, presented his measured drawings to Atatürk.[90] In 1932, with the mediation of Yunus Nadi Abalıoğlu (1879-1945) the owner of the *Cumhuriyet* (Republic) newspaper, Çetintaş had an opportunity to meet Atatürk and to share his work on the Sokollu Mehmet Pasha Mosque in Kadırga.[91] Promptly, the progressive leader recognized the merit of Çetintaş's draftsmanship and requested Çetintaş to devise a timeline for making measured drawings of all monuments in Turkey, along with an estimated budget for repairs and restoration treatments. In the same year, Atatürk commissioned Çetintaş to produce the measured drawings of the sixteenth-century Şehzade Mosque, in Istanbul for the 1933 Chicago World's Fair, Century of Progress (Figure 2.22).[92] Çetintaş rented a two-bedroom apartment next to the historic mosque and prepared twelve plates of measured drawings within six months.[93]

---

[89] Bozdoğan and Akcan, *Turkey: Modern Architectures in History*, 99.

[90] Çetintaş, *Türk Mimari Anıtları*, 5.

[91] Ödekan, *Yazıları ve Rölöveleriyle*, 90.

[92] Çetintaş, *Türk Mimari Anıtları*, 6.

[93] Ödekan, *Yazıları ve Rölöveleriyle*, 91.

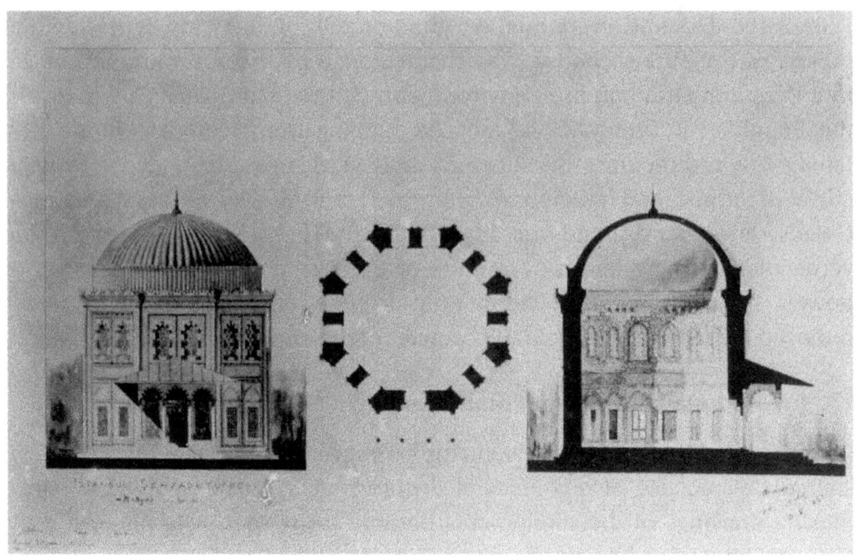

Figure 2.22. Photograph of the measured drawing sheet of the Tomb of Şehzade Mehmet, delineated by Sedat Çetintaş, May 5 1933. SALT Research, Ali Saim Ülgen Archive, TASUH0890.

The weight of measured drawings as a scientific tool for the protection of monuments can be felt through the architectural texts written at the time. In "*Tarihi Anıtların Korunması ve Onarılmasına ait Prensipler*" ("Principles of Preservation and Maintenance of Historic Monuments"), Ülgen describes measured drawings as *mimari tavsif* (architectural portraiture) of a building.[94] The flow of information in these graphic illustrations would be fundamental to safeguard the authentic qualities of historic properties. In his tenure at the *Office of Monuments,* Ülgen vehemently advocated for the methodical documentation of the built heritage and pursued state funds to implement a rigorous scientific program of architectural surveying nationwide. Significantly, in 1956 Ülgen petitioned the General Directorate Antiquities and Museums, to authorize the documentation of the entire body of museum buildings and monuments under

---

[94] Ali Saim Ülgen, "Tarihi Anıtların Korunması ve Onarılmasına ait Prensipler," (Manuscript, SALT Research, Ali Saim Ülgen Archive, TASUDOCA0224, date unknown). https://archives.saltresearch.org/handle/123456789/69124 (accessed September 20, 2021).

their stewardship.[95] Considering his demanding work-load as a restoration-architect and his teaching responsibilities at Ankara University, Ülgen's notable request indicates the significant role of architectural documentation to create a lasting record of the built environment.

Translated into the practice of historic preservation, without a question, measured drawings were seen as essential mediums of communication and representation. In fact, Hamit Kemali Söylemezoğlu's 1944-dated postcard to Ülgen exhibits the central role of architectural documentation in the practice. When Söylemezoğlu (1909-1965), an architect and academician, came across the run-down Aydınoğulları İsa Bey Mosque during his travels to İzmir in western Anatolia, he promptly wrote to Ülgen asking if the historic structure had been surveyed and a thorough measured drawing set had been compiled. Söylemezoğlu enthusiastically inscribed the postcard, "How nice it would be to see the mosque repaired and restored." [96]

Copious contracts and reports of surveying tasks created at state-agencies exhibit the growing professionalization of a specialized practice of architectural documentation. For the 1956-dated repairs of the portal of the Bursa Great Mosque, for instance, the measured drawings were to be drafted with a 1:5 scale. Concurrently, the exact deterioration patterns and their dimensions had to be replicated on the drawings, all annotated with construction estimates for repairs.[97] The 1959-dated bidding contract for the documentation of the Divriği Great Mosque and Hospital shows the official emphasis on the caliber of measured drawings. After enlisting a strict job order, the state agency limited the applications to only experienced surveyors, firmly stating any measured drawings put together by an incompetent drafter would be rejected right away without further review. [98]

---

[95] Ülgen, "Maarif Vekaletine" (Letter, SALT Research, Ali Saim Ülgen Archive, TASUDOC043 8040, July 9 1956).https://archives.saltresearch.org/handle/123456789/78739 (accessed September 20, 2021).

[96] Hamit Kemali Söylemezoğlu, "Sevgili Kardeşim," (Postcard, SALT Research, Ali Saim Ülgen Archive, TASUDOC0281045, April 2 1944). https://archives.saltresearch.org/handle/123456789/77682 (accessed September 20, 2021).

[97] GEEAYK, "Karar," (Memorandum, SALT Research, Ali Saim Ülgen Archive, TASUDOC0437040-41, August 3 1956). https://archives.saltresearch.org/handle/123456 789/70246 (accessed September 20, 2021).

[98] In 1963, the previous surveying regulation of 1959 was still in use; the selected contractor would be awarded 80,000TL. Anonymous, "Sivas Divriği Ulu Cami 1959 Yılı Onarımına ait Rölöve Şartnamesi," (Memorandum, SALT Research, Ali Saim Ülgen Archive, TASUDOC0709054, TASUDOC0437, and TASUDOC1407, March 7 1963).

The establishment of the Surveying Bureau at the General Directorate of the Antiquities and Museums in 1936 and the materialization of in-house surveying offices at *Vakıflar Genel Müdürlüğü* (General Directorate of Endowments) in 1952 and 1961 highlights the prominence of measured surveys to inform physical interventions. To meet the procedural needs of repairs, in 1952, an Istanbul surveying office, and in 1961, a central branch in Ankara were established within the General Directorate of Endowments.[99] Signed by Cahide Aksel Tamer (1915-2005), a restoration-architect and a leading historic preservation advocate, miscellaneous project memorandums pertaining to the fiscal year of 1959 exemplify the nature of surveying fieldwork. Amid the repairs of Istanbul's Topkapı Kara Ahmed Pasha Mosque, Tamer, for example, requested the surveying office to prepare detailed measured drawings of the ablution fountain before the contractor could proceed with the restoration.[100] Likewise, Tamer requested the documentation of the portico of the elementary school in the mosque complex of Sultan Selim, as the basis of information for the physical treatments. In addition to these, Tamer assigned individual surveying tasks for Edirnekapı Mihrümah Sultan Mosque, Bali Pasha Mosque, and Şah Huban Hatun Tomb and School to the surveying office in the same fiscal year.[101]

---

https://archives.saltresearch.org/handle/123456789/70246 (accessed September 20, 2021).

[99] Tuba Akar, "Vakıflar Genel Müdürlüğü ve Vakıf Kültür Varlıklarının Korunması," Erdem 59 (2011): 26. Akar, "The Role of Vakıf Institution in the Conservation of Vakıf based Cultural Heritage," (PhD diss., Middle East Technical University, 2009), 83.

[100] One of Sinan's designs, Kara Ahmed Pasha Mosque became a heated discussion at the intersection of Turkish nationalism and formalism, see, Akboy-Ilk, "Building the Architectural Narrative of the Topkapı Kara Ahmed Pasha Mosque Complex in Early Republican Turkey," YILLIK: Annual of Istanbul Studies 2 (2020): 81–102.

[101] Ülgen, "Sultan Selim Camii 1959 Yılı Onarımı Hakkında," (Memorandum, SALT Research, Ali Saim Ülgen Archive, TASUDOC0481111, October 27 1959). https://archives.saltresearch.org/handle/123456789/85567 (accessed September 20, 2021); Cahide Tamer, "Abide ve Yapı İşleri Şubesine," (Memorandum, SALT Research, Ali Saim Ülgen Archive, TASUDOC0481112, October 1 1959). https://archives.saltresearch.org/handle/123456789/85567 (accessed September 20, 2021); Ülgen, "Topkapı Ahmed Paşa Camii 1959 Yılı Onarımı Hakkında," (Memorandum, SALT Research, Ali Saim Ülgen Archive, TASUDOC0481113, November 4 1959). https://archives.saltresearch.org/handle/123456789/85567 (accessed September 20, 2021); Tamer, "Abide ve Yapı İşleri Şubesine," (Memorandum, SALT Research, Ali Saim Ülgen Archive, TASUDOC0481114, October 1 1959). https://archives.saltresearch.org/handle/123456789/85567 (accessed September 20, 2021); Ülgen, "Rölöve Yapılmak İstenilen Onarımlar Hakkında," (Memorandum,

1959-dated memorandum to hire seven surveyors for the Istanbul surveying office of the General Directorate of Endowments exhibits the rising demand in architectural surveys. To gauge the level of draftsmanship and the expertise with technological tools, the applicants would go through a two-step examination. First, the search committee including Ülgen (the chair), Cahide Tamer, Ertuğrul Eğilmez, Hasan Rıza Ergezen, and Burhanettin Tansun would interview the candidate. Second, to be completed within eight hours, the applicant would measure and draw one of the assigned tombs for the Ambassador to Berlin Ahmed Tevfik Pasha, Governor of Egypt Halim Pasha, Calligrapher Osman Zeki, Captain Osman, Grand Vizier Said Pasha, and Ziya Gökalp. Due to the anticipated high number of applicants, the state agency warned the committee members to keep an open agenda for re-scheduling of interviews and field examination sessions.[102]

Despite the growing professional interest in architectural documentation, the end-of-the-fiscal year report of 1962, written by Ülgen, presents the other side of the coin. Ülgen firmly stated that the repairs and the physical interventions conducted within the General Directorate of Endowments did not culminate in the desired results. Ülgen enlisted the diminishing state funds as the major cause. To

---

SALT Research, Ali Saim Ülgen Archive, TASUDOC0481115, October 27 1959). https://archives.saltresearch.org/handle/123456789/85567 (accessed September 20, 2021); Şevket Özden, "Rapor, 11. Gurup Şefliğine," (Memorandum, SALT Research, Ali Saim Ülgen Archive, TASUDOC0481116, October 7 1959). https://archives.saltresearch.org/handle/123456789/85567 (accessed September 20, 2021).

[102] Vakıflar Umum Müdürü, "Vakıflar Baş Müdürlüğüne, İstanbul," (Memorandum, SALT Research, Ali Saim Ülgen Archive, TASUDOC0481121, October 26 1959). https://archives.saltresearch.org/handle/123456789/85567 (accessed September 20, 2021); Vakıflar Umum Müdürü, "(2)," (Memorandum, SALT Research, Ali Saim Ülgen Archive, TASUDOC0481122, unknown date).
https://archives.saltresearch.org/handle/123456789/85567 (accessed September 20, 2021); Vakıflar Umum Müdürü, "Vakıflar Baş Müdürlüğüne, İstanbul," (Memorandum, SALT Research, Ali Saim Ülgen Archive, TASUDOC0481123, October 26 1959). https://archives.saltresearch.org/handle/123456789/85567 (accessed September 20, 2021); General Manager, Vakıflar Umum Müdürü, "Vakıflar Baş Müdürlüğüne, Istanbul," (Memorandum, SALT Research, Ali Saim Ülgen Archive, TASUDOC0481124, unknown date). https://archives.saltresearch.org/handle/123456789/85567 (accessed September 20, 2021); Vakıflar Umum Müdürü, "Vakıflar Baş Müdürlüğüne, İstanbul," (Memorandum, SALT Research, Ali Saim Ülgen Archive, TASUDOC0481125, unknown date, Examination Topics). https://archives.saltresearch.org/handle/123456789/85567 (accessed September 20, 2021)

generate lean project budgets the general directorate was purging the travel expenses of the surveying fieldwork. Coupled with the understaffed surveying offices and the shortage of architects assigned to the headquarters in Ankara, the most significant part of a restoration project, the architectural documentation, could not be realized. Without the scientific records of documentation to guide the historic preservation treatments, the efforts to maintain the historic properties were to no avail. Ülgen firmly stated that the monuments were already vanishing at a dizzying pace and they should never be sacrificed to budget contingencies. He petitioned to seek financial measures to resume the surveying campaigns.[103]

Besides the state agencies, the establishment of *Gayrimenkul Eski Eserler ve Anıtlar Yüksek Kurulu* (Supreme Council of Immovable Antiquities and Monuments, GEEAYK) in 1951, the first legal institution in republican Turkey to regulate the practice of historic preservation as an autonomous entity outside the institution of the state, enhanced documentation efforts. The independent Supreme Council consisted of lifelong members working at universities and state-agencies who were predominantly academic and bureaucratic authorities. Some of the members included, Arseven, Söylemezoğlu, Ülgen, Ünsal, Ekrem Akurgal, Mithat Yenen, Orhan Alsaç, Orhan Çapçı, Tahsin Öz, and Zeki Faik İzer. The members' reception and reasoning for the preservation rationale acted as a mechanism of review and judgement.[104] Significantly, GEEAYK expanded the protection efforts for monuments to vernacular architecture and landscapes. Hence, many historic buildings and structures that were not deemed a "masterpiece" were able to be documented and protected.[105]

Compiling a scientific review of built works

Archival building documentation, intrinsically, became a by-product of the theory and practice of historic preservation. Preservation professionals frequently authored formal texts about the historic properties that they were already working on. They published their field notes pertaining to architectural heritage at risk, or on monuments that were becoming

[103] Ülgen, "Vakıflar Genel Müdürlüğü Abide ve Yapı İşleri Dairesi Reisliğine," (Report, SALT Research, Ali Saim Ülgen Archive, TASUDOC0437035, unknown date). https://archives.saltresearch.org/handle/123456789/70246 (accessed September 20, 2021)

[104] Madran, "Cumhuriyet'in ilk Otuz Yılında (1920-1950) Koruma Alanının Örgütlenmesi-II," in ODTU MFD 17, no.1-2 (1997): 77.

[105] In 1983, GEEAYK was replaced with Kültür ve Tabiat Varlıklarını Koruma Kurulu (Conservation Council of Cultural and Natural Properties).

vulnerable. In these publications, however, authors were mainly concerned with the perception of architectural forms in a purely conceptual space. Construed as a scientific methodology, measured and drawn lines allowed the aesthetic attitude to accompany formalist representation of architecture.

Concerning formalism, the study of art has to focus on its form, the way it is made and what it looks like. In this representational matrix, works of art tend to omit political or social comments. Imagery, often abstracted or distorted, becomes subordinate to composition. Instead, the harmony of visual elements becomes the form of art. [106] Borrowed from formalist art theory, republican authors conceived works of historic architecture as spontaneous, internalized (outside circumstantial reality), and an assimilable pure idea. Translated into archival building information, measured drawings included the scientific apparatus to reflect on historic building forms that are both balanced and aesthetically pleasing within the unity of an image. The abstraction of forms with measured and drawn lines became integral to deliver explanations between different parts of architectural works, although the subject properties were distributed in a large chronological and geographical terrain. The depicted pure forms of architecture, were self-explanatory, regardless of cultural symbolism or social purpose.

A formalist review probes the purely visual aspects of the work and the architects' ability to accomplish order and balance in the composition. In this respect, in his book review for Yetkin's *Türk Mimarisi,* the French scholar Gabriel celebrated its author's formalist comparative approach. Gabriel praised Yetkin's thorough analysis of plan types and basic forms, which clearly exhibited the linear and self-contained artistic development of Turks. Although Yetkin was not trained as an architect, Gabriel acknowledged the Turkish scholar's distinguished scientific gaze, pertaining to the discovery of meanings in architecture independent from the contingencies of place and time, "The author directly engages with the building and does not occupy

---

[106] Roots of formalism can be traced to nineteenth-century, "when artists began to make works of art that shied away from political or social comments. Modern artists were concerned with the harmony of visual elements as a form of art. Called "Formalists" or "Modernists," these artists prioritized the autonomy of an art object. Concurrently, they highlighted the processes of art, for instance, application of paint, arrangement of shapes and selection of colors. Sally Everett, *Art Theory and Criticism: An Anthology of Formalist, Avant-Garde, Contextualist and Post-Modernist Thought* (Jefferson, NC: McFarland & Company, Inc., 1991), ix–x. Also, see, Serra Akboy-İlk, "Measured drawing: A Nationalist Reaction in Early Republican Turkey," *Drawing: Research, Theory, Practice* 5, no. 2 (2020): 374-375.

with the intentions of the builder at all. The first [condition] to evaluate a structure is to understand the meaning [embodied in the edifice]. Suut Kemal Yetkin manifests his mastery in understanding [architecture] in numerous examples of [analysis]." [107]

On the basis of scientific documentation, a strict hierarchy of building typologies (mosques, followed by madrasas, tombs, and public architecture) and their morphological configurations (e.g. building plan, courtyard, dome, fenestration, portal) dominated the published measured surveys. In its blanket application to a larger chronological and geographical terrain from Central Asian steps to Anatolia, the morphological and typological comparisons of building types echoed the scientific explanation to declare the qualities of national architecture. In *Türk Mimarisi,* Yetkin's formalist investigation of fragmented floor plans of dynastic architecture (e.g. Ghaznavids, Seljuks, Timurids, Mamluks, Indians, *Beyliks,* and Ottomans), in the vast scale of Islamic art schools from tenth-century to nineteenth-century came as no surprise. Although the historical context is not entirely ignored in *Türk Mimarisi,* Yetkin relegated historical anecdotes to the categorization of individual buildings and their structural units, utterly disconnected from the discussion of built works.

What has been determined as scientific documentation to understand historic architecture, however, was context-independent and a historically fabricated interpretation of architectural heritage. History hardly played any role in archival building documentation. Neither the cultural milieu of the architectural patronage, nor the ethnic diversity of users, their social status, customs, or lifestyles were deemed significant. Thousands of historic properties, from public fountains to mosques were diligently surveyed, then evaluated under the gaze of a modern professional to serve as objects of formal analysis to be classified and labelled (Figure 2.23).[108] Through this dense and tremendously influential analysis, historic properties were weighed by "universal" ideals of beauty and aesthetics, framed in terms of major and minor periods of art, and judged for their conformance to the ideal.

---

[107] Gabriel, "Türkiye'de Türk Mimarisi," trans. A. Fırtınalı, *Ankara Üniversitesi İlahiyat Fakültesi Dergisi* (1963): 1.

[108] Baydar Nalbantoğlu, "Between Civilization and Culture," 66-74.

Figure 2.23. Measured survey for Sivas' Güdük Minare, delineated by Ali Saim Ülgen, undated. SALT Research, Ali Saim Ülgen Archive, TASUDOC1073026.

Although republican authors agreed in their understanding of national character of Turkish architecture through formalist measured surveys, they had nuances when it came to historical analysis. For example, Ayverdi's interest in the methodic documentation of national architecture was rooted in the outright hostility against Ottoman culture,[109] "...Someone would come out and declare, 'The Ottoman period was the darkest assault for Turks.' At that, ..., a red flag should immediately rise. Because it is impossible to consider the Ottoman period, established by Turks, as said; Ottomans could be strict invaders, yet the Muslim-Turks, who formed the state, embodied

[109] Ayverdi, "Büyük Emanet," *Makaleler* (İstanbul: İstanbul Fetih Cemiyeti, 1985), 407-408.

wisdom, morals, character, and faith… The works of literature, calligraphy, music, and architecture constitute the material evidence of the Turkish style."[110] Set to defy the systemized mistreatment of Ottoman monuments and spiritual belongings in the dizzying pace of revolutionary modernization in the early republic, Ayverdi wrote "the music, language, literature, style, faith and belief of the nation have been severely disrupted, all their sacred affinities from their mosques to their houses have been scorned. Then, the massacre of the monuments and sanctity began." [111] To uphold a vanishing imperial legacy, Ayverdi attributed the Ottoman visual culture as a unified whole, to which he owed his lifelong passion for collecting, documenting, restoring, and writing.

Ayverdi's mission of architectural documentation aimed to counter the misjudged and underappreciated qualities of Ottoman architecture. Ayverdi stressed that there were minimal studies of Ottoman architecture about societal mentalities and major concepts that brought forward built works, of form, proportion, volume, harmony, and of unity with decoration. Instead, a limited review on the technical elements and construction had lingered. To Ayverdi, particularly, the built environment cultivated in the early beginnings of the Ottoman Empire, had suffered from this mono-lateral reading. These architectural reviews, to a large extent, revolved around the built environment of the former imperial capital Bursa, the use of Roman and Byzantine spolia materials in new construction and the pedigree of alternating brick and stone walls in Ottoman buildings.[112] To expand the knowledge on national building forms, Ayverdi turned to measured drawings as a scientific account of the built environment, "without documents and evidence, certainly one cannot refute the old allegations [of the Byzantine roots of Ottoman architecture] and such an unsubstantiated act would damage [the understanding of architecture].[113]

In contrast, Eldem's interest in architectural documentation echoed the idea that the Turkish house had been essentially modern. From the turn of the twentieth century and until the 1980s, modern design dominated the practice

---

110 Ibid., 362-363.

111 Ibid., 407.

112 Ayverdi, "Bursa Orhan Gazi Camii ve Osmanlı Mimarisinin Menşei Meselesi," *Vakıflar Dergisi* 6 (1965): 69.

113 Ayverdi, "İlimde Millî Basîretin Ehemmiyeti," *Makaleler* (İstanbul: İstanbul Fetih Cemiyeti, 1985), 367.

of architecture with an emphasis on functionalism, minimalism, along with the use of state-of-the-art materials and construction technologies. In support of the "inherent modernity" of traditional, timber-frame Turkish houses, Eldem epitomized studying the built heritage by making drawings of historical precedents. With the students of the National Architecture Seminar at the Academy, Eldem undertook an extensive documentation campaign to record the vernacular architecture in Istanbul as well as in the provincial towns of Anatolia. By doing so, the students enrolled in the seminar could transcribe the authentic form, proportion, and construction elements of the Turkish house to new design.[114]

Despite peer scholars' preoccupation with the Turkishness of the built environment, Eldem was not so interested in the symbolic genealogy of the elements of the Turkish house. Instead, Eldem strived to create a genuine modern architecture inspired by Turkish national traditions. Eldem esteemed the folk wisdom of traditional constructions, as he recognized these assemblies to have a simplicity and rationality reflected in a series of modern elements.[115] These features comprised of the floor plan, lightness, transparency and ventilation, sensitivity to the site, and relationship to nature.[116] As such, Eldem's publications of archival building documentation exhibit his primary focus to analyze the traditional plan types and constructional systems in order to abstract transhistorical and transregional architectural types.[117] In *Türk Evi*, Eldem stipulated a typological matrix of floor plans on the basis of the *sofa* (hall). Cataloguing the configuration, location, and shape of the halls in residential architecture across Turkey, Eldem concluded that a rudimentary rural house was no different than an imperial palace in Istanbul. In terms of

---

114 Eldem, "Önsöz," *Rölöve I: İstanbul Boğaziçi Köyleri Yerleşmesi, Resmî ve Kültürel Taş Binalar, İstanbul ve Anadolu Evleri, Çeşmeler ve Selsebiller*, ed. Eldem, Feridun Akozan, and Köksal Anadol (İstanbul: Millî Eğitim Basımevi, 1968), 5-6.

115 Carel Bertram, *Imagining the Turkish House: Collective Visions of Home* (Austin: University of Texas Press, 2008), 208-209.

116 Tchavdar Marinov, "The 'Balkan House': Interpretations and Symbolic Appropriations of the Ottoman-Era Vernacular Architecture in the Balkans," *Entangled Histories of the Balkans*, vol. 4, Concepts, Approaches, and (Self-)Representations, ed. Roumen Daskalov, Marinov, Diana Mishkova, and Alexander Vezenkov (Leiden & Boston: Brill, 2017), 582.

117 Bozdoğan, "The Legacy of an Istanbul Architect: Type, Context and Urban Identity in the Work of Sedad Eldem," *Modern Architecture and the Mediterranean: Vernacular Dialogues and Contested Identities*, ed. Jean-François Lejeune and Michelangelo Sabatino (London: Routledge, 2010), 131.

their floor-plans, both forms were a result of the modular arrangement of the rooms around the hall. Given this, Eldem assigned priority to floor plans over decoration, which secured the continuation of the essence of the Turkish house regardless of its style or its scale.[118]

Despite Eldem's focus on the hall as the core of the Turkish house, the vernacular heritage in Anatolia differed significantly. In the southwest of Anatolia existed stone dwellings associated with the Aegean Greek architectural heritage. In the central, south and southeastern Anatolia, there were stone-built dwellings along with houses built of sundried bricks. Along the mountainous regions wooden-log houses were common. Eldem identified the geographical borders of the Turkish house, "[In eastern and southern Anatolia] the Turkish house could not expand beyond Anatolia. On one side, the Persian influence stretched to the Caucasus, Iraqi Arabia, on the other side, the Arabic house in Syria created a natural border to the region of the Turkish house. Beyond this border, only the localization and the infiltration of the Turkish house can be observed… The influence of the Turkish house on the Aegean islands, although the islands were inhabited by the Turks, was limited to certain construction features and decorative motifs."[119] In this quest, Eldem focused on the Ottoman timber-framed dwellings in a defining moment of Turkish national architecture. These timber and infill houses were common in the north and the west Anatolia, along with the former Ottoman provinces in the Balkans.

Nevertheless, one can ask why Eldem chose the timber-framed Ottoman houses as the essence of Turkish architecture and led a diligent formal analysis of its constituents. Laden with nationalist and Modernist motives, his quest can be explained by the historic moment in which he lived and worked. Eldem's highly academic transaction was partly due to the early republican presentation of the Turkish architectural heritage as inherently western and modern. In this regard, any relationship to Arabian and Persian architectural heritage was deemed "irrational" and "backward." On the margins of Europe, Eldem positioned the boundary of the "Oriental" eastwards and focused on the timber constructions that were widely available in Anatolian centers that were socially and culturally closer to Europe. Eldem's preference of the timber

---

118 Eldem, *Türk Evi, Osmanlı Dönemi = Turkish Houses, Ottoman Period*: 3 vols (İstanbul: Türkiye Anıt Çevre Turizm Değerlerini Koruma Vakfı, 1984–1987); Bozdoğan, "The Legacy of an Istanbul Architect," 134.

119 Eldem, *Türk Evi Plan Tipleri* (İstanbul: İstanbul Teknik Üniversitesi, 1954), 11.

frame, was also due to his projection of the contemporary architectural features in the traditional Turkish house. For Eldem, this particular architectural type carried similar features to the concept of a modern house. Utilization of ample windows, lightness, transparency, flexible floor-plan, and modular units in traditional forms lent themselves to a skeleton construction, which was the structural basis of the Modern Movement in design[120] executed through glass, steel, and reinforced concrete.[121]

Eldem's sustained efforts for architectural documentation and his teaching at the National Architecture Seminar cultivated a generation of architects with a quest of documentation as an analysis and learning tool. For example, a student of the seminar, Ülgen prepared measured drawings for the Köprülü Mansion (*Köprülü Konağı*) in Vezirköprü, Samsun, the Şemaki House (*Şemaki Evi*) in Yenişehir, Bursa and the Siyavuş Pasha Pavilion, in Bakırköy, Istanbul (Figure 2.20). From his early years at the Academy, Ülgen read Turkish architecture as a timeless source of the national identity and focused on the epistemological grounds of the Turkish architecture within other building traditions. Ülgen epitomized building documentation as a means of

---

120 Modern Movement, came to be called as "International style," and dominated the architectural production in Turkey from the 1930s and onwards. Coined as *Yeni Mimari* (New Architecture) in Turkey, also known as "cubic style", the international style became prevalent in the early republican architectural practice, since its modern design represented a forward-looking attitude. A major irony in the history of modernism was, however, the reconciliation of the international style during the domination of strong nationalist sentiments in the practice of architecture. Modernist Turkish architects vehemently opposed the term "international style" and insisted on the name, "new architecture," which was neither "international" nor "a style." "New architecture" was believed to be the most rational response to site, program, climate, and context, and thus it was "national." Yet, the dispute between the anti-stylistic taste of modernism and the domination of elements of modern design (cubic form, flat roofs, horizontal window bands, and the like) created an ongoing tension; see Bozdoğan and Akcan, *Turkey: Modern Architectures in History*, 18–19. For Bozdoğan, from the beginning the genuine critical and creative potential of modern design was compromised in early republican Turkey due to its top-down formulation through cultural policies of the nation-state without thorough conceptualization. See, Bozdoğan, "The Predicament of Modernism in Turkish Architectural Culture," *Rethinking Modernity and National Identity in Turkey*, ed. Bozdoğan and Kasaba (Seattle: University of Washington Press, 1997), 135 & 136-147.

121 Marinov, "The Balkan House," 584; Acciai, "The Ottoman-Turkish House According to Architect Sedad Hakkı Eldem," 4.

protecting the built works of the nation, but also of conveying the national qualities of architecture to a broader populace. In 1938, the same year of his graduation from the Academy, Ülgen reflected, "Our aim is to inform the new generation [of the nation] about our architecture and to show its glorious place in the world of civilization..."[122]

The reasoning of scientific documentation was deep-rooted in refuting the biases of the Orientalist European scholarship, which advocates a stagnant East in contrast to a dynamic and progressive West.[123] At the heart of this Orientalist view was that the "sedentary" schools of Islamic architecture represented superiority until nomadic Turks arrived as they had no distinct and authentic art or architecture, and owe their achievements to Arab, Persian, and Byzantine precedents.[124] Halim Baki Kunter (1900-1971), a historian and an author, fervently refuted the Western Orientalist categorizations of Islamic building traditions, "Turkish art has always been repudiated. It has been appropriated with other [schools] of [Islamic] arts. However, Turkish art and architecture have [always] existed."[125]

Nearly all republican authors countered the statements of the Orientalist architect and historian Charles Texier (1802-1871). Texier notoriously denigrated Turks as "a nomadic tribe of tents"[126] without a distinct architectural tradition of their own. "...As known for a long time, the Ottomans do not have any unique architectural styles of their own, since being a nomadic tribe these [people] have been dissociated with the building arts, and all their buildings include foreign

---

[122] Ülgen, "Türk Mimarisi," *Gençlik* 2 no.38, May 19, 1938, I.

[123] Bozdoğan, "Reading Ottoman Architecture Through Modernist Lenses: Nationalist Historiography and the 'New Architecture' in the early Republic," ed. Bozdoğan and Necipoğlu, *Muqarnas* 24 (2007): 202; Bozdoğan and Necipoğlu, "Preface: Entangled Discourses," ed. Bozdoğan and Necipoğlu, *Muqarnas* 24 (2007): 3.

[124] James Fergusson, *The Illustrated Handbook of Architecture: Being a Concise and Popular Account of the Different Styles of Architecture Prevailing in all Ages and all Countries,* 2 vols. (London: J. Murray, 1855), I:464.

[125] Halim Baki Kunter, "[Letter about the Turkish Architecture Exhibition in London, April 1960,"] (Letter, SALT Research, Ali Saim Ülgen Archive, TASUDOC0484, May 9 1959). https://archives.saltresearch.org/handle/123456789/86640 (accessed September 20, 2021)

[126] Charles Texier, *Asie Mineure: Description Géographique, Historique et Archéologique des Provinces et des Villes de la Chersonnèse d'Asie,* 1842, 59-68.

works conducted by the Arab, or Persian, and later Byzantine architects."[127] In response to Texier's skewed assertion, Çetintaş stated, "I. Turkish architecture: without seeking foreign provisions, has risen through the spirit of its own nation and has flourished in the hands of its own [people], II. Turkish architecture: without any Byzantine, nor Arab, or Persian influences, has prevailed autonomous and original."[128]

Likewise, Ayverdi built a case for the national roots of Ottoman architecture on the basis of his own documentation findings of Bursa's fourteenth-century Orhan Gazi Mosque. Texier, notoriously, claimed that the historic building, due to its inverted "T" plan, resembled a church.[129] Furthermore, the use of spolia materials in the body of the mosque entailed Byzantine-inspired design solutions. To dissolve Texier's claims, Ayverdi took into account a taxonomical gaze that natural scientists would have been equipped with and dissolved the elements of the historic mosque in five clauses: (a) the plan of the mosque was derived from one-*eyvan* Seljuk madrasas with a covered courtyard, (b) the monumental five-bay porch fronting the entrance solidified the tradition of a *son cemaat yeri* (narthex gallery) in later mosques, (c) the authentic arrangement of windows on the floor level presented exterior views when worshipping, (d) the subordination of decorative elements to structural rationalism is originated, and (e) the harmonious volumetric composition of its domes and arches paved the way for the sixteenth-century imperial mosques devised by Sinan.[130] To provide material evidence for his scientific vision, Ayverdi noted that he annotated a substantial amount of dimensions in the measured drawings of the mosque (Figure 2.24).[131, 132]

Regardless of an academic quest to provide scientific evidence for national forms, the formalist measured drawings perceptually merge in the primary and unquestionable role of drawing as a teaching tool to depict the theory of Turkish architecture. In terms of referentiality, the body of illustrations aimed to serve a wide circle of native and international audiences: academics, art theorists, practicing architects, students, teachers, and lay-people who would

---

[127] Texier, *Asia Minor, Geographical, Historical and Archaeological Descriptions of its Provinces and Cities*, 1862, 227.

[128] Çetintaş, *Türk Mimari Anıtları*, 15.

[129] Texier, *Asie Mineure*, 1842, 227; also see, Çetintaş, *Türk Mimari Anıtları*, 15.

[130] Ayverdi, "Bursa Orhan Gazi Camii ve Osmanlı Mimarisinin Menşei Meselesi," 80-81.

[131] Ibid., 77.

[132] Çetintaş, *Türk Mimari Anıtları*, 15.

gain insight on the collective artistic achievement of the Turks. A closer look at the drafted lines shows the formal correlation of pieces of building information which aimed to relate the viewers to the visual presence of the built heritage.

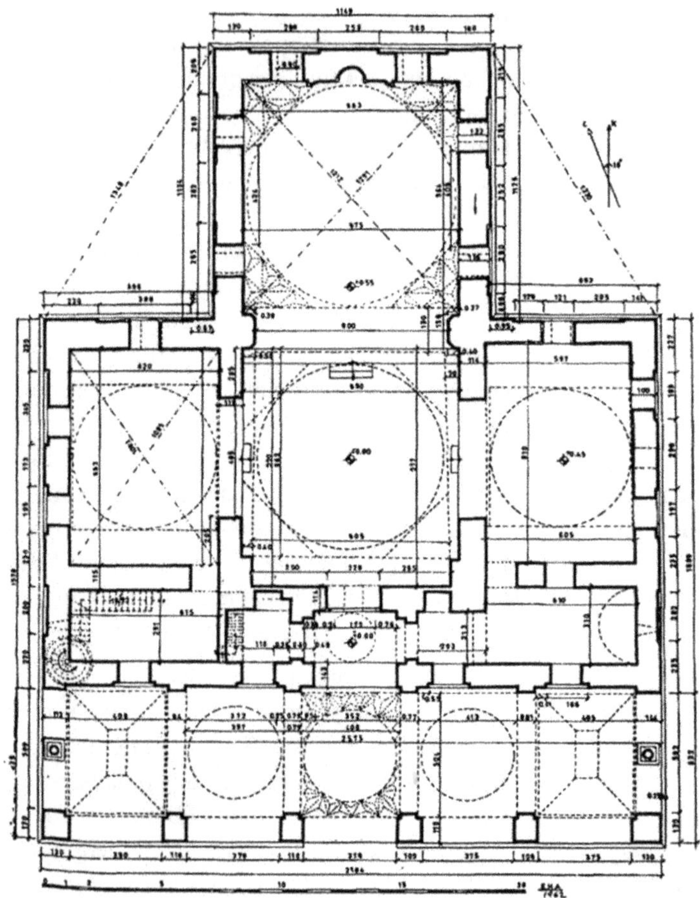

Figure 2.24. Floor plan of the Orhan Gazi Mosque, delineated by Ekrem Hakkı Ayverdi, 1962. Ekrem Hakkı Ayverdi, "Bursa Orhan Gazi Camii ve Osmanlı Mimarisinin Menşei Meselesi," *Vakıflar Dergisi* VI, 1965.

Chapter 3

National cultivation of the built environment

> Monuments are the witness of our belonging to these lands, which we call homeland (*vatan*)...We do not engage in platonic love, but we love our homeland for framing our consciousness. For this reason, we are obliged to love our monuments, protect them, preserve them like a sacred memory, and transfer them to future generations.
>
> Ali Saim Ülgen[1]

Ali Saim Ülgen's appraisal of historical monuments stems from an object-oriented framing of cultural heritage, which was rooted in the desire to connect past and present in a continuous trajectory within the modern borders of Turkey. Ülgen formulated monuments, whose forms came to be seen as the arbiter for artistic truth and beauty of the Turkish creativity, in the context of unbroken cultural continuity. With the same token, Ülgen sought to preserve a moment in the consciousness of future generations, which would presumably make the protection of monuments vital and significant in the perpetuity of the nation-state. Ülgen's definition was in tune with the imposed trajectory upon a bounded landscape of common destiny which had been in operation since the Enlightenment era. The emerging concepts of historical progress and continuity along with romantic notions of attachment to places, extensively, set forth the modern understanding of heritage in the world of nation-states.[2]

---

[1] Ülgen, "Türkiye Anıtları ve Bugünkü Feci Durumları," (Memorandum, SALT Research, Ali Saim Ülgen Archive, TASUDOC0486025, date unknown). https://archives.saltresearch.org/handle/123456789/82564 (accessed September 20, 2021)

[2] Atakuman, "Shifting Discourses of Heritage and Identity in Turkey: Anatolianist Ideologies and Beyond," in *In Search of Pre-Classical Antiquity: Rediscovering Ancient Peoples in Mediterranean Europe (19th and 20th c.)* vol.13, ed. Antonino de Francesco (Leiden: Brill, 2017), 166-167.

Alois Riegl (1858-1905), Austrian art historian, famously wrote, "We, modern viewers, rather than the works themselves by virtue of their original purpose, assign meaning and significance to a monument. In both cases – that of deliberate and of unintentional monuments– a commemorative value exists, and for that reason we think of both as 'monuments.'"[3] Riegl did not witness the transition from empires to nation-states following WWI,[4] but his words deeply echoed the rigorous efforts of the young countries to craft an official-agenda of national monuments. Appropriating architectural heritage into state ideologies, the nation-states sought historical legitimacy in the twentieth century. Selected monuments served to provide a sense of history and a collective awareness of the national past. Together, a consciousness of the value of historical monuments materialized as a testimony of the past achievements of the people who formed a nation.

To Riegl, the present value of most historical monuments did not stem from their original commemorative connotation. The meaning of monuments and the memories they were intended to commemorate change over time. Today, to a large extent, historic properties (for example, Istanbul's Hagia Sophia or Topkapı Palace Museum) are valued for associations that were acquired long after their construction.[5] The events and details of these monuments deemed important deeply resonated with how and when these facets had been interpreted and by whom, along with the criteria for judging those values at the time. In the redemption of the Turkish nation within the modern history of civilizations, the authentic artistic expressions of nation entailed diverging readings in the course of transforming political tendencies. In the Late Ottoman Era, from the shared identity of *Osmanlıcılık* (Ottomanism) in the wake of westernizing *Tanzimat* reforms to the rise of Turkish nationalism with

---

[3] Alois Riegl, "The Modern Cult of Monuments: Its Essence and its Development," in *Historical and Philosophical Issues in the Conservation of Cultural Heritage*, ed. Nicholas Stanley Price., M. Kirby Talley Jr., and Vaccaro, Alessandra Melucco Vaccaro (Los Angeles: The Getty Conservation Institute, 1996), 72.

[4] Four empires collapsed due to WWI: Austro-Hungarian Empire, German Empire, Ottoman Empire and Russian Empire; new countries were formed: Austria, Czechoslovakia, Estonia, Finland, Hungary, Latvia, Lithuania, Poland, Turkey and Yugoslavia.

[5] Another example to national appraisal of architecture includes the WWI military sites in the Gallipoli Peninsula. The sites have endured conflicting readings of history in the course of changing political tendencies. Lucienne Thys-Şenocak, *Divided Spaces, Contested Pasts: The Heritage of the Gallipoli Peninsula* (London: Routledge, 2019).

Young Turks, the architectural heritage across the empire reflected the spiritual aspiration of the empire in a modern world. The same monuments met alternating titles through the lens of ruling ideologies while they were forged a prestigious lineage oscillating between the civilization of Islam or Turks. With the same token, the early republican leaders' emphasis on the ethnized history of Turks transformed the architectural heritage in the modern borders of Turkey into an unconcealed means of nationalist manifestation and resistance against the European cultural exploitation. Yet, with the rise of Islam in the aftermath of Atatürk the pedigree of the same monuments was once again charged, this time reflecting the chronicle of Muslim-Turks.

Negotiating a binding architectural identity in the Late Ottoman Empire

In the late nineteenth century, the Ottoman Empire got entangled with European colonialism and the rise of nationalism, both shrinking its territories. Between the intense westernizing *Tanzimat* reforms and the political turmoil, imperial authorities sought for a new identity that would support the shared interests with the European stakeholders and would assure a national coherence in the remaining territories.[6] In the wake of the *Tanzimat* reforms to achieve equality and unity for all the citizens of the empire, the imperial authorities promoted Ottomanism as the shared identity of the empire. The imperial interest in the search of a national identity within the multi-religious and multi-ethnic seams of the empire culminated in a highly academical reading of the built environment. *Usūl-i Mi'mārī-i Osmānī* (1873), a compilation of written histories and measured drawings of historical monuments, demonstrates the academical formulation of a collective consciousness on national art and architecture in the empire. Prepared by a highly diverse team of Ottoman architects, bureaucrats, and scholars, the production team itself mirrored the shared identity of been Ottoman in the nineteenth-century imperial lands. The authors coming from different ethnic and religious backgrounds, concentrated on the formal analysis of iconic monuments across the country to plead for the genuine Ottomanness of the visual culture.[7]

---

[6] Wendy M. K. Shaw, "Islamic Arts in the Ottoman Imperial Museum, 1889-1923" *Ars Orientalist* 30 (2000): 57.

[7] Ersoy, *Late Ottoman Historiography*, 27.

Figure 3.1. Pertevniyal Valide Sultan Mosque, Aksaray, Istanbul, ca. 1890, street view. Library of Congress, LOT 13428, no. 016 [item] [P&P].

In retrospect, the authors of *Usūl* reflected on the national progress of architecture from the dynastic beginnings embodied in the Bursa monuments, which was then crowned with Sinan's classical age. The authors hoped that the elements of the early Ottoman national monuments could become a model for contemporary architects, both native and European, to devise a new synthesis for the new architecture.[8] Not surprisingly, in this evolutionary path of Ottoman style, the architectural patronage of the reigning Sultan Abdülaziz was labeled as "Ottoman Renaissance" in architecture. The authors noted that the monuments of the Abdülaziz era, Istanbul's Pertevniyal Valide Mosque (c.1869–71) and Çırağan Palace (c.1864–71), with their mixture of Ottoman, Orientalist, and Gothic forms represented the essence of the dynastic architecture and constituted a formative stage for the assembly of future national forms (Figure 3.1).[9] This reconciliation of Ottoman revivalism with Islam can be read through the idealistic association between Gothic revivalism with Christianity. After the turn of the twentieth-century Turkish nationalists progressively recharged Ottoman forms with Turkishness, not unlike the means in which later Victorians looked upon Gothic revivalism as much as a symbol of "Englishness" as that of the good Christian society that Augustus Welby Northmore Pugin (1812-1840) and John Ruskin (1819-1900) promoted.[10]

The collective Ottoman identity celebrating the democratic tendencies of the *Tanzimat* era did not last, however. Sultan Abdülhamid II abolished the parliament along with the charter of the First Constitutional Era using the ongoing Russo-Turkish War as a political excuse. Abdülhamid II reinstated the authoritarian regime and foregrounded Islamism as the new entity for the empire.[11] Through his role as caliph, which the sultanate had assumed in 1517, the Sultan associated Ottomanness with Islam and reiterated himself as the leader of the Muslim world. Accordingly, Abdülhamid II solidified the use of Islamic symbolism to compete with the nationalist symbols emerging across the empire. [12] Architectural heritage signifying the essence of Islam became integral to the rhetoric of the Ottoman identity. Such, in 1906, the incumbent *Asar-i Atika Nizamnamesi* (Antiquities Law) was revised to

[8] Ersoy, "The Search for Ottoman Origins," 122.

[9] Montani et. al., *Usūl,* 7.

[10] Bozdoğan and Akcan, *Turkey: Modern Architectures in History,* 23.

[11] Kemal H. Karpat, "Historical Continuity and Identity Change or How to be Modern Muslim, Ottoman, and Turk," in *Ottoman Past and Today's Turkey,* ed. Karpat (Leiden: Brill, 2000), 15.

[12] Mardin, *Religion and Social Change in Modern Turkey: The Case of Bediüzzaman Said Nursi* (Albany: State University of New York, 1989), 129.

incorporate Islamic and Ottoman artworks.[13] In respect, the Islamic heritage gained legislative interest for legal protection and preservation.[14]

Following the 1908 Young Turk Revolution, CUP reinstated the parliament and began to dominate the political helm. This time, CUP emphasized the nation of Turks united with Islam, replacing the collective Ottoman identity embodied in the *Tanzimat* era and the subsequent Islamized Ottomanness of the Abdülhamid II era. The dominance of "Turkishness" culminated in a growing interest when reading the Ottoman. The iconic monuments that had been brought forward in the multi-cultural structure of the empire became to be seen as examples of the Turkish civilization.

Kemalettin Bey, although was not an official member of the CUP, he was a fervent supporter of the liberal ideas implemented by the Young Turks.[15] A reverent Muslim and a nationalist, Kemalettin Bey interpreted Turkish architecture within the civilization of Islam. He probed that the Turkish civilization was initiated in Central Asia, then moved to the West elevating the architectural culture in Asia and Europe. After the acceptance of Islam, the system of Turkish architecture pursued the implementation of a scientific system of construction and decoration, which constituted the crowning products of the civilization of Muslims.[16] To study examples of Turkish architecture, Kemalettin Bey traveled to Konya and Bursa despite Abdülhamid II's strict travel regulations. There, he documented and studied "the beginning phase of the rise of Turkish architecture," the Seljuk heritage. [17] Unfortunately, none of these Kemalettin Bey's field drawings survived to day.

---

[13] The previous regulations were largely confined to the Hellenic antiquities, in order to prevent smuggling of artifacts out of the empire and to establish an imperial collection of art comparable with museums in Europe.

[14] Madran, *Tanzimattan Cumhuriyete Kültür Varlıklarının Korunmasına ilişkin Tutumlar ve Düzenlemeler: 1850-1950* (Ankara: ODTÜ Mimarlık Fakültesi Yayınları, 2002), 199-200.

[15] Kemalettin Bey wrote that the destructive ramifications of wars upon architectural heritage was deepened with the travel restrictions during the rule of Abdülhamid II. The restrictions hampered his efforts to inspect the conditions of the historic properties across the empire. Kemalettin Bey, "Türk ve Müslüman Mimarlığı," in *Mimar Kemalettin'in Yazdıkları*, 154.

[16] Ibid., 155; Kemalettin Bey, "Türk Mimarlığı," in *Mimar Kemalettin'in Yazdıkları*, 150.

[17] Kemalettin Bey, "Bulgarların Ahval-i Medeniye-i Hazırası," in *Mimar Kemalettin'in Yazdıkları*, 79.

Figure 3.2. Drawing for the Ottoman revivalist styled Bezmialem Valide Sultan Hospital, drawn by Mehmet Nihat Nigizberk, undated. Koç University, Suna Kıraç Library Special Collections and Archives, Mehmet Nihat Nigizberk Collection of Architectural Drawings and Photographs, MNN_NB_01, 536.

A prolific advocate of Turkish architecture, Kemalettin Bey, was highly critical of the architectural culture that was infiltrated with foreign conducts and Western architectural styles. He contended that the "soul" of Turkish architecture, "the elaborate and the pure" forms, was abandoned in favor of Western idioms.[18] He rejected the eclectic revivalist style (an amalgamation of native and foreign forms) as promoted in the *Usūl*. Instead, he celebrated a more purist Turkish expression inspired by Seljuk and Ottoman elements. Hence, Kemalettin Bey became one of the founders of the First National Style that turned to historic monuments for inspiration for modern buildings. Yet, reading Kemalettin Bey's portfolio solely through Ottoman revivalism, namely Seljuk and Ottoman rudiments, dismisses the diversity of his designs.[19] True, Kemalettin Bey was a proponent of celebrating the purity of the national architecture of Turks in new forms. His neo-classical styled Third Vakıf Han in

---

[18] Kemalettin Bey, "Eski İstanbul ve İmar-ı Belde Belası," in *Mimar Kemalettin'in Yazdıkları*, 113.

[19] Paolo Girardelli, "Re-thinking architect Kemalettin," *Abe Journal: Architecture beyond Europe* 2 (2012): 5. (accessed April 1, 2022)

Beyoğlu and his Art Nouveau styled Ahmet Ratib Pasha Mansion in Çamlıca, however, exhibits that Kemalettin Bey did not display professional bias against the stylistic trends in Europe. His office at the Ministry of Endowments operated as a school for young architects and craftsmen who deployed revivalist designs across the empire (Figure 3.2).[20]

Figure 3.3. "Formerly it was the servants who swept the ministries, but now it is the ministers who clean them up." *Kalem*, September 3, 1908, delineated by Esad Arseven, Celâl and Cimcoz, Selah, University of Texas Libraries, Kalem Cartoon Satire Collection.

---

[20] In fact, one of Kemalettin Bey's proposals for his work at Haram, resonated with introducing classical Ottoman motifs to Masjid Al-Aqsa. See, Yavuz, "The Restoration Project," 149-164.

Celâl Esad (Arseven), too, sympathized with the rhetoric of Young Turks.[21] Arseven periodically contributed to *Kalem*, a recognized Ottoman satirical magazine, which was published right after the 1908 Young Turk Revolution and was in circulation until 1911. With his cartoons, Arseven ridiculed the dysfunctional old Ottoman rule, and brought to the fore poignant illustrations of the political and social reforms of the Young Turks (Figure 3.3). In these years, Arseven formulated the conceptual framework of Turkish art and architecture. His *Constantinople de Byzance à Stamboul* (1909) became the earliest book by a Turkish writer on the Byzantine and Ottoman monuments of the imperial capital, Istanbul.[22] His subsequent publication, *Türk San'atı (Turkish Art,* 1928), then became the first survey compiled by a Turkish scholar to probe the eastern Turkic origins of the art and architecture of Turkey.[23] To Arseven, the Turkish art included formative phases spanning from the ancient and medieval Asiatic origins to the present. The latest Anatolian stage, embracing the Seljuk and Ottoman periods, constituted an unbroken national style culminating with Sinan's masterworks, which doubtless attested to the greatest achievement of Turkish art.[24]

In context with the enactment of the 1906-Antiquities Law, the Ministry of Public Education established a commission in 1910 to investigate the best methods for the preservation of Islamic and Ottoman arts. Given this, the Ottoman state differentiated religious from dynastic in the museum context. As a result, the Imperial Museum was assigned to house mosaics, tiles, and other removable ornaments while the Ministry of Endowments was to conserve consecrated buildings.[25] The 1908-constitutional revolution raised Kemalettin Bey to prominence as an architect and restorer since he was assigned as the head of the newly founded department, *İnşaat ve Tamirat Heyet-i Fenniyesi* (the Technical Commission for Construction and Repairs) within Ministry of Endowments in 1909. Thus, Kemalettin Bey became the

---

[21] F. Dieter Kickingereder, "Celâl Esad Arseven's Memoirs of his Life as an Artist and a Man of Politics: Sanat ve Siyaset Hatıralarım (1993)", in *Many Ways of Speaking About the Self: Middle Eastern Ego-Documents in Arabic, Persian and Turkish (14th-20th century),* ed. Ralf Elger and Yavuz Köse (Wiesbaden: Harrassowitz Verlag 2010), 41.

[22] Celâl Esad (Arseven), *Constantinople de Byzance à Stamboul* (Paris, 1909), 151–55.

[23] Necipoğlu, "Creation of a National Genius," 161.

[24] Arseven, *Türk San'atı* (İstanbul, 1928), 7–11.

[25] Zarif Orgun and Serap Aykaç, "La fondation du Musée turque et le Musée des Arts turcs et Islamiques," *Travaux et Recherches en Turquie* 1 (1982): 135–41; Altınyıldız, "The Architectural Heritage of Istanbul," 281-305.

main authority for the restoration of historic monuments along with the construction of modern buildings.

Although the enactment of the 1906-Antiquities Law recognized Islamic monuments as antiquities, a legal agenda for their preservation could only be attained by the passing of *Muhafaza-i Abidat Hakkinda Nizamname* (the Regulation for the Preservation of Monuments) in 1912.[26] This new regulation stated that monuments could not be vandalized or destroyed by any means. Yet, if demolition was deemed an option, then a commission of experts would examine the case.[27] Consequently, *Asar-i Atika Encümeni* (the Commission for the Preservation of Monuments) was established in 1915 as an advisory body for the implementation of the law in Istanbul. The council became a permanent body in 1917: *Asar-i Atika Encümen-i Daimisi.* The founding members included Kemalettin Bey, Celâl Esad (Arseven), and Halil Edhem (Eldem) the director of the Istanbul Archaeological Museums. The council was in charge for the implementation of the 1912 law and dedicated their efforts to create an inventory of monuments in Istanbul, to register them, and to supervise their restorations. The law, however, put forward a schedule of demolition rather than actual protection of monuments. By appealing to the council, a local government would seek a schedule for demolition of a historic building. If a building was in a hazardous condition, then it could be torn down immediately, omitting the bureaucratic process, ensured that any decorated and inscribed parts of it were preserved.[28] The preservation of the salvaged items prompted the creation of a museum where articles from mosques, masjids, tombs, and convents would be collected and exhibited. The public kitchen of the sixteenth-century Süleymaniye Mosque Complex (Figure 3.4) operated as the building for *Evkaf-i İslamiye Müzesi* (Islamic Endowments Museum), founded in 1914.[29]

---

[26] Pınar Aykaç, "The Commission for the Preservation of Antiquities and Its Role in the Appropriation of Istanbul's Diverse Heritage as National Heritage (1939–1953)," *New Perspectives on Turkey* 62 (2020): 79.

[27] Osman Nuri Ergin, *Mecelle-i Umur-ı Belediye,* 9 vols. (İstanbul: İstanbul Büyükşehir Belediyesi, 1995), 3:1228–35.

[28] Altınyıldız, "The Architectural Heritage of Istanbul," 286.

[29] The imperial museum was renamed *Türk ve İslam Eserleri Müzesi* (Turkish and Islamic Arts Museum) in 1923 with the proclamation of the Republic of Turkey. In 1983, the museum was moved from the Süleymaniye Mosque Complex to the newly restored Ibrahim Pasha Palace, Sultanahmet, Istanbul.

Figure 3.4. Aerial photograph of Istanbul's Süleymaniye Mosque Complex, undated. SALT Research, AHISTEMIN035.

Kemalettin Bey's article pertaining to the seventeenth-century Ebu'l Fazl Mahmud Efendi Madrasa in Istanbul reveals the heated tension between demolition and protection at the time. The Mayor of Istanbul and Construction Minister, Cemil Topuzlu (1866-1958), was ardently implementing urban transformation projects in order to create a modern city. Amid the prioritization of tramlines over monuments, the city designated to demolish the Ebu'l Fazl Mahmud Efendi Madrasa, which was then in a dilapidated condition. The city repudiated that the Ministry of Endowments was working overtime to preserve an ailing monument and criticized the overzealousness of the office to perpetuate the lifespan of the structure. In a newspaper op-ed dated 1913, Kemalettin Bey, the head of the Technical Commission for Construction and Repairs, countered these criticisms, "...We haven't heard this kind of statement neither from ones oblivious to our civilization nor ones spiteful of our civilization. To preserve the historic monuments is the most important duty of the Ministry of Endowments and it is also the governing law of humanity and our new civilization…" [30, 31]

Figure 3.5. İstanbul's Fourth Vakıf Han, designed by Kemalettin Bey, street view, undated. SALT Research, Harika and Kemali Söylemezoğlu Archive, TSOH126002.

---

[30] Kemalettin Bey, "Yeni Camii'nin Tamiri Münasebetiyle bir iki Söz," in *Mimar Kemalettin'in Yazdıkları*, 110.

[31] Stefanos Yerasimos, "Tanzimattan Günümüze Türkiye'de Kültürel Mirası Koruma Söylemi," *İstanbul* 54 (2005), 48. In this context, founded in 1912 *İstanbul Muhipleri Cemiyeti* (Friends of Istanbul Association), a civil initiative to cultivate awareness of historical monuments also formed an oppositional voice against the modernization projects of Istanbul devised by Cemil Topuzlu.

Ironically, numerous buildings designed by Kemalettin Bey brought forth the demolition of national monuments that were under his protection at the Ministry of Endowments. To open space for his First Vakıf Han near Eminönü, the seventeenth-century Vani Efendi Madrasa was torn down and a substitute madrasa constructed nearby.[32] Similarly, for the construction of his Fourth Vakıf Han (Figure 3.5), Sultan Abdülhamid I's public kitchen and school were pulled down; its fountains were dismantled and assembled elsewhere, while the madrasa and tomb survived across the road. The substitute for Sultan Abdülhamid I's public kitchen was built on a site emptied by tearing down Sultan Selim I's older building with the same function.[33] The Fethiye Madrasa, which had been built as an annex to the Pammakaristos Church when it was converted to the Fethiye Mosque in 1588, was demolished by the Ministry of Endowments between 1911 and 1915; for which Kemalettin Bey designed a new madrasa. Another replacement included his Harikzedegan Apartments for fire victims, constructed in the place of the decaying eighteenth-century Laleli Madrasa.[34, 35]

To a large extent, the Ottoman institutional and legal infrastructure was maintained in republican Turkey, upon which the nation-state built an elaborate system of agencies and regulations to counter the expanding interest in architectural heritage in the new political context. The 1906-Antiquities Law, along with the 1912-Preservation of Monuments law, was effective until 1973. Likewise, the Commission for the Preservation of Monuments, was ratified by the republican government in 1925 and was renamed *Muhafaza-i Asar-i Atika Encümeni* (*Eski Eserleri Koruma Encümeni*) with the same founding members, Kemalettin Bey, Halil Edhem (Eldem), and Celâl Esad (Arseven). The committee operated as the main advisory body on preservation in Istanbul until 1951.

In the march towards a secular country, republican authorities' principal decree to dismantle the legal framework, which was underpinning the *vakıf* (endowments, in Ottoman *evkaf*) system, rendered the condition of the historic properties very vulnerable. The first tactical move of the founding

---

[32] Yavuz, "The Restoration Project," 147–48.

[33] Ibid., 173, 227.

[34] Ibid., 222, 271, 314, 232.

[35] Nigizberk, an architect of the Ministry of Endowments, supervised most of these new construction projects including the Vakıf Hans. See, Cengizkan, "Mehmet Nihat Nigizberk Katkıları, Evkaf İdaresi ve Mimar Kemalettin," 179.

leaders included decapitating the Orthodox Islamic hierarchy with the abolition of the caliphate in 1924 and invalidating the legal jurisdiction. In 1926, the new Medeni Kanun (Turkish Civil Code) recast the endowment system by secularizing it, removing its perpetual immunities. In 1928, the New Endowments Law centralized the administrative and fiscal functions of all endowments nationwide under the auspices of the newly established General Directorate of Endowments, which demoted the endowment system into an agency operating directly under the office of the Prime Minister.[36]

In this consequential move to secularize the state the endowment facilities were closed down and individual buildings were allocated to different agencies based on their functions. Madrasas were closed down in 1924, followed by tombs, convents, and *zaviyes* (dervish lodges) in 1925. The General Directorate of Endowments became in charge of the mosques; the Ministry of Education took over the madrasas and tombs[37] and municipalities assumed the management of fountains and cemeteries. Within this scheme, any building material with historical and aesthetic value was to be kept, but the rest of the facilities were to be sold for the construction of new school buildings and the new capital Ankara.[38] Pertaining to the restoration of individual facilities that were once contributing to a *külliye* (mosque complex), the allocation of monuments to different institutions generated financial and logistical contingencies when coordinating preservation interventions.[39] While an individual building would be repaired by the

[36] Zeynep Kezer, *Building Modern Turkey: State, Space, and Ideology in the Early Republic* (Pittsburgh, Pa: University of Pittsburgh Press, 2015), 90-91.

[37] The Ministry of Education restored some of the madrasa and *mevlevihane* (convent for Mevlevi dervishes) buildings in Istanbul to use these facilities as elementary schools. See, Anonymous, "Bu Sene İstanbul'da 11 İlkmekteb Yapılacak," *Son Posta*, July 18, 1939, 3.

[38] For example, many bathhouse owners put their facilities up for sale. See, Anonymous, "İstanbullular ve Temizlik: Birçok Hamamcılar Ziyan Ettikleri İddiası ile Mallarını Satılığa Çıkarmışlar," Son Posta, July 11, 1935, 5. Likewise, many unused mosque buildings were opened to the real estate market. Anonymous, "Satılığa Çıkarılacak Camiler," *Son Posta*, October 23, 1937, 3.

[39] Anonymous, "Yeni Bir Komisyon Kuruluyor," *Son Posta*, February 18, 1937, 4.

responsible agency, the rest of the properties in the complex would be left untouched for years.[40, 41]

The demand of preservation professionals for the establishment of a supervising council to orchestrate the preservation work and to ensure scientific repairs went unresolved, however. In a report drafted as late as 1947, Ülgen complained that the nationwide historic preservation agenda regulated by the Conservation Council of Monuments in 1933, unfortunately, had not been fulfilled. Ülgen considered the distribution of monuments among the hands of diverse state agencies, legal entities, and individuals as a major obstacle.[42] Regardless of the stewardship of the guarantors, the monuments were in ruins across the country and they were doomed to disappear unless a scientific council was formed to orchestrate the preservation work of the agencies.[43]

Lending a voice for monuments in the Turkish History Thesis

Inspired by the theories of Ziya Gökalp (1876-1924), the leading nationalist ideologue, in the early years of the republic the Turkish History Thesis constituted the driving rhetoric in constructing a cohesive and Westernized national identity. Gökalp differentiated "nationality," rooted in the Ural-Altaic group of Turkic people from "religion," the Islamic community that had transnational qualities. Although Seljuk and Ottoman cultures represented Islamic community, which Turks belonged to by religion, it was specifically an individual Turkish culture, distinct from other cultures of nations in the

---

[40] Ümit Fırat Açıkgöz, "On the Uses and Meanings of Architectural Preservation in Early Republican Istanbul (1923–1950)," *Journal of the Ottoman and Turkish Studies Association* 1, no. 1/2 (2014): 174.

[41] To provide consistency and standardizations in the methods of repairs, some agencies sought to merge their projects. In 1937, thus, Directorate of the Endowments, Board of the Istanbul Museums, and the City of Istanbul prepared a joint inventory of the historic properties under their stewardship. The agencies assigned the Istanbul Museums as the manager of the historic preservation work. Anonymous, "Eski Eserlerin Tamirine Bundan sonra Müzeler İdaresi Nezaret Edecek," *Son Posta*, May 5, 1937, 4.

[42] Ülgen, "Rapor," (Memorandum, SALT Research, Ali Saim Ülgen Archive, TASUDOC1311126, 1940). https://archives.saltresearch.org/handle/123456789/75853 (accessed September 20, 2021); also, see, Ülgen, "Rapor," (Memorandum, SALT Research, Ali Saim Ülgen Archive, TAS UDOC0486009, 1947). https://archives.saltresearch.org/handle/123456789/82564 (accessed September 20, 2021)

[43] Ibid., "Rapor,"1947.

Islamic community.[44] Based on this narrative, the Thesis implied that the Turkish nation established its civilization, even before the Western nations existed. Rooted in the Turkic tribes in Central Asia, Turks migrated to the West bringing their civilization and transforming other cultures.[45] The Turkish identity, therefore, resonated with the ancient people of Hittites in Anatolia, the Greek culture of the Classical Antiquity, and even with Roman society through the Etruscans.[46] The Mediterranean cultures, or even native American cultures across the Pacific Ocean, consequently, were considered as born from the Turkish civilization.[47] Seen in this light, the Thesis, placed the "Turkish race," at the forefront of world-historical development through the ages and portrayed it as being related to the region's ancient civilizations to which European nations also traced their cultural ancestry.

In the implementation of the Turkish History Thesis as the state propaganda, Atatürk was one of the few, if not the only intellectual, to reject Pan-Turkism with its focus on the cultural and political unification of all Turkic peoples. Instead, Atatürk affirmed Anatolia as being the homeland of Turks. To authenticate this new concept, the ancient Hittites and Sumerians were integrated into the ethnohistorical framework as the ancestors of Turks. Pan-Turkists did not concur with the pre-Turkish history Anatolia; rather they accentuated the Central Asian origins. Yet, they were content with the association of Hittites and Sumerians with the origins of Turks. The texts written in the 1930s, under the impact of nationalist trends, and Atatürk's perception of summoning all the pasts of Anatolia, regardless of ethnic origin, were integrated into the ideology of the modern state.[48]

This national history also aimed to counter the classification of Turks as a "yellow race" and to present a white protagonist nation superior to the Indo-European peoples. In 1928, the dissent brought forward when Afet İnan (1908-1985), the oldest of Atatürk's adopted daughters, confided her concerns about a history textbook she had read at the French convent school, Notre

---

44 Bozdoğan, Modernism and Nation Building, 35.

45 Nilüfer Öndin, Cumhuriyet'in Kültür Politikası ve Sanat 1923–1950 (İstanbul: İnsancıl Yayınları, 2003), 56 and 58.

46 Etienne Copeaux, *Tarih Ders Kitaplarında (1931–1993), Türk Tarih Tezinden Türk İslâm Sentezine,* trans. Ali Berktay (İstanbul: İletişim Yayınları, 2006), 56.

47 İnan, "Türk Tarih Kurumunun Arkeoloji Faaliyeti," Belleten 2, no.5-6 (January 1938):5.

48 Mehmet Özdoğan, "Ideology and Archaeology in Turkey," Archaeology under Fire: Nationalism, Politics and Heritage in the Eastern Mediterranean and Middle East, ed. Lynn Meskell (London: Routledge, 2002), 116.

Dame de Sion in Istanbul, categorizing Turks among the yellow races.[49] Subsequently, in 1929 Atatürk showed İnan a monograph, Joseph de Guignes' the *Histoire générale des Huns, des Mongoles, des Turcs, et des autres Tatares occidentaux* (4 volumes, 1756-1758). Atatürk pointed to a passage that stated that the Turks were a "yellow" race sharing a common origin with the Mongols in Mongolia. İnan replied, "Let's work on this." [50]

The attempt to differentiate from the "yellow race" the white "Turkish race," continued during the lifetime of Atatürk. As late as 1937, the year before the passing of Atatürk, Şemseddin Günaltay (1883-1961), historian and politician, wrote an article in the *Tarih Semineri Dergisi* (*The Journal of History*) of Istanbul University, confronting the narrative of the long-dead de Guignes. The Turks were not yellow but white; their home was not Mongolia but the Altay Mountains of Turkistan. Günaltay heralded, "We are determined to reveal our own history with our own intellect and our own efforts while [walking along] the scientific path of the TTK commenced by Atatürk."[51] Within the same year, in a lecture for the Turkish History Congress, İnan stressed that the scholars of the TTK were zealously working to share "the solid foundation" of the nation with the rest of the world. Their inspiration for this national cause was none other than documenting the forebears of the "white and brachiocephalic Turkish race" who also founded the ancient civilizations of Anatolia.[52]

Not surprisingly, the racial emphasis of the Thesis accompanied the reading of historic architecture. Ülgen, for example, located evidence for the unity of Turkish architecture in the pure, rational, and austere forms of the tents of the nomadic Turkic tribes in Central Asia, the Buddhist Temples in Turkestan, the tombs of the Seljuks in Anatolia, and the mosques of the Ottoman-Turks. Amid this lengthy history of the nation, the purity of Turkish architecture has not weakened due to the centuries-long exchange of different nations. Quite the reverse, the Turkish spirit infused different schools of architecture, including Arabic, Gothic, Persian, and Roman Ülgen wrote.[53]

---

[49] Andrew Mango, *Atatürk* (Woodstock N.Y.: Overlook Press, 2000), 468–69.

[50] Redford, "What Have You Done for Anatolia Today?" 243.

[51] Şemsettin Günaltay, "Türklerin Ana Yurdu ve Irkı Meselesi," *Tarih Semineri Dergisi* 13 (1937): 13.

[52] İnan, "Türk Tarih Kurumunun Arkeoloji Faaliyeti," 5.

[53] Ülgen, "Türk Mimarisi," *Gençlik* 2, IV.

Atatürk's confidence in Anatolia as the homeland of Turks also brought a retrospective view to the built environment within the modern borders of Turkey. In 1933, the Ministry of Education[54] initiated a comprehensive state program to formulate a scientific basis for the protection of monuments in Turkey.[55] Through its several state departments, the Ministry directed research programs, restoration projects, along with educational actions. Concurrently, the Ministry introduced a bill to regulate the preservation of monuments and published a booklet in 1933 named *Tarihi Abide ve Eserlerimizi Korumağa Mecburuz (We are obliged to Protect our Historical Monuments and Antiquities)*. The booklet included a draft of the bill,[56] an article written by Halil Edhem (Eldem), and accompanying visual materials. Halil Edhem (1861-1938), the recognized museum director, historian, and politician, blamed the lack of resources as the main reason for deficiencies in the upkeep of architectural heritage. Edhem acknowledged the severe destruction of monuments, admitting that works from the Turkish era, like others, were in a "despicable state" of disrepair.[57] The booklet, moreover, included two maps portraying locations of historic properties in the modern borders of Turkey. One map covered antiquities of the Hittite, Phrygia and Classical Antiquity, while the other presented the Turkish dynastic periods of *Beylik*, Seljuk, and Ottoman. The inclusion of antiquities to be worthy of protection confirmed the official recognition of the "other" historical patrimony in the nation-state. Nevertheless, a separate list in the booklet indicating solely Turkish monuments for immediate repairs, revealed the ideological split in the appraisal of monuments.

TTK, Ministry of Education, General Directorate of Endowments, General Directorate of Antiquities and Museums, and other state agencies encouraged scholars to study diverse topics, from a single building type to an architectural landscape. Ülgen's, *İznik'te Türk Eserleri (The Turkish Architectural Works in İznik) and Mimar Sinan Yapıları (The Buildings of Mimar Sinan)*, Sedat Çetintaş's, *Türk Mimari Anıtları: Osmanlı Devri (Turkish Architectural*

[54] The Ministry of Education was organized under the name "The Ministry of Culture" from December 28, 1935 to September 21, 1941.

[55] Giorgio Gasco, "Bruno Taut and the Program for the Protection of Monuments in Turkey (1937-38)/Three Case Studies: Ankara, Edirne, Bursa," *METU JFA* 27 no.2 (2010): 15.

[56] The bill was never brought to parliament for ratification, thus, never enacted.

[57] Halil Ethem Eldem, *Tarihi Abide ve Eserlerimizi Korumağa Mecburuz*, (İstanbul: Devlet Matbaası, 1933), 5 and 8.

Monuments: Ottoman Period) and *Sivas Darüşşifası, 614-1217*,[58] [59] Albert Gabriel's *Monuments Turcs d'Anatolie*, Ülgen and Hikmet Turhan Dağlıoğlu's *Ankara'da Cenabî Ahmed Paşa Camii ve Türbesi (Cenabî Ahmed Pasha Mosque and Tomb in Ankara)*, Ülgen and Şerefüddin Yaltkaya's *Topkapı'da Ahmed Paşa Heyeti (The Complex of Ahmed Pasha in Topkapı)*, Ülgen and Halim Baki Kunter's *Fatih Cami ve Bizans Sarnıcı (Fatih Mosque and Byzantine Cistern)*, and Yusuf Akyurt's (Figure 3.6) *Türk Asar-ı Atikası Binalarına ait Tarihi Mecmua (Historical Review of Buildings of Turkish Antiquities)* exemplify the swelling archival building documentation work.

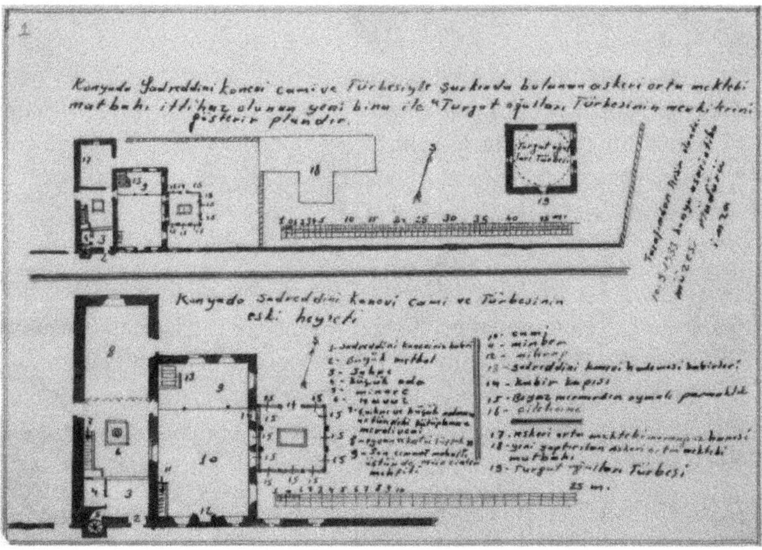

Figure 3.6. Measured drawing sheet for Konya's Sadrettin Konevi Mosque and Tomb, delineated by Mehmet Yusuf Akyurt, 1933. SALT Research, Ali Saim Ülgen Archive, TASUDOC1146.

58 Between 1937 and 1938, Çetintaş surveyed the thirteenth-century Şifaiye hospital and madrasa in Sivas. Çetintaş, later published his findings in proceedings along with his book, Sivas Darüşşifası, 614-1217. See, Çetintaş, "Türk Tarih Kurumu Tarafından Sivas Sifaiyesinde Yaptırılan Mimari Hafriyat," *Belleten* 3, no.9 (January 1939): 61-67; Çetintaş, *Sivas Darüşşifası: 614-1217* (İstanbul: İbrahim Horoz Basımevi, 1953).

59 In 1935, Çetintaş was tasked with the documentation of the Turkish buildings in Edirne. The resulting measured drawings were exhibited in domestic and international exhibitions. Anonymous, "Edirnedeki bütün Tarihi Abideler Tetkik Ediliyor," *Akşam*, March 24, 1935, 5.

Selecting monuments to be surveyed

With the profound state support in the early republic, making measured drawings of architecture promptly became an institutional practice, to which prominent architects and scholars, individually or collectively, contributed. Even for personalities who fell short on fully explaining their drive to document or the contents of their measured drawings, their work clearly indicates a strong belief in the drafted lines and the growing specialization in archival building documentation.

As a result of the dense and tremendously influential Turkish History Thesis, the growing collection of archival drawings became a way to outline the sense of history and a collective awareness of the national past in the context. Yet, the Thesis itself embodied diverging nuances in terms of the Central Asian or Anatolian roots of Turks. Sided with either view, drafters created a diplomatic way to put historic properties in context of the history of Turks. The resulting work was heavily used for identifying various values and interests concerned, and for institutional restructuring of the protection of the delineated monuments.

In *İznik'te Türk Eserleri* (1938), Ülgen explained his interest in documenting the Turkish built environment of İznik (Nicaea), to alleviate the lack of publications on the Ottoman history of the ancient city and to secure restoration funds.[60] Due to the Greek occupation (1919-1922) of İznik, destructions and disruptions already took their toll on monuments and not only of buildings ruined at the time, but of their urban and topographic settings. Ülgen compiled measured drawings of the Turkish monuments within the citadel with the anticipation that these published illustrations would garner interest for the repairs and restoration of these properties. Interestingly, among the mosques, tombs, madrasas, *imarets* (hospices), and public baths constructed under the Turkish rule, Ülgen included the Ayasofya Mosque, a sixth-century Byzantine church, which had been converted into a mosque (Figure 3.7, Figure 3.8, and Figure 3.9).[61]

---

[60] Ülgen, "İznik'te Türk Eserleri," *Vakıflar Dergisi* 1 (Ankara, 1938): 53.

[61] Ibid., 55.

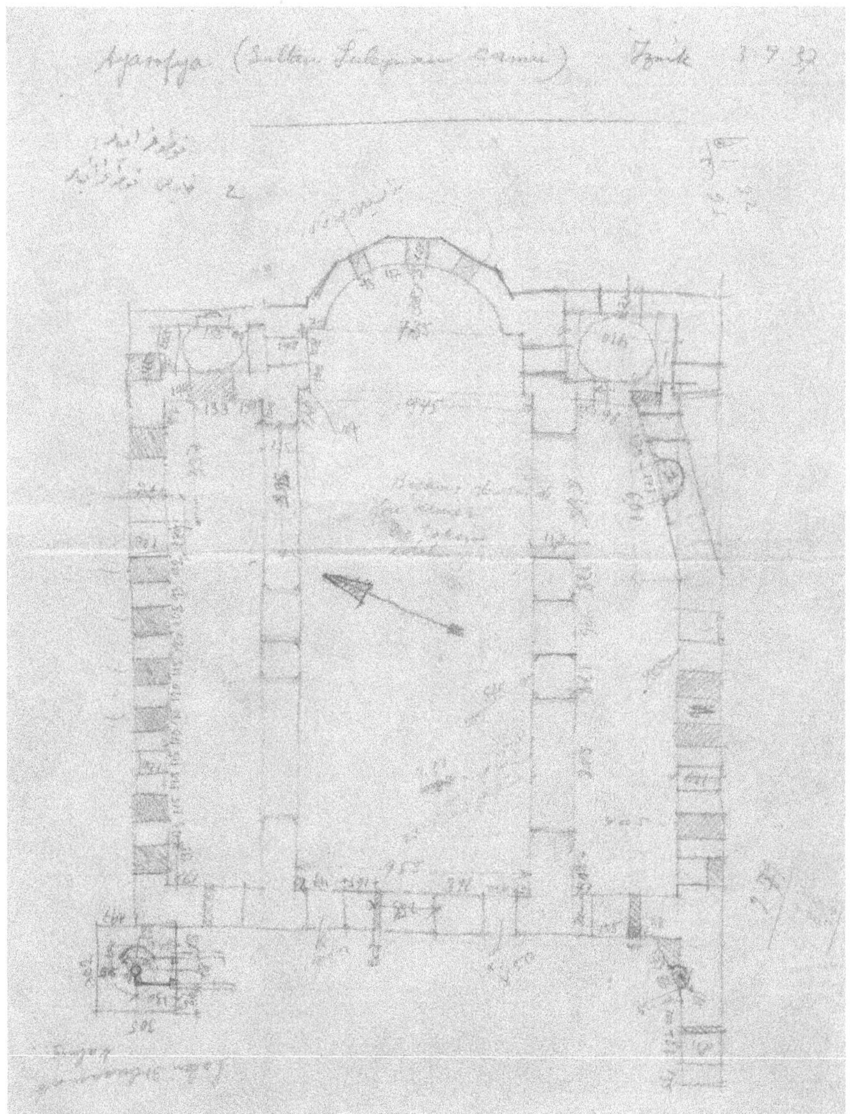

Figure 3.7. Field note for the survey of İznik's Ayasofya Mosque, delineated by Ali Saim Ülgen, September 3, 1937. SALT Research, Ali Saim Ülgen Archive, TASUDOC171001.

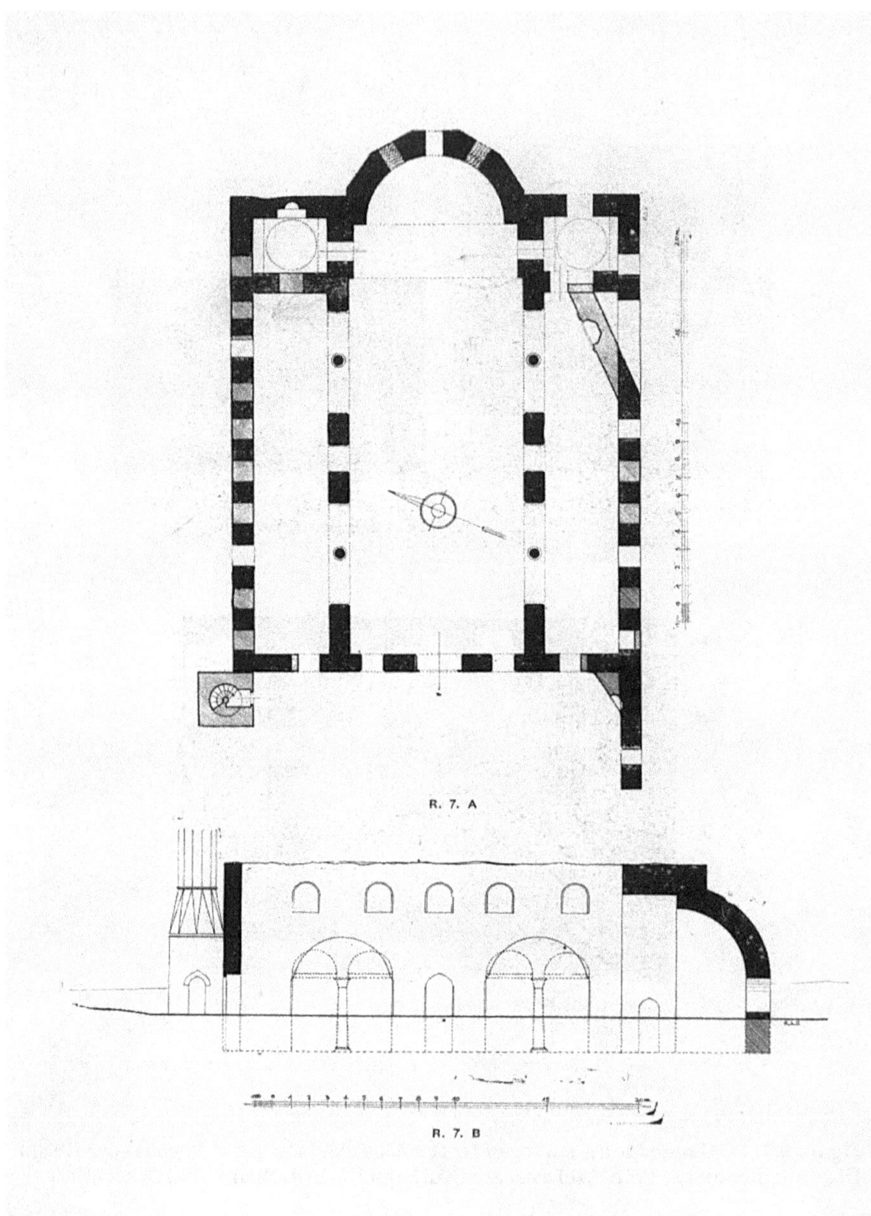

Figure 3.8. Measured drawing of İznik's Ayasofya Mosque, delineated by Ali Saim Ülgen. Ali Saim Ülgen "İznik'te Türk Eserleri," *Vakıflar Dergisi* 1, Ankara, 1938.

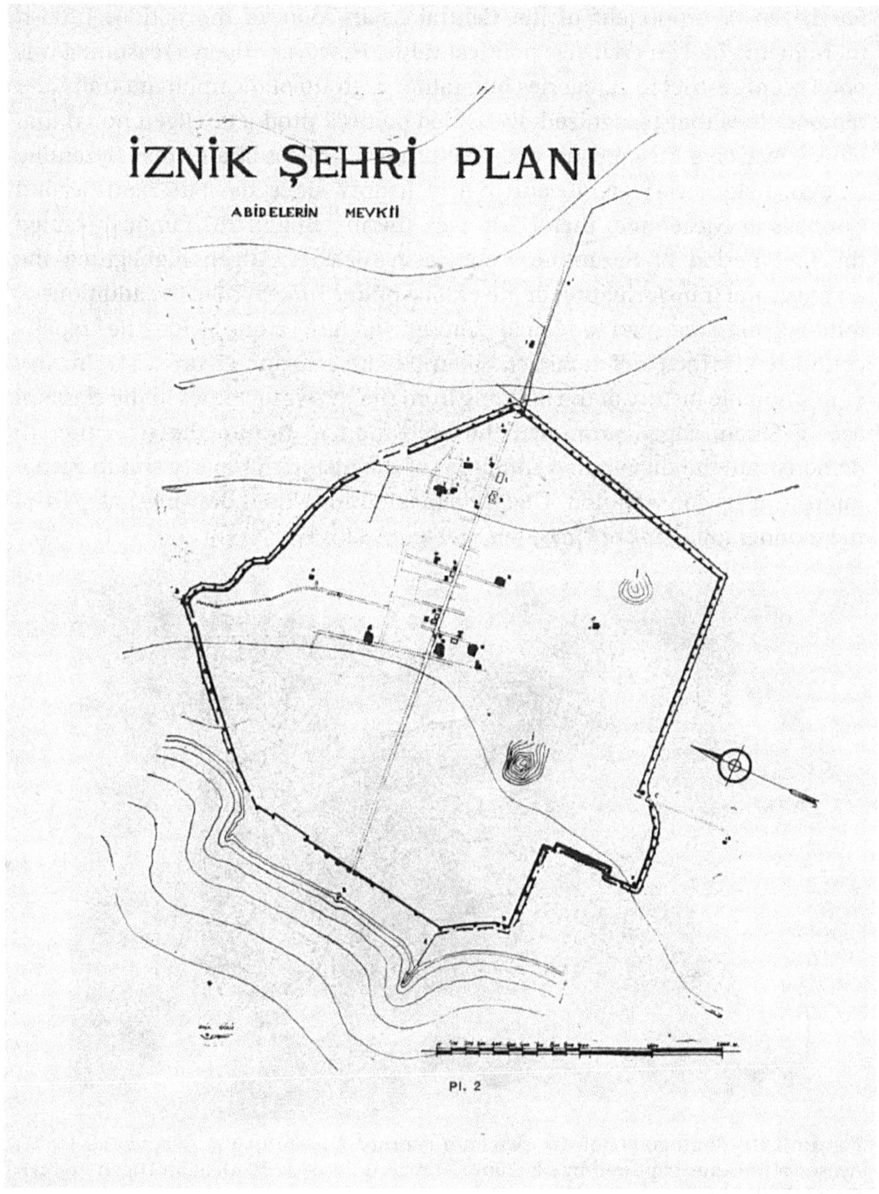

Figure 3.9. Site plan of the monuments within the citadel of İznik, delineated by Ali Saim Ülgen. Ali Saim Ülgen, "İznik'te Türk Eserleri," *Vakıflar Dergisi* 1, Ankara, 1938.

For Ülgen, a proponent of the Central Asian roots of the nation, Turkish monuments had an exclusive political value. However, Ülgen's reasoning was not a set of restricted categories but, rather, a group of recombinant traits and temporalities that recognized diversified cultural products. Ülgen noted that İznik's Ayasofya Mosque, an adaptive re-used project of a former Byzantine church, held a very significant role in history since the First and Second Councils of Nicaea met there. [62] In fact, the meeting in 787 famously ended the first period of Byzantine Iconoclasm. Besides, Ülgen highlighted the architectural transformation of the edifice under Turkish rule: the additions of minbar, minaret, and widened interior arches, along with the repairs conducted by the chief architect, Sinan (Figure 3.10 and Figure 3.11). In view of this notable history of the building from the Byzantine times to the classical age of Sinan, Ülgen promoted the obligation to restore the structure. To demonstrate the dilapidated condition of the historic property and to garner interest in its conservation, Ülgen delineated measured drawings, as part of the monograph, *İznik'te Türk Eserleri* (Figure 3.8). [63]

Figure 3.10. Photograph of the sixteenth-century mihrab of the dilapidated İznik's Ayasofya Mosque, captured by Ali Saim Ülgen. SALT Research, Ali Saim Ülgen Archive, TASUH7391002.

---

62 Ibid.

63 Ibid., 53.

Figure 3.11. Image of the sixteenth-century minaret of the İznik's Ayasofya Mosque, taken by Ali Saim Ülgen. SALT Research, Ali Saim Ülgen Archive, TASUH7391.

When it came to creating a permanent record of heritage at risk, Ülgen was not the only architect addressing the urgency of measured surveys. Kemal Altan (unknown -1948), a restoration-architect and historian who also worked at the Istanbul Archaeological Museums, was one of the historical figures devoted to archival building documentation. Altan predominantly focused on Turkish art and architecture, and extensively published his documentation findings. For Altan anchor monuments had been receiving funds for repairs and maintenance. Yet, small-scale structures contributing to the cultural landscape were doomed to dilapidation due to public negligence and lack of resources, if they had not been already sacrificed to new development.[64] On many occasions, Altan regretted that an inexorable tide of destruction had already taken its toll, and buildings that he knew dearly were wiped out before he could compile an archival record. Most significantly, Altan underscored the

---

[64] H. Bedir Ülgen, "İstanbul'da Tarihi Eserler: Bu Ne Tezat?" *Kurun*, May 13, 1936, 3.

duty of architects to capture these unrecorded legacies before they faced the wrecking ball.[65]

Unfortunately, the corpus of Altan's field drawings has not survived to day. However, his publications indicate his emphasis on measured surveys as a form of insurance for historic properties. For example, as early as 1935, Altan wrote about the duty to save Istanbul's sixteenth-century Siyavuş Pasha Pavilion, designed by the chief architect, Sinan (Figure 1.9 and Figure 2.20). Located on the outskirts of the city the building was in a derelict condition since it was used as a storage facility.[66] To describe the pavilion, Altan added his own measured drawings and photographs to the editorial piece. Altan noted that, in fact, it was Ülgen, at the time a student-architect at the Academy, who initiated the formal interest in the historic structure. [67] For the National Architecture Seminar, Ülgen compiled measured drawings and a preliminary report on the Siyavuş Pasha Pavilion, a rare example of a residential building designed by Sinan. Plausibly, after Altan saw Ülgen's documentation work at the student exhibition at the Academy, the senior architect embarked on his own documentation campaign of the structure.

If it had been Byzantine architecture that was either re-used with a different function or annexed to new construction in the Turkish city, a detailed documentation work materialized within the operational scheme of the Turkish History Thesis. In the orbit of the rise of Turkish architecture, the historiography of repurposed historic properties directly included the institutionalized mix of old and new building forms. Altan confirmed that Turkish architects did not hesitate to embrace the Byzantine monuments and to bless them with the architectural program of Islam. He stressed that these architectural "mementos had been carved with the beauty of the Turkish spirit."[68] Despite Altan's sustained efforts to preserve, unfortunately, most of

---

[65] For example, the İmrahor Mosque, Ahmed Pasha Mosque, and Manastır Masjid had to be documented. Kemal Altan, "Bizans Eserleri Üzerinde Türk Mimarlarının İşleri," *Arkitekt* 8 no. 68 (1936): 224-226.

[66] Altan, "Siyaveş Paşa Kasrı," *Arkitekt* 9 no. 57 (1935): 268-269.

[67] In the editorial piece, Altan congratulates Ülgen, then a student-architect at the Academy, to garner interest in the protection of the historic pavilion. Altan, "Mimari Kıymeti olan Binalarımız: Sinan'in Siyavuş Paşaya Yaptığı Kasır," *Zaman*, May 25, 1935, 5.

[68] Ibid., 226.

the architectural fabric[69] has been lost and no known documentation records exist apart from the few photographs and field drawings that Altan had published.

In fact, one of the historic buildings at risk, to which Altan voiced the urgency for its documentation, faced demolition during the boom in new construction, and thus became the subject of a heated discussion. The now-lost seventeenth-century Tulumcu Hüsam Mosque (also known as Tulum Hüsameddin Masjid) in Fatih, Istanbul, was demolished in 1945 by the order of the General Directorate of Endowments and its ashlar stones were ransacked to be used in the restoration of the fifteenth-century Sultanahmet Firuzağa Mosque and in the construction of Istanbul's new Şişli Mosque (c. 1949).[70] Çetintaş condemned the loss of the Tulumcu Hüsam Mosque "...Bestowed to the history of [Turkish] civilization, our fathers entrusted the protection of their monuments to us. Certainly, we cannot forgive these offensive hands demolishing [this Turkish monument]." [71] Similarly, Ülgen disapproved of the General Directorate's fervent action and wrote a petition signed by community members and preservation professionals.[72] Ülgen scorned the irrevocable loss of "this unprecedented example of national architecture," as he was about to secure provisions to document the mosque as part of his forthcoming book, *Türk Mimarisine Giriş* (*Introduction to Turkish Architecture*).[73]

Ayverdi's reasoning in archival building documentation, in this context, aligned with peer professionals, who assigned the highest priority to document historic properties of national significance, particularly those in

---

[69] In 1936, by the time he was writing "Bizans Eserleri Üzerinde Türk Mimarlarının İşleri," Altan noted that Istanbul's Odalar Mosque, Kandili Güzel Masjid, and Toklu Ibrahim Masjid already got demolished.

[70] Ülgen, "Zabıt," (Memorandum, SALT Research, Ali Saim Ülgen Archive, TASUDOC04 71007, October 23 1945). https://archives.saltresearch.org/handle/123456789/78741 (accessed September 20, 2021)

[71] Çetintaş, "Tulumcu Hüsameddin Kimdir, Tulumu nasıl bir Şeydir?" in *İstanbul ve Mimari Yazıları*, ed. Dervişoğlu (Ankara: Türk Tarih Kurumu Basımevi, 2011), 300.

[72] Ülgen, "Zabıt," (Memorandum, SALT Research, Ali Saim Ülgen Archive, TASUDOC04 71007, October 23 1945). https://archives.saltresearch.org/handle/123456789/78741 (accessed September 20, 2021)

[73] Ülgen, "Rapor," (Memorandum, SALT Research, Ali Saim Ülgen Archive, TASUDO C0476021, date unknown). https://archives.saltresearch.org/handle/123456789/735 33 (accessed September 20, 2021)

danger of demolition or mutilation. Yet, his documentation work vibrated with an academic focus on Turkish - Ottoman architecture. Ayverdi was a proponent of the Central Asian roots of the Thesis; Turks came from Central steps and settled in Anatolia. Ayverdi, nonetheless, diverged from Gökalp's concept on Central Asia as the true homeland of Turks. Ayverdi stressed that the exodus constituted the essence of the history of the nation. Yet, the yearning for these far lands in Central Asia would prove futile in a political capacity, since it was impossible for the republican government to virtually and legally claim those lands.[74] Instead, Ayverdi supported "the civilization of Anatolia and Rumelia of the Ottoman country," encompassing all the Anatolian and European lands under imperial rule.[75] The Turkish architecture brought forward in this far-fetched landscape, then, constituted the only material evidence for the artistic creativity of the nation.

Coined as "The Tale of Anatolian Civilization," Ayverdi ridiculed the concept that all the architectural landscape layered in Anatolia (Hittite, Phrygian, Lydian, Roman, or Byzantine), exhibited the building traditions of the Turkish race. Ayverdi stressed that these ancient peoples disappeared from the surface of the earth centuries ago and only some archaeological remnants prevailed as a proof of their existence. Turks, on the other hand, belonged to a different ethnic race who came from the East, and honored these archaeological remains as a memento.[76] When Turks settled in the new frontiers, they brought their own cultural, economic, and political institutions from Central Asia. Turks' capacity to develop autonomous architecture without imitating Byzantine building traditions, and to arrive at "the world's only pure and genuine architecture" confirmed an astonishing phenomenon.[77]

Ayverdi's archival building documentation heavily focused on the identification of the civilization of Anatolia and Rumelia.[78] His earlier documentation work on the dynastic beginnings of Ottoman architecture and then his corpus on the architectural patronage of Sultan Mehmed II (Figure 3.12 and 3.13), mirrors his interest in capturing the Turkish architectural heritage in unity, spanning from the modern borders of Turkey to former provinces of the Ottoman Empire. His later work, understandably was

[74] Ayverdi, "Anadolu Medeniyeti Masalı," *Makaleler,* 394.

[75] Ibid., 373.

[76] Ibid., 376-377; 380-389.

[77] Ibid, 388.

[78] Ibid., 373.

dedicated to mapping the architectural works in the Balkans, including Albania, Bulgaria, Greece, Hungary, Romania, Yugoslavia. Ayverdi sought out the architectural heritage in these regions to prove the civilization of Anatolia and Rumelia, in particular against the critical eyes who did not believe in its existence. Ayverdi regretted that the architectural evidence located abroad was bound to disappear due to the political hostility to Ottoman civilization. Hence, documentation was essential to capture the footprints of the creativity of the Turkish nation before they vanished altogether.

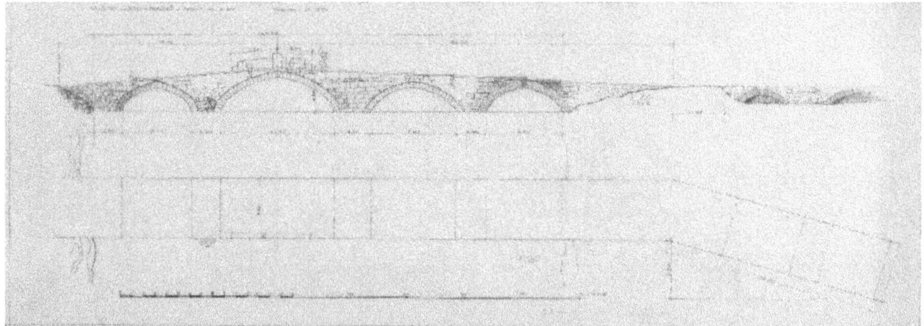

Figure 3.12. Elevation and plan of the Nilüfer Hatun Bridge, delineated by Ekrem Hakkı Ayverdi, 1963. Ekrem Hakkı Ayverdi Institute Archive, Kubbealtı Waqf Collection, Istanbul.

Çetintaş, the founding chief of the Surveying Bureau, interpreted archival building documentation to get access to the composition of historic works and to acquire an understanding of the builder's cognitive hierarchy. With documentation findings, categorization and periodization of artworks would be automatically achieved and the historiography on Turkish architecture could be written, "This operative surgery [a.n. Çetintaş habitually coins *rölöve* as *ameliyat*] puts forward the mentality of the master on art and technics in a very detailed manner, to which we owe for recognizing and reading the enthusiasm and the professional identity of the creator. Once the persons' artistic identity became visible, with the aid of [measured drawings] the periods and stages of art history get innately revealed."[79]

[79] Çetintaş, "Maruz Maldığımız Müşkilat ve Tek Çare," in *Istanbul ve Mimari Yazıları*, 36.

Figure 3.13. Section drawing of Bursa's Hamza Bey Mosque, delineated by Ekrem Hakkı Ayverdi, 1968. Ekrem Hakkı Ayverdi Institute Archive, Kubbealtı Waqf Collection, Istanbul.

A fervent supporter of Atatürk and his ideals on the study of Turkish history, Çetintaş acknowledged the origins of the Turkish civilization in the Central Asian steppes, with the republican Turkey been the latest phase.[80]

> We all know, our Republic is secular. There is not an individual [citizen] left [in our country], who has still not inscribed this to their head and heart. Even a modest building is a page written on stone, [representing] the Turkish history and civilization, our secular Republic protects all these buildings with utmost respect. In the eye of the Republic, there does not exist a class difference between a mosque, a tomb, or a

[80] Çetintaş, "Kör Kazma," in *İstanbul ve Mimari Yazıları*, 14.

> madrasa, but prevails "Turkish monuments" prevail, which represent separate patronages in the history of the Turkish culture...[81]

Çetintaş drew a parallel between conducting archival research and building documentation; for those who know how to read these books made of stones, bricks, and mortars, to discover its chronology and its architect from the embodied expression in an arch, window, and cornice was child's play.[82] Under his supervision, the Surveying Bureau became instrumental to read the formal components of Turkish architecture and to coordinate documentation, registration, and provisions for their protection. As early as 1940, Çetintaş and his colleagues at the bureau completed the registration of historical works in miscellaneous cities across Turkey including Ankara, Amasya, Diyarbakır, Edirne, Istanbul, Kayseri, Sivas, and Trabzon, and catalogued these with maps, measured drawings, and written histories.[83]

Despite his comments on the overarching stewardship of the republican state and the protection of all the architectural patrimony, Çetintaş favored monumental and classical example of the Ottoman heritage over "lesser" and later specimens.[84] The folios of measured drawings prepared at the Surveying Bureau operated to weigh monuments against each other. On the basis of architectural and historical value, the selected monuments worthy of preservation would be maintained while the rest was doomed to be demolished. Çetintaş clarified the principle of selection at the bureau on the basis of a strict division of architectural significance: masterpieces followed by first, second, and third tiers. In this matrix, the unnecessary cluster of buildings in the third category could be demolished without further notice. Çetintaş noted that with their cleanup, Istanbul Public Works would breathe a sigh of relief. [85]

Eldem's analysis of the evolutionary path of Turkish architecture rested on the exodus from Central Asia to Anatolia. Eldem acknowledged the Central Asian origins of Turkish architecture and classified the Anatolian Seljuk built

---

[81] Ibid., 15.

[82] Çetintaş, "Mimar Sedat Çetintaş'la bir Konuşma," in *İstanbul ve Mimari Yazıları*, 111.

[83] Ibid., 113.

[84] Altınyıldız, "The Architectural Heritage of Istanbul and the Ideology of Preservation," in *Muqarnas*, 24, (2007), ed. Bozdoğan and Necipoğlu, p. 293; Madran, "Cumhuriyet'in ilk Otuz Yılında (1920-1950) Koruma Alanının Örgütlenmesi-I," p.81.

[85] Şevket Rado, "Mimar Çetintaş'la bir Konuşma," *Akşam*, 10 October 1940, *İstanbul ve Mimari Yazıları*, 112.

heritage as the predecessor of Ottoman forms.[86] Eldem emphasized that the regional building materials culminated in the original character of Seljuk forms in Anatolia. Unlike the more primitive structures in Asia, the great majority of Anatolian Seljuk buildings were built of ashlar stone. The specific construction techniques of stone masonry culminated in the authentic Anatolian Seljuk building forms. Notably, the purification of architectural compositions and scale was evident in Anatolian Seljuk forms, which in fact paved the way for the modern attributes of Ottoman architecture. Eldem defined the emergence of the Ottoman building forms in medieval Anatolia as "a miraculous birth" due to the decline of the architectural styles at the time. The Seljuk architecture, with the disintegration of its state, was in decline and their essential form now a purely decorative state. Byzantine architecture was also in its final stages. In contrast to earlier inspiring structural solutions, their late buildings resembled figurines buried in decorative elements and frescoes. The emergence of modular, purified, and rational Ottoman forms in this relapsed design culture should be regarded as a miracle, according to Eldem.

Eldem's documentation work, in this context, can be interpreted in the context of formal and stylistic reappropriations of Turkish architecture in modern design. Despite the strong ideological association with the terms of modern and national in the architectural culture of the early republic, Eldem had a strong position against a universally postulated avant-garde modernism that discards culture, context, and history. Instead, Eldem believed that the most viable sources of modern, thus national, Turkish architecture were deep-rooted in the country's own building traditions. Unlike his fellow scholars' focus on monumental architecture, Eldem turned to houses, residential pavilions, and palaces as an inspiration. For Eldem, the functional, structural, and formal rationality was the defining character of the Turkish house.[87]

Eldem cultivated a formal interest in building documentation when he was a student-architect at the Academy. Over the weekends, Eldem's excursions in the streets of Istanbul led him to the traditional neighborhoods of the historic peninsula. There, Eldem realized the human scale embodied in the wooden houses. Despite the subtle motifs and rhythms of individual houses, to his amazement, overall, the architectural composition was unified. To probe the harmonious character of residential architecture, Eldem began making

---

[86] Eldem, *Türk Mimari Eserleri (Works of Turkish Architecture)* (İstanbul: Binbirdirek Matbaacılık Sanayii A.Ş. Yayınları, 1975).
[87] Bozdoğan, "The Legacy of an Istanbul Architect," 133.

sketches in-situ.[88] Eldem's prioritization of documentation as a tool of analysis continued in his post-graduate studies in Europe.[89] Eldem spent two years traveling and making sketches of his surroundings. His illustrations, often juxtapositions of actual forms and design concepts, exhibit a prolific repertoire from white Mediterranean cubes to Central Anatolian dwellings. Eldem truly believed that the vernacular architecture of the Balkans, Anatolia, and the Mediterranean were already modern. Building documentation, thus, became a compelling agenda for Eldem to achieve his theoretical and methodological premises.

Later, teaching the National Architecture Seminar at the Academy, Eldem embarked on an elaborate program of archival building documentation. Over the years, his students enrolled at the seminar documented and studied vernacular architecture across the country. Eldem's primary legacy entails the codification and theorization of this monumental documentation work to define the rational characteristics of the Turkish house. For Eldem, the Turkish house was a recognizable cultural artifact in the former territories of the Ottoman Empire in Balkans, Middle East, and from North Africa to Anatolia. Although regional variations existed in the Turkish house, constant features made it a distinct architectural type. These features included the lifting of the main floor above a service/storage floor on the ground, a clear differentiation between the rooms upper floor projections supported by brackets, circulation spaces, rows of windows reflecting the wooden structure, and a roof with overhanging eaves.[90]

Building Anatolian humanism in the aftermath of the Turkish History Thesis

Subsequent to Atatürk's passing in 1938, which deprived TTK and TDK of patronage at the highest level, the republican polity strengthened the early thesis of national origin into an officially sanctioned identity, and the state was overtly committed to cultural westernization. Albeit sustained for a very brief period, the rise of humanism overlapped with the appointment of Hasan Âli Yücel (1897–1961) as the head of the Minister of Education between 1938-1946. Then, a new generation of cultural theorists, called Blueists, including Cevat Şakir Kabaağaçlı (*Halikarnas Balıkçısı*) (1886-1973), Nurullah Ataç (1898–1957), Sabahattin Eyüboğlu (1908-1973), and Azra Erhat (1915-1982)

88 Yenal and Özkan, *Sedad Eldem ile Söyleşiler*, 38-39.

89 Ibid., 43-52.

90 Bozdoğan, "The Legacy of an Istanbul Architect," 134.

separated themselves from the racial proclivities of the 1930s and stipulated the organization of a Western-oriented "humanism" in Turkey. *Tercüme Bürosu* (State Translation Bureau), founded in 1940, significantly, contributed to the dissemination of humanist ideas, through the translation of world classics into Turkish. While a few non-Western pieces were included in the portfolio of translations, the majority of the works were chosen from ancient Greek and French literature. The state's fervent commitment to establish a classical culture also reverberated with the introduction of ancient Greek and Latin curricula in some high schools. In 1940, the launch of *Köy Enstitüleri* (the village institutes) entailed a monumental manifestation to reach out with "humanist" educational reform to a largely agricultural society.[91]

To Blueists, Anatolia was the cradle of civilization, which formed an indigenous cultural expression on Anatolian soil from the prehistoric times to the present day. Regarding the Anatolian past as a culturally and socially cohesive nation, Blueists translated a modernizing ideological project of Turkey. Blueists followed up earlier attempts of the Ministry of Education in the mid-1930s to teach the stratified built environment of Anatolia at schools and to claim all historical works exhibited the building traditions of Turks.[92] Nonetheless, the Blueists diverged from the Ministry's racial focus on the Turkish people as the precursor of the civilizations in Anatolia. Instead, they presented the current stewards of the land, Turks, a discourse that had taken root in the expressions of their cultural ancestors, Greeks, Romans, Byzantines, Seljuks, Ottomans, and others. With the noteworthy contribution of all the civilizations to the culture of Anatolia, the Blueists amplified three chapters in the history of Turkey; the Hittites since they formed a bridge between the lands of Mesopotamia and the Aegean coast; the Trojans, because they fought against the Greeks; and the Ionians as they were the birthplace of Homer's legends and the first philosophers.[93]

Blueists crafted a wide collection of intellectual works in anthropology, architecture, art, cinema, and literature. These works, to a large extent, aimed to establish that the people of Anatolia, although not ethnically homogenous,

---

[91] Can S. M. Bilsel, "Our Anatolia": Organicism and the Making of Humanist Culture in Turkey," ed. Bozdoğan and Necipoğlu, *Muqarnas* 24 (2007), 228.

[92] Madran, "Cumhuriyet'in ilk Otuz Yılında (1920–1950) Koruma Alanının Örgütlenmesi-I," *ODTU MFD* 16, no. 1-2 (1996):74; Gülekli, *Eski Eserler ve Müzelerle ilgili Kanun Nizamname ve Emirler*, 85-88.

[93]Bilsel, "Our Anatolia," 223–224.

were the solitary inheritors of an indivisible and authentic culture. Eyüboğlu's torrent of words mark the gist of Anatolian humanism,

> The history of our nation is the history of Anatolia. Once we were pagans, then we became Christians, after that Muslims. It is this nation who erected temples, churches, and mosques. It was us who went to snow-white theaters and then to dark caravanserais. At times, we stretched to the steppes, at times, to the blue sea. Countless states, civilizations raised from our backbones, and then collapsed. We spoke seventy-two languages before deciding on Turkish. We still remember all these flavors... [94]

With the rise of Islamism in Turkey, the humanist version of the republic's myth of origin was abruptly deleted from the rhetoric of the nation-state. Blueists' uniting nationalism did not stand a chance against a foundation myth that consecutively pledged patriotism with Islamic symbols and promoted the ethno-centric definition of the nation as Muslim-Turks. In 1954, the village institutes were closed and some of the prominent Blueists were incarcerated in the following years. Under these circumstances, the short-lived state philosophy of the Blueists, unfortunately, could not thoroughly transliterate to the official agenda of archival building documentation.

Celebrating the quincentenary of the Ottoman conquest of Constantinople

The seeds of Islamism can be formally traced as early as 1939, just a year after Atatürk's passing, when the republican authorities concurred to celebrate the five hundredth anniversary of the Ottoman conquest of Constantinople in May 29, 1953. Overseen by the President İnönü, the Ministry of Education and TTK established an organization committee. Hasan Âli Yücel became the chairperson of the committee, which consisted of representatives from respective ministries along with representatives from Istanbul Municipality. The committee planned conferences and publications for Istanbul and Sultan Mehmed II along with organizing international exhibitions at universities. The Commission for the Preservation of Monuments was then tasked to organize the provisions for the historic preservation of the monuments of Istanbul. With these preparations, the glorification of the Ottoman-Islamic past became a convenient charter to re-formulate the national monuments of the Turks. While

---

[94] Sabahattin Eyüboğlu, *Mavi ve Kara: Denemeler* (İstanbul: Ataç Kitabevi, 1961), 1.

the Ottoman conquest of the city became publicized through printed media, the associated architectural heritage (both Ottoman and Byzantine) was inaugurated as part of the nationalist discourse. The essentialist tenet of the Turkish History Thesis, a conspicuous de-emphasis on the Ottoman past, quickly waned with the advent of the imperial and the Islamic past now seen as the roots of the nation.[95]

Çetintaş, who was known for his commitment to the documentation and conservation of the Turkish built environment, in 1939 founded *Güzideler Komisyonu* (Commission for the Distinguished) with intellectual elites of the time. In accordance with his learning under Kemalettin Bey's mentorship at the Ministry of Endowments, Çetintaş prioritized the restoration of Turkish architectural heritage as the beacons of the celebrations. Çetintaş fervently opposed erecting new memorial statues across the city while most of the historic properties associated with the conquest were in a dilapidated condition or had become subject to poor preservation treatments.[96]

Against the background of "Turkish Istanbul," a slogan of Yahya Kemal Beyatlı (1884-1958), author, poet, and diplomat, Çetintaş heavily criticized the destruction of Turkish monuments.[97][98] Çetintaş openly favored the upkeep of the early and classical Ottoman built environment. In return, Çetintaş demanded the authorities cleanse Istanbul from the "non-Turkish" buildings that had been erected in the Late Ottoman Era. For example, Çetintaş openly suggested the demolition of the nineteenth-century Istanbul Archaeological Museums building, the first museum facility constructed in the Ottoman Empire. Located in the outer gardens of the Topkapı Palace Museum, Çetintaş noted that the timber ceiling and flooring of the archaeological museum were susceptible to the ravages of fire. The late-imperial building was, therefore, putting the fifteenth-century examples of the Turkish built heritage, including *Çinili Köşk* (the Tiled Kiosk, also known as the Tiled Pavilion) and the

[95] Aykaç, "The Commission for the Preservation of Antiquities," 82.

[96] Çetintaş, "Fatih Evvela Bizi Fethetmeli," in *İstanbul ve Mimari Yazıları*, ed. Dervişoğlu (Ankara: Türk Tarih Kurumu Basımevi, 2011), 391-392; Çetintaş, "Fatih'i Tahkir mi yoksa Kutlamak mı? Tavı Geçmiş Demire Çekiç Vurulursa Kırılır," in *İstanbul ve Mimari Yazıları*, ed. Dervişoğlu (Ankara: Türk Tarih Kurumu Basımevi, 2011), 444-447.

[97] Yahya Kemal Beyatlı, "Kör Kazma," in *Aziz İstanbul* (İstanbul: Milli Eğitim Basımevi Devlet Kitapları, 1969), 152-155.

[98] Proponent of the architectural heritage of Turks over "lesser" and later specimens created by foreigners in the Late Ottoman Era, Yahya Kemal had written that "the new generation of Turks had been infected with the microbe of newness." Ibid.,153.

structures in the adjacent Topkapı Palace Museum in imminent danger. Most significantly, Çetintaş asserted that the Neo-Greek style of the Istanbul Archaeological Museums building was a disgrace to Kemalettin Bey's Turkish revivalist architecture (for example, his First and Fourth Vakıf Hans) located in the historic neighborhood.[99]

Çetintaş was not the only preservation professional proposing the demolition of the Neo-Greek-styled building. Tahsin Öz, historian and director of the Topkapı Palace Museum, was also favoring the demolition of the museum facility in order to restore the Tiled Kiosk to its fifteenth-century setting (Figure 3.14). Öz stated that Mehmet II had commissioned the Tiled Kiosk as a recreational structure for archery and javelin-throwing events, for which practice fields had been constructed on the premises. To meet the Turkish Istanbul setting of the conquest, the original form of the site had to be retrieved, Öz justified.[100]

Figure 3.14. Tiled Kiosk in the Late Ottoman Empire, when the building was used as the imperial museum, view from the courtyard. Koç University, Suna Kıraç Library Special Collections and Archives, Mehmet Nihat Nigizberk Collection of Architectural Drawings and Photographs, MNN_ALB18_phg_060.

---

[99] Çetintaş, "Fatih'i Tahkir mi," 446; Çetintaş, "Topkapı Sarayını Tehdit eden Binayı Yıkmalıyız," in *İstanbul ve Mimari Yazıları*, ed. Dervişoğlu (Ankara: Türk Tarih Kurumu Basımevi, 2011), 351-354.

[100] Cemaleddin Bildik, "Fatih'in Çiniliköşkü eski hale getiriliyor," *Akşam*, October 16, 1949, 4 and 6.

Although Çetintaş and Öz's request for the demolition of the Istanbul Archaeological Museums building did not materialize, their pursuit indicates the solidifying interest for a classical Ottoman architectural heritage. In 1950, the celebration committee formed an institute, named *İstanbul Fetih Cemiyeti* (Istanbul Conquest Association), which still actively participates in the ceremonies of the Ottoman capture of the city.[101] The aim of the association included contributing to the annual conquest celebrations and supporting historic preservation projects, research, and publications. Ayverdi, a student of Kemalettin Bey at the Ministry of Endowments, served as the director of the society between 1955-1984. In fact, Ayverdi's monograph, *Fatih Devri Mimarisi,* was published by the Istanbul Conquest Association to accommodate the quincentenary celebrations of 1953 (Figure 1.10). The rich repertoire of measured drawings in the volume was the outcome of Ayverdi's documentation campaigns between 1943 and 1952 to the previous territories of the Ottoman Empire.[102] With this volume, Ayverdi became the first native scholar to study and classify the corpus of the Turkish building traditions during the period of the conquest.

In a scale reminiscent of the colossal publications of the early republic, *Fatih Devri Mimarisi* is distinguished in the aftermath of the Turkish History Thesis. Ayverdi followed the basic formula of a formalist study: a lengthy inventory of individual properties across the late imperial lands (including repurposed Byzantine monuments and new Turkish assemblies) and a monographic analysis of monuments. Then, in a separate chapter, Ayverdi utilized this architectural and historical information to address the characteristics of the architectural patronage during the reign of Sultan Mehmed II. Ayverdi read the continued existence of an autonomous national art, which was rooted in Central Asia, carried with Anatolian Seljuks, and then culminated in "the magnificent Ottoman branch of Turkish art."[103] This progression of architecture including the Sultan Mehmed II "era was distinguished with its purity of forms without any foreign influence.

When it came to acknowledging the evident sources of influence on the architecture of Turkish Istanbul, however, Ayverdi pursued a somewhat

---

[101] Anonymous, "500üncü Fetih Yılı: Bir Kutlama Derneğinin Teşkiline Karar Verildi," *Akşam,* December 28, 1949, 3; Anonymous, "Beşyüzüncü Fetih Yılı: Istanbulun Fethini Kutlamak için bir Dernek Kuruluyor," *Akşam,* January 21, 1950, 3.

[102] Ayverdi, *Fatih Devri Mimarisi* (İstanbul: İstanbul Fetih Cemiyeti Neşriyatı, 1953), 6-7.

[103] Ibid., 481.

speculative approach. His discussion of the formation of the Tiled Kiosk, which has an architectural style, the so-called International Timurid style of Iran and Turan, exhibited this dilemma (Figure 3.15).[104] Simply isolating the historic structure from the architectural culture of the era, Ayverdi paid heed to Mehmed II's personal request to introduce a foreign style into a purely Turkish palace,

> How could [the royal architects] hesitate to grant the Conqueror's own request to build an exotic kiosk with a scenic view? This example is only one of a kind; it does not have an antecedent or an apex.[105]

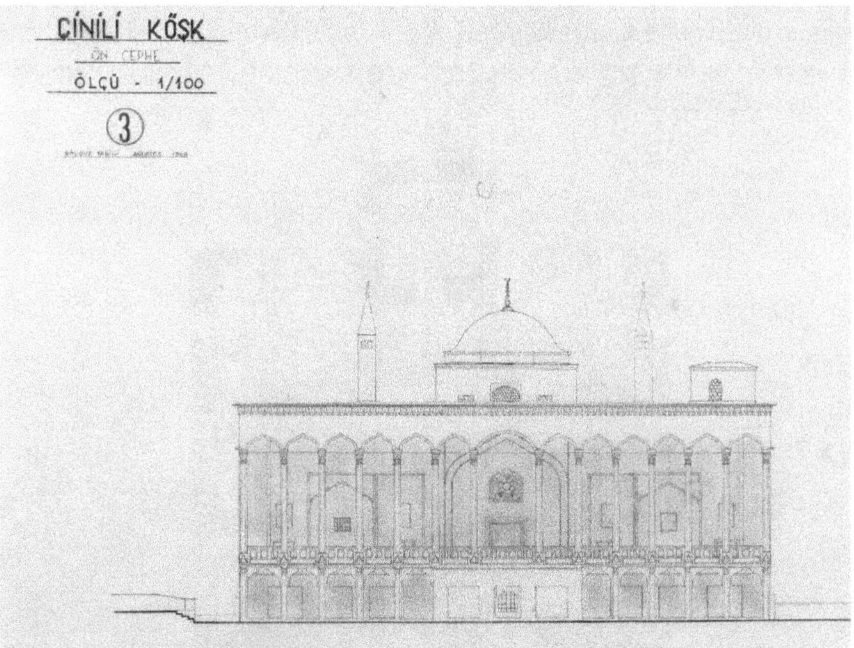

Figure 3.15. Façade of the Tiled Kiosk, delineated by Ekrem Hakkı Ayverdi, 1948. Ekrem Hakkı Ayverdi Institute Archive, Kubbealtı Waqf Collection, Istanbul.

---

104 Necipoğlu, *Architecture, Ceremonial, and Power: the Topkapı Palace in the Fifteenth and Sixteenth Centuries* (New York, NY: Architectural History Foundation, 1991), 213.
105 Ayverdi, *Fatih Devri Mimarisi*, 482.

The rhetorical weight of the primary ordinates can be felt in the measured drawings of the Tiled Kiosk, which was then repurposed as the Museum of Mehmed II to meet the preparations for 1953. Ayverdi included two subsequent measured plans of the historic structure in the volume. A measured drawing (Figure 3.16) compiled by Altan, then an architect at the Istanbul Archaeological Museums, demonstrates the nineteenth-century configuration of the structure when the facility operated as an imperial museum. In contrast, a 1948-dated measured drawing (Figure 3.17) delineated by Reşid Bey, an architect at the Department of Public Works, portrays the ongoing restoration campaign. The comparison between these two drawings reveals the restoration path on the basis of its fifteenth-century configuration. While the repairs focused on the walls, roof, and the foundation; the adjunct staircase was replaced with internal steps, the concealed niches, windows, and hearths were revealed, and the later opened doors were sealed.

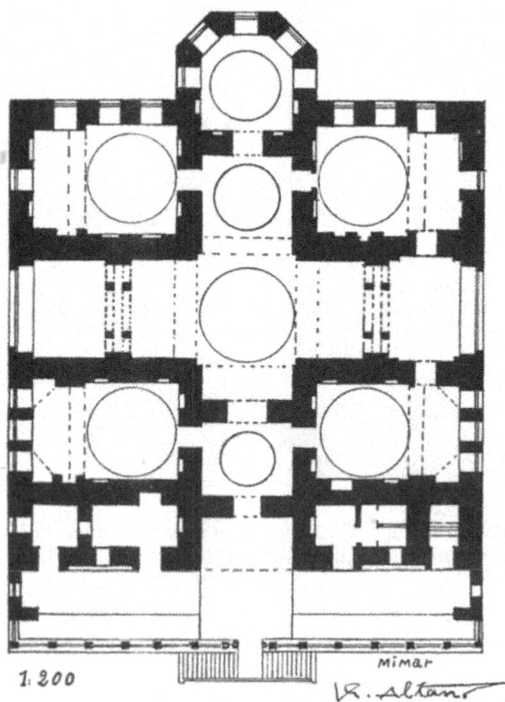

Figure 3.16. Drawing of the Tiled Kiosk, exhibiting the floor-plan when used as an imperial museum, delineated by Kemal Altan. Ekrem Hakkı Ayverdi, *Fatih Devri Mimarisi,* İstanbul: İstanbul Fetih Cemiyeti Neşriyatı, 1953.

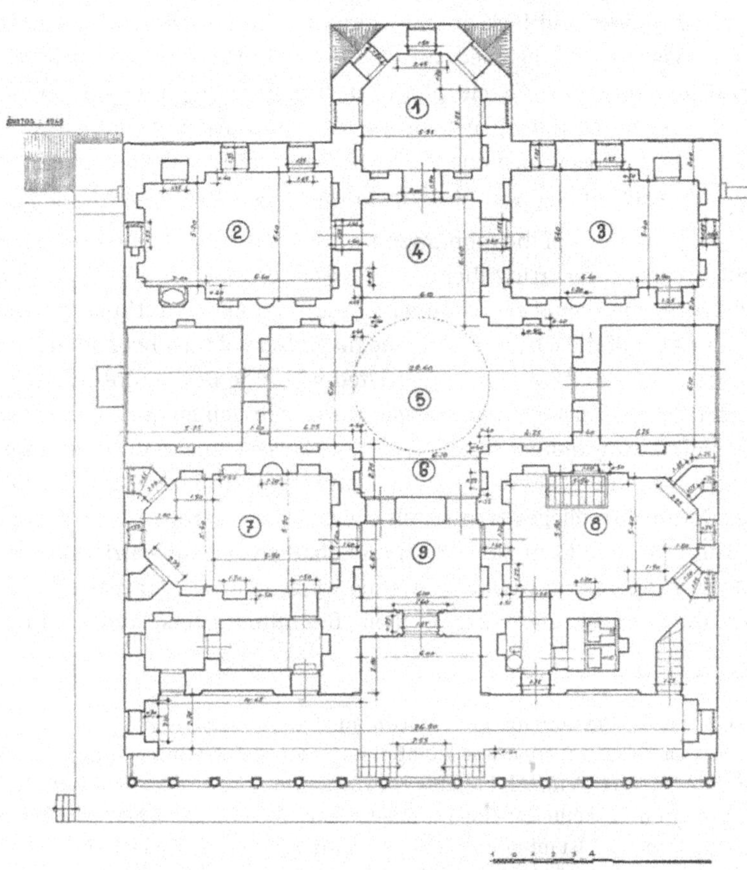

Figure 3.17. Measured drawing of the Tiled Kiosk, 1948, delineated by Reşid Bey. Ekrem Hakkı Ayverdi, *Fatih Devri Mimarisi,* İstanbul: İstanbul Fetih Cemiyeti Neşriyatı, 1953.

The purpose of the 1953 celebrations was to draw attention to the Ottoman heritage in Istanbul, yet repairs for the city walls and the Byzantine monuments converted to mosques were also considered. In 1941, the Commission for the Preservation of Monuments prepared an agenda for the documentation and preservation of the historic monuments including the Hagia Sophia Museum, Hagia Irene, Kariye Museum (Chora Church), and İmrahor Mosque (Monastery of Stoudios). By 1949, the commission compiled a detailed inventory of both existing and demolished monuments.[106] Yet, due to a limited budget and lack of state support, the members of the Istanbul Conquest Association resigned in 1951 followed by the dismissal of the preservation program.[107] None of the documentation or repairs could be achieved, except for the upkeep of the Tiled Kiosk certain facilities at the Topkapı Palace Museum, along with the intermittent repairs of the Fatih Mosque Complex and with some of the burial sites of martyrs.[108]

The poor conditions of the monuments against the background of a neglected Istanbul became a recurring theme in newspapers and tabloids. With a daily countdown to the day of the commemoration, popular print media began to share snapshots of the city, ridiculing the magnitude of the uncompleted public works. In a Turkish city which is associated with one of the most momentous events in the world history, many neighborhoods remained quite literally mired in mud.[109] The irony did not escape Çetintaş, "This cannot be the quincentenary of the conquest. Today, Rumelihisarı [a.n. also known as Boğazkesen Castle] is a garbage dump, the colleges of the Fatih University are in ruins. The caravanserai of the Fatih Mosque Complex, which once had served the carriages, was just recently torn down and public restrooms were built in their place."[110, 111, 112] Besides the Turkish monuments, their Byzantine peers were sharing an

[106] Aykaç, "The Commission for the Preservation of Antiquities," 84.

[107] By 1951, all the members of the Istanbul Conquest Association resigned. See, M. R. E., "İstanbul 500üncü Fetih Yılı Kutlama Hazırlığı Aksıyor," *Akşam*, May 17, 1951, 3 and 7; also, Anonymous, "Fetih Kutlama Derneğindeki Istifalar," *Akşam*, May 23, 1951, 3.

[108] Müjgan Cunbur, "İstanbul'un 500üncü Fetih Yıldönümü Dolayısiyle Tertiplenen Sergilere, Yapılan Kültür, San'at ve Neşriyat Hareketlerine dair," *Vakıflar Dergisi* 4 (1958): 265; Altınyıldız, "The Architectural Heritage of Istanbul," 293.

[109] Anonymous, "İşte Turist Şehri Istanbul: Tarihte yeni bir Devir Açan Fethin 500üncü Yıl Dönümüne Tam 766 Gün Kaldı," *Akşam*, 24 April, 1951, 3; also see Anonymous, "İşte Turist Şehri Istanbul: Tarihte yeni bir Devir Açan Fethin 500üncü Yıl Dönümüne Tam 743 Gün Kaldı," *Akşam*, May 17, 1951, 4.

[110] Çetintaş, "Fatih'i Tahkir mi," 468.

[111] Surprisingly, as late as 1951, authorities were still sorting the derelict neighborhoods of Istanbul to jump start the revitalization of the built environment. Anonymous, "Süleymaniye: Caminin Manzarasını Bozan Enstitü Binasının Kaldırılması Muhtemel," *Akşam*, January 29, 1951, 3 and 6.

[112] A. Adnan Adıvar, "Fetih Yılı", *Akşam*, 1952, August 24, 1 and 2. Approximately a year before the quincentenary event, Adıvar (1882-1955), the prominent author and politician, ridiculed the failure of organizing "even a modest celebration," and humorously stated the commemoration should be limited to "101-gun salute."

unfortunate destiny. In a field report, Ülgen inscribed the "tragic conditions" of the Byzantine monuments listed in the inventories for the quincentenary of the conquest. Due to regular maintenance, only the museums of Hagia Sophia and Kariye (Figure 3.18) were in a relatively reasonable condition, but the rest of the monuments were barely standing.[113]

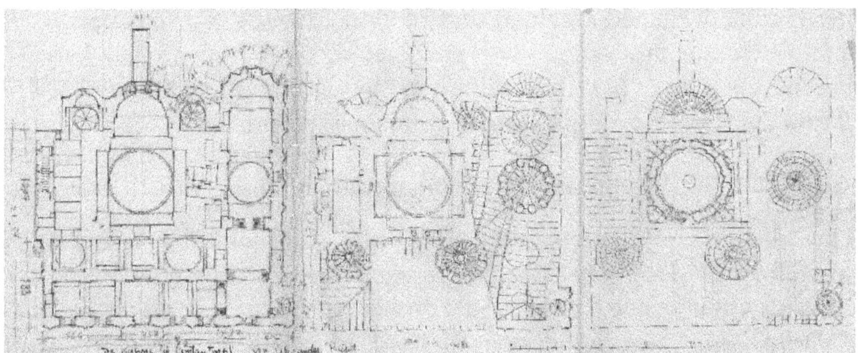

Figure 3.18. Field drawing of the Kariye Mosque during the repairs of 1946, delineated by Cahide Tamer. Koç University, Suna Kıraç Library Special Collections and Archives, Cahide Tamer Historic Buildings Restoration Projects Collection, S102_D02_jpg, CTA_S102_D02_dra_03.

By the time of the five hundredth anniversary, the celebrations had already fallen out of favor. The official ceremony was more modest than projected, organized with two separate programs in Istanbul and Ankara.[114] The commemorative events focused on the organization of art contests, conferences, exhibitions, public lectures, publications, radio shows, school events, and theater plays.[115] The emerging historiography from the published corpus, however, indicates the growing synthesis of the Ottoman past with the nationalist milieu, where the shared memories of May 29, 1453, became

---

[113] Ülgen, "İstanbul'daki Bizans Eserleri Hakkında Rapor," (Report, SALT Research, Ali Saim Ülgen Archive, TASUDOC1323, September 5 1953). https://archives.saltresearch.org/handle/123456789/75855 (accessed September 20, 2021)

[114] Neither the president Mahmut Celâl Bayar nor the prime minister Adnan Menderes attended the actual inauguration.

[115] For the resulting events and historiography, see, Cunbur, "İstanbul'un 500üncü Fetih Yıldönümü," 265-281.

integral to the national identity of Turks.[116] Evidently, the contents of all these events repetitively accentuated Sultan Mehmed II's Turkish national identity, his revolutionary, pro-Western outlook, and his secularism. Hence, Sultan Mehmed II was not an Ottoman emperor, but the "great Turkish ruler" of a "great Turkish empire" who bestowed Istanbul, his "eternal gift," to the Turkish nation.[117] Among many academic texts, the recurring theme was the portrayal of the superior military and political authority of Sultan Mehmed II and the cultural production of the era. That said, the Ottoman built heritage became the imprint of Turkish culture and the academic focus transitioned to the fifteenth and sixteenth centuries of architectural production.

Becoming the "other" monuments

The Islamized narrative subsumed an ethnically homogenous nation of Muslim-Turks. From the standpoint of the rise of modern Turkey, the religious-ethnic reading channeled a tunnel vision, focusing on the Battle of Manzikert in 1071 as the milestone for Turkish Anatolia. After the defeat of the Byzantines in Manzikert (Figure 3.19), the Seljuk-Turks poured into the Asia Minor and made the lands their home, while proceeding westward to Istanbul and the Balkans. Under the rubric of Muslim-Turks, then the formation of the state included the neat sequence of the Seljuk Turkish Anatolia, followed by the *Beylik* Period, the empire of the Ottoman Turks, and then the Republic of Turkey. Within this linear progress of history, the conquest of Constantinople in 1453 provided the decisive motor of turning the Turkish state into a world empire. The historical moments embedded in the Anatolian past of Turks, in turn, provided points of departure and reference when defining architectural heritage of the nation and excluding others. In the orbit of the rising Ottoman classical architecture, the built environment created during the *Beyliks*, Seljuks, and Late Ottoman Era became tangential.

---

[116] Gavin D. Brockett, "When Ottomans Become Turks: Commemorating the Conquest of Constantinople and Its Contribution to World History," *The American Historical Review* 119, no. 2 (2014): 403.

[117] Nicholas Danforth, "Multi-Purpose Empire: Ottoman History in Republican Turkey," *Middle Eastern Studies* 50, no. 4 (2014): 661.

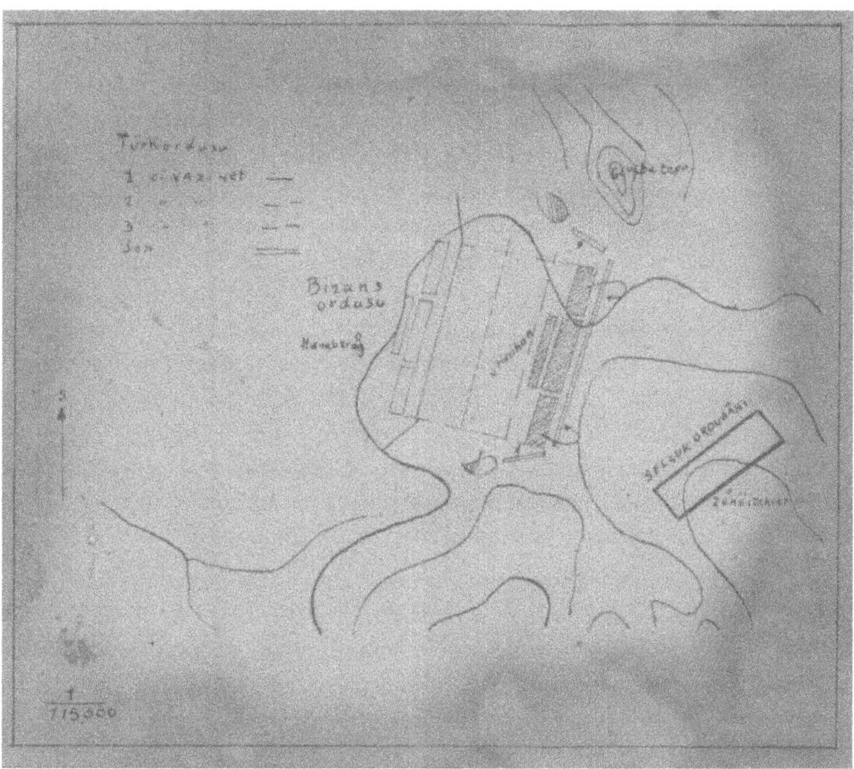

Figure 3.19. Map showing the armies of Byzantine and Seljuk in Battle of Manzikert. SALT Research, Ali Saim Ülgen Archive, TASUDOC0802003.

Against the background of the Turkified Anatolia, the post-Manzikert reading included a direct encounter between the "Turkish settlers" and "autochtonous" others.[118] Coined as "Seljuk," in its blanket application to the medieval Anatolia, the historicist appraisal simply excluded non-Turkic or non-Muslim cultures and polities living in the lands. Hence, the Byzantines (located in Istanbul, Nicaea and Trebizond) along with the Kingdom of Armenian Cilicia became the

[118] Cemal Kafadar, "A Rome of One's Own: Reflections on Cultural Geography and Identity in the Lands of Rum" ed. Bozdoğan and Necipoğlu, *Muqarnas* 24 (2007): 10.

"other cultures," for which the Turkish settlers, with their worldly pragmatism, provided modernity and democracy.[119, 120]

In fact, the Turkish lenience to other cultures and their ritual observance dominated the narrative of the Ottoman conquest of Constantinople. The encounters of the two cultures was marked by the tolerance of Mehmed II to treat the defeated Byzantines humanely after the fall of the city and to declare provisions for the protection of their works of art. No sooner had Mehmed the Conqueror occupied Constantinople than he set about founding the city as Istanbul, the rundown Byzantine capital soon to be synonymous with the prosperity and prominence of Islamic civilization. Succumbing to the stewardship of the Muslim-Turkish nation, the Byzantine built heritage could outlive for centuries. Çetintaş simply put it, if Turks did not conquer Istanbul, the site of Hagia Sophia would be no different than the dilapidated Byzantine neighborhoods that were once home to the Great Palace of Constantinople. Since the conquest, Turks spent more money to uphold Hagia Sophia in comparison to its initial construction costs under the Byzantine reign.[121]

Yet, the Byzantine architectural heritage already became the academic, stylistic, and obsolete "other" to exhibit the rise of Islamized Turkish architecture. Öz stated that a thorough review of other schools of art in Turkey was the only way to map the autonomous development of Turkish architecture.[122] The last of these cultures, the advanced Byzantine works of

---

[119] Feridun Fazıl Tülbentçi (1912-1982), noteworthy journalist, author, and poet, mirrored this teleological reading of Turkish history. Tülbentçi wrote that after the defeat of the Byzantines in Manzikert, the ruling Christian elites became more hostile to their own people in Anatolia. Therefore, the Byzantian populaces began to see the Turkish settlers as their saviors, stating "It is not Turks who are tyrannizing us, but our dukes in Istanbul." Tülbentçi, "Anadolu'nun Fethi," (Manuscript, SALT Research, FFTDOC00382, date unknown). https://archives.saltresearch.org/handle/123456789/19096 (accessed September 20, 2021)

[120] Ibid. When it came to the Turkish capture of the Armenian territory around Antakya, Tülbentçi used a nationalist lens. Armenian people were drained because of the torments of the reigning landlords. Concurrently, Armenians, themselves, invited the Turks to their cities to save them from the vicious native dukes.

[121] Çetintaş, "İstanbul'un Yıldönümü," in *Istanbul ve Mimari Yazıları*, ed. Dervişoğlu (Ankara: Türk Tarih Kurumu Basımevi, 2011), 379.

[122] Öz, "Bizans Sarayları," (Circular, FFT273001, SALT Research, November 1947). https://archives.saltresearch.org/handle/123456789/25581 (accessed September 20, 2021)

architecture, had to be protected and studied; hence, the differences between the Turkish and Byzantine built environment could be attested. That said, Byzantine Istanbul became a symbol to attest to the greatness of the Turkish struggle to defeat and replace it.[123] Upholding the defeated Byzantine structures was a necessary act to draw attention to the maturity and prominence of Turkish monuments. Concurrently, Altan noted that the Turkish people indisputably formed a more glorious civilization than the Byzantines. Coupled with a deep passion for the protection of arts, Turks did not hesitate to consecrate the ancient works of the Byzantines next to the pure forms of Turks, however. Altan highlighted the Fethiye Mosque, which was converted from the Church Pammakaristos Monastery (Figure 3.20) to present the layered history of Istanbul. Altan celebrated the recent restoration work conducted by architect Vasfi Egeli and his colleagues at the Ministry of Endowments, honoring the authentic configuration of the edifice.[124]

Figure 3.20. Photograph of the Fethiye Mosque (Church Pammakaristos Monastery) during the repairs of 1956, delineated by Cahide Tamer. Koç University, Suna Kıraç Library Special Collections and Archives, Cahide Tamer Historic Buildings Restoration Projects Collection, S098_D01, CTA_S098_D01_phg_01.

---

123 Kültür Bakanlığı, Antikiteler ve Müzeler Dairesi, Anıtları Koruma Komisyonu, *Anıtları Koruma Komisyonunun 1933–1935 Yıllarındaki Çalışmaları* (İstanbul: Devlet Basımevi, 1935), 9, 17-20.

124 Altan, "Fethiye Camii," *Arkitekt* 10-11 no. 94-95 (1938): 296-297.

Surveying Byzantine Istanbul

Studying Byzantine architecture, even for the purpose of legitimizing the attributes of the Turkish built environment, was a topic of enduring unease. The propensity for examining Byzantine architecture often reflected a purely academical quest and in the practice of archival building documentation such extension was a low priority. To meet the celebrations of the 500th anniversary of the Ottoman conquest of Constantinople, few studies were published dedicated to the study of Byzantine architecture. Feridun Dirimtekin (1894-1976), soldier, teacher, and director of the Hagia Sophia Museum, published *Fetihten önce Marmara Surları* (*The Walls of Marmara before the Conquest,* 1953),[125] followed by *Fetihten önce Haliç Surları* (The Walls of the Golden Horn, 1956).[126] For these studies, Dirimtekin surveyed the existing city walls and delineated site maps using previously published monographs. Not an architect or a historian by training, the contents of Dirimtekin's drawings, thus, were more aligned to an antiquarian's quest for creating an account of history. In this respect, his illustrated survey served to substantiate the additions and subtractions to the historic walls at the time of his documentation campaign.

In the stratified landscape of Istanbul, professionals often came across unnoticed pieces of Byzantine built heritage and incorporated those surveys to the monographs. One example includes *Fatih Camii ve Bizans Sarnıcı* (Fatih Mosque and the Byzantine cistern, 1939) written by Ülgen and historian Halim Baki Kunter. Mehmed II commissioned the imperial mosque complex, which was built on the ruins of *Havariyyun Kilisesi* (the Church of the Holy Apostles). The mosque was completed in 1463, yet had to be rebuilt in 1771 following a severe earthquake.[127] In response to the deficiency of

---

[125] Feridun Dirimtekin, *Fetihten önce Marmara Surları* (Ankara: Kanaat, Feyz ve Güzel Sanatlar Matbaası, 1953), 76.

[126] Dirimtekin, *Fetihten önce Haliç Surları* (İstanbul: İstanbul Fetih Derneği, 1956).

[127] Art historian Mehmed Ağaoğlu (1896-1949) depicted the original form of the Fatih Mosque with a smaller space and a five-domed narthex. See, Ağaoğlu, "Fatih Camiinin Şekl-i Aslisi ve Türk San'at-i Mimarisindeki Yeri," *Hayat Mecmuası* 45, 1927. To Kunter and Ülgen, the lateral walls of the mosque and wall of the mihrab were extended. Also, the tombs were relocated. See, Kunter and Ülgen, *Fatih Camii ve Bizans Sarnıcı* (İstanbul: Cumhuriyet Matbaası, 1939). For Ayverdi, however, only the lateral walls were moved closer. See, Ayverdi, "İlk Fatih Camii Hakkında yeni bir Vesika," *Vakıflar Dergisi* 6 (1965): 63-68. Also, see, Aslanapa, *Fatih Devri Âbideleri,* Güzel Sanatlar Akademisi Türk San'atı Tarihi Enstitüsü Yayınları 1, İstanbul: Berksoy Matbaası, 1963).

information on the mosque building, Kunter and Ülgen noted the shortage of the state-of-the-art surveying technologies in the past to bring forth an accurate replica of the mosque.[128] Coupled with the ignorance of the European scholars to thoroughly examine the structures in situ, the existing literature culminated in misconceptions about the whereabouts of the Byzantine church. The duo emphasized that the endowment of Mehmed II did not include any reference to the Church of the Holy Apostles, which was unusual in the format of deed records at the time. [129] The footprint of the existing building did not align with a previous Byzantine church either. Concurrently, the authors nullified the idea that the mosque had been directly built on the ruins of the church. Yet, during the documentation campaign they located an overlooked Byzantine cistern between the two madrasas of the mosque complex, which they measured and drew. The authors suggested that this cistern could have been the basement of the long-sought Church of the Holy Apostles, but it had to be clarified with further research.[130]

Nationalist historiography informed the built environment as independent strands of cultural products that had emerged from the lands of Turkey. Concurrently, preservation circles did not use art and architecture as a means of constructing links between these cultures either. Officially compiled state archives, catalogues, and collections exhibit a strictly hierarchical and categorical framework of facilities, distinguishing between Byzantine, Seljuk, or Ottoman works of architecture.[131] To this end, itemized expenses of state-agencies, end-of-year reports, heritage-at-risk lists, and emergency funds did include a corpus of Byzantine architecture across the country.[132] For example,

---

[128] Kunter and Ülgen, *Fatih Camii ve Bizans Sarnıcı*, 12.

[129] Ibid., 15.

[130] Ibid., 16.

[131] Ülgen's proposal includes the assembly of maps, archives, and collections. Pertaining to the classification of architectural heritage, he divides these into separate camps: Byzantine architectural heritage, Seljuk, Ottoman, and *Beylik* architecture, Turkish castles, and military sites. Ülgen, "Türkiye'de Yapılması Gerekli Haritalar, ve Gerekli Görülen Arşiv, Atölye, ve Müeyyedeler," (Manuscript, SALT Research, TASUDOC1311111 and TASUDOC1311112, date unknown). https://archives.saltresearch.org/handle/123456789/75853 (accessed September 20, 2021)

[132] For example, see the itemized list of the facilities across Turkey to be repaired and their estimated budget, Ülgen, "Vakıflar İdaresinin Elindeki Anıtlar Hariç Bilcümle Korunması Gerekli Eski Eserlerin Durumu ve Takribi Keşif Tutarları," (Memorandum, SALT Research, Ali Saim Ülgen Archive, TASUDOC1311116-TASUDOC1311124, date unknown). https://archives.

in an official report Ülgen noted that under the ruins of the seventeen-century Yayla Kambur Mustafa Pasha Mosque in Fatih, Istanbul, he located a Byzantine cistern with ten colonnades (Figure 3.21). Ülgen warned that a wall had to be built around the cistern to protect the Byzantine structure which had architectural and historical value.[133]

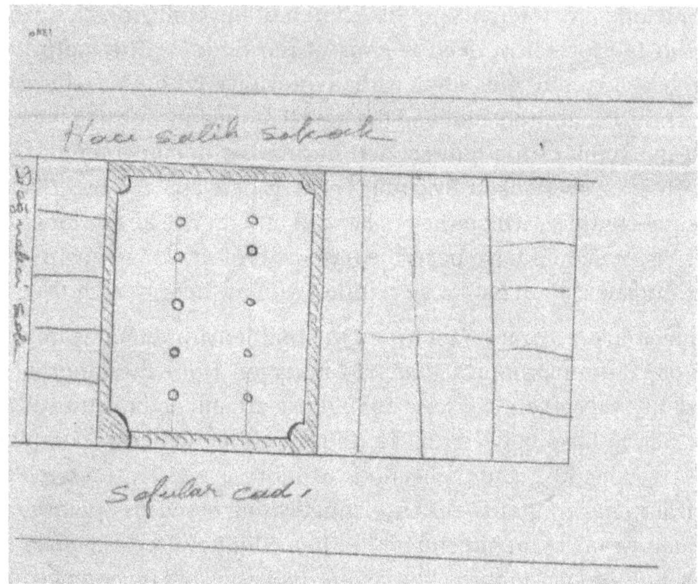

Figure 3.21. Field note showing the map of a Byzantine cistern under the Yayla Kambur Mustafa Pasha Mosque, Istanbul, delineated by Ali Saim Ülgen, undated. SALT Research, Ali Saim Ülgen Archive, TASUDOC0437006.

When it came to the allocation of limited preservation funds to the properties in need, however, the prioritization of Turkish monuments would be felt. Drafted in 1949, the 3-year master plan for the revitalization of museum

---

saltresearch.org/handle/123456789/75853 (accessed September 20, 2021); also see, Ülgen's list of itemized monuments classified by towns and cities, Ülgen, "Vilayetlere ve Kazalara göre Sınıflandırılmış Onarımları veya Kurtarılmaları elzem Başlıca Anıtlarımız," (Memorandum, SALT Research, Ali Saim Ülgen Archive, TASUDOC1311133-TASUDOC1311150, date unknown). https://archives.saltresearch.org/handle/123456789/75853 (accessed September 20, 2021).

[133] Ülgen, "Rapor," (Memorandum, SALT Research, Ali Saim Ülgen Archive, TASUDOC0 437005, date unknown). https://archives.saltresearch.org/handle/123456789/70246 (accessed September 20, 2021)

facilities across the country, for example, exhibits the regulated inclusion of Byzantine monuments in Istanbul. Compared to the adaptive-reuse project of Ankara's Museum of Anatolian Civilizations, which had been repurposed from *Mahmud Pasha Bedesteni and Kurşunlu Han* (a total of 770.936 Turkish Liras, TL), the cluster of Byzantine monuments in Istanbul received limited state-funds (679.901 TL), mainly focusing on the museums of Hagia Sophia and Kariye (Church of the Chora Monastery). Moreover, the same list includes the request for additional funds of 1.000.000 TL for the Museum of Anatolian Civilizations and 1.250.000 TL for the Byzantine museums.[134] With the same token, compiled in 1950, the estimated costs for the preparations of the quincentenary anniversary of the conquest attested to a larger budget for Byzantine monuments in Istanbul (350,000 TL), tailing the upkeep of the Topkapı Palace Museum and the madrasas of the Fatih Mosque Complex (500.000 TL, each).[135]

In this context, the preparations for the International Congress of Byzantine Studies, 1955- Istanbul, facilitated the allocation of resources to the repairs of the monuments. To exhibit the Byzantine monuments as clean and well-kept to the participants of the congress, the General Directorate of Antiquities and Museums, Endowments, and Public Works, along with Istanbul Municipality appointed a technical committee to determine the monuments to be maintained and to enlist the physical interventions.[136] In 1955, Cahide Aksel Tamer, a restoration architect at the General Directorate of Antiquities and

---

[134] See the projected expense reports between 1949-1951 for individual monuments, Ülgen, "Türkiye Müzelerinin Geliştirilmesi için Üç Yıllık Program (Müze olarak kullanılan binaların %70'i Tarihi Anıttır.)" (Memorandum, SALT Research, Ali Saim Ülgen Archive, TASUDOC1311080, date unknown). https://archives.saltresearch.org/handle/123456789/75853 (accessed September 20, 2021); also, see, repair expenses for monuments, Ülgen, (Memorandum, SALT Research, Ali Saim Ülgen Archive, TASUDOC1311042, date unknown). https://archives.saltresearch.org/handle/123456789/75853 (accessed September 20, 2021).

[135] Ülgen, "1950 Yılı Bütçesinden İstanbul Fethinin 500üncü Yıldönümü Dolayısıyla Onarılması Gerekli Anıtlar" (Memorandum, SALT Research, Ali Saim Ülgen Archive, TASUDOC1311044, date unknown). https://archives.saltresearch.org/handle/123456789/75853 (accessed September 20, 2021)

[136] Tamer, "Bizans anıtlarında bakım ve onarım," (Photograph and document, Koç University, Suna Kıraç Library Special Collections and Archives, Cahide Tamer Historic Buildings Restoration Projects Collection, S108 _A01_doc_01 and S108_A01_doc_02, 1955). https://libdigitalcollections.ku.edu.tr/digital/collection/CTA/id/928/rec/3 (accessed September 20, 2021)

Museums supervised the projects for the Mosques of Kariye, Fethiye (Church of Pammakaristos Monastery), Imrahor Ilyas Bey (Stoudios Monastery), Fenari Isa (Church of Constantine Lips Monastery), Bodrum (Church of Myrelaion Monastery) along with the Tekfur Palace (Figure 3.20 and 3.22). Tamer requested a budget of 81.528.15TL for all the monuments, which was used for repairs and consolidation work.

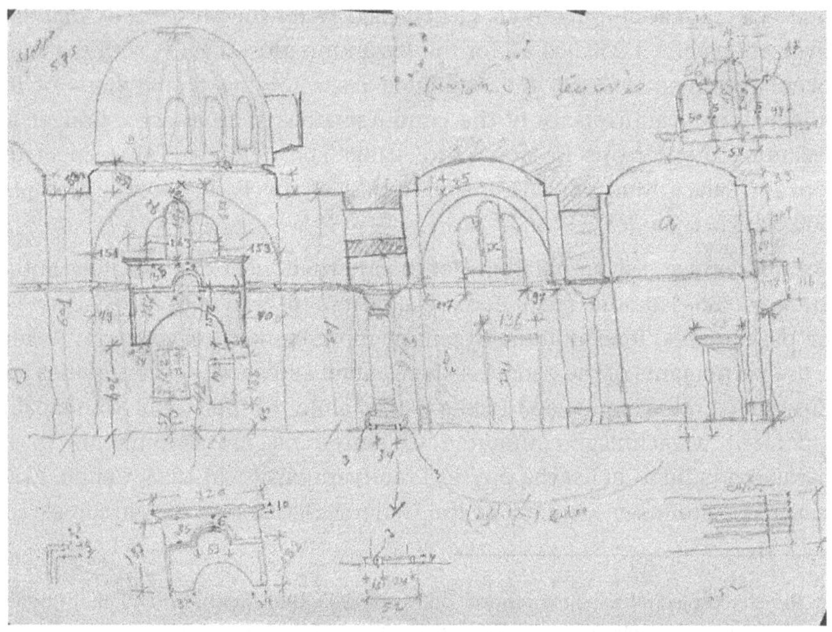

Figure 3.22. Field note for the 1946-repairs of the Kariye Mosque (Church of the Chora Monastery), delineated by Cahide Tamer. Koç University, Suna Kıraç Library Special Collections and Archives, Cahide Tamer Historic Buildings Restoration Projects Collection, S102_D02_jpg, CTA_S102_D02_dra_12_02.

Turkifying Byzantine architecture

In the idiosyncratic scale where Turkish monuments had an additional political value, to justify the upkeep of the Byzantine architectural heritage within the limited resources, preservation circles pursued intriguing narratives. In many cases, the "Turkishness" of the Byzantine built environment became a topic. Ülgen, for example, referred to Istanbul's Hagia Sophia, as a "Turkified

Byzantine monument," noting the improved state of the structure due to the maintenance and repairs under the Turkish rule. [137] Enlisting the preservation treatments commissioned by subsequent Ottoman sultans, Ülgen concluded that the Byzantine building had achieved "a new identity and meaning" infused with the Turkish creativity.[138] Ülgen extended his doctrine of Turkified Byzantine monuments to İznik's Ayasofya Mosque, a former Byzantine church.[139] In the monograph on the Turkish works of İznik, Ülgen included an architectural and historical description of the mosque, which was then in ruins. With a brief connotation on its Byzantine past and a relatively larger section on structural and decorative modifications under the Ottoman rule, Ülgen clearly attested to the Turkish pedigree of the historic architecture with future restoration work in mind.

Ülgen was not the sole scholar building on the Turkish characteristics of Byzantine architectural heritage. Likewise, Halil Edhem Eldem defended the upkeep of the Istanbul city walls against attempts at demolition. Eldem stated that the Turkish repairs made them more Turkish than Byzantine, so these monuments could not be discarded by any means.[140] Concurrently, Altan probed that the once-derelict Istanbul's Hagia Sophia had flourished aesthetically and structurally after the Ottoman conquest. In fact, the modifications (minarets, external buttresses, calibration of the uneven dome, and marble surface materials) introduced by Turkish architects, had surpassed the experimental configuration brought forward by the Byzantine peers; the deteriorating structure became an architectural manifestation of modular and volumetric forms. Interestingly, Altan read Hagia Sofia together with the later edifices[141] commissioned by Sultan Mahmud I (r.1730-1754) as a complex that had to be documented and conserved in totality. To harvest official interest in the protection of the facilities of the Hagia Sophia Mosque

---

[137] Ülgen, "Türkleşmis bir Bizans Abidesi, Ayasofya, (Manuscript, SALT Research, Ali Saim Ülgen Archive, TASUDOCA0255, date unknown). https://archives.saltresearch.org /handle/123456789/89733 (accessed September 20, 2021)

[138] Ibid.

[139] Ibid., 53.

[140] Altınyıldız, "The Architectural Heritage of Istanbul," 292.

[141] Sultan Mahmud I had commissioned a public fountain, elementary school, and a soup kitchen in the courtyard of Hagia Sofia.

Complex, Altan made measured drawings of individual buildings in the premises, such as the eighteenth-century elementary school facility.[142]

One interesting case includes the preservation efforts for Istanbul's Bodrum Mosque (also known Mesih Pasha Mosque), formerly the Church of the Monastery of Myrelaion "the place of myrrh."[143] The Turkified attributes of the historic structure came to the fore when the General Directorate of Endowments decided to put the dilapidated mosque building for sale in 1935. Commission for the Preservation of Monuments vehemently opposed selling the Bodrum Mosque or its building materials. To secure its protection, the commission members highlighted the patrimonial value of its minaret and the memory of the sixteenth-century grand vizier Mesih Pasha (also known as Misac Pasha, d. 1501) who endowed the conversion of the tenth-century Byzantine church into a mosque.[144]

Mesih Pasha's interest in re-purposing the Byzantine building was part of the Ottoman policy of *şenlendirme* (revitalization), where dilapidated and deserted smaller churches were either reused as neighborhood masjids or annexed to convents to avoid their total dereliction.[145] In 1501, with the addition of an ashlar stone minaret, mihrab, and a wooden minbar, the Church of the Monastery of Myrelaion became the Bodrum Mosque.[146] Its conversion to a mosque involved minimal physical transformation; the existing narthex gallery still served as the porticoed courtyard for the congregation to perform their daily prayers. Even its name in Turkish embodied a memento from its former use. *Bodrum* means basement, which directly referred to the crypt at the church, a burial place for the family members of the Byzantine emperor.[147] The historic building served as a mosque for centuries, although its lifecycle was disrupted by destructive fires in

---

[142] Altan, "Ayasofya Etrafında Türk San'at Ekleri," *Arkitekt* 9 no. 57 (1935): 264-265.

[143] Raymond Janin, *Constantinople Byzantine: Développement Urbain et Répertoire Topographique* (Paris: Institut Français D'études Byzantines, 1964), 394.

[144] Anonymous, "Rapor" (Rapor, Eski Eserleri Koruma Encümeni Arşivi, İstanbul, GN 115, June 24 1935).

[145] Altınyıldız, "The Architectural Heritage of Istanbul," 282.

[146] Cecil L. Striker, *The Myrelaion (Bodrum Camii) in Istanbul* (Princeton NJ: Princeton University Press, 1981).

[147] Janin suggests that the cistern, a former rotunda located in the site of the mosque, could also be an ancient tomb due to its irregular form and columns of various origins. See, Janin, *Constantinople Byzantine,* 213.

1784, 1906, and 1911.[148] In the latter catastrophe, the authentic sixteenth-century additions of the mosque (minbar and mihrab) along with the original calligraphy work were demolished.[149] After 1911, the building was abandoned.

To preserve the Bodrum Mosque, in 1936, Ülgen, then a student-architect at the Academy and a collaborator at the Commission for the Preservation of Monuments compiled an inventory of the historic building and registered the vestige as a historic landmark.[150] In-situ, Ülgen observed that the remaining Byzantine structural parts were solely "a skeleton of brick and stone capped with a dome."[151] The only residual Ottoman addition included the shaft of the minaret made of Bakırköy ashlar stones. Notably, Ülgen defined the monument as a representative work of Byzantine art and confirmed its eligibility as a historic landmark.[152] Interestingly, Ülgen highlighted the memory of its Byzantine patrons, who were also buried there. In this vein, Ülgen issued an emergency order to preserve the monument.

Ülgen's plea to save the Bodrum Mosque, did not immediately materialize, however. In 1946, Aziz Ogan (1888-1956), a classical archaeologist who became the director of the Izmir Museum, then the director of the Istanbul Archaeological Museums, submitted a petition to the district governor of Eminönü to prevent a neighborhood resident from keeping his chickens on the premises of the Bodrum Mosque, the former church of Myrelaion. Then working both as the director of the commission and the Istanbul Archaeological Museums, Ogan requested the governor to save the historic building from the chicken manure and stop the disgrace for the domestic and foreign tourists.[153]

---

[148] Striker notes the destructive fires of 1784 and 1911 as the cause of the ailing edifice, while Ülgen confirms the fire of 1906 which engulfed the mosque with its entire neighborhood. See, Striker, 1981; Ülgen, "Tescil 165," (Manuscript, Koç University, Suna Kıraç Library Special Collections and Archives, Cahide Tamer Historic Buildings Restoration Projects Collection, CTA_S106_D01_doc_06_01, July 17 1936).

[149] Striker, *The Myrelaion.*

[150] Ülgen certified the Bodrum Mosque on July 17, 1936 with the registration number 165 and the record of 13. Ülgen, "Tescil 165," CTA_S106_D01_doc_06_01, CTA_S106_D01_doc_06_02, and CTA_S106_D01_doc_06_03. https://libdigitalcollections.ku.edu.tr/digital/collection/CTA/id/857/rec/43 (accessed March 29, 2022).

[151] Ibid., CTA_S106_D01_doc_06_02.

[152] Ibid., CTA_S106_D01_doc_06_03.

[153] Aziz Ogan, "Eminönü Kaymakamlığına" (Letter, Eski Eserleri Koruma Encümeni Arşivi, İstanbul, GN 115, September 14 1946).

In retrospect, in the 1950s, the entire Byzantine building stock of Istanbul became the object of fleeting attention due to the International Congress of Byzantine Studies which was to meet in 1955. Despite the professional willingness to restore the Byzantine heritage, due to budgetary constraints, the physical interventions remained superficial. Under Tamer's supervision, who was working as a restoration-architect at the General Directorate of Endowments, monuments that scholars would visit were cleaned and patched up to avoid embarrassment.[154] The Bodrum mosque was included in the program of repairs. Tamer's itemized construction estimates in 1953 clearly exhibits her pursuit of thoroughly consolidating the existing structure and replacing the damaged or missing building materials.[155] Tamer enlisted the work order as covering the structure to protect it from external damage, adding windows, reclaiming the minaret, cleaning the structure and its site, and assigning a guard.[156] These repairs had to wait until subsequent years, nevertheless. In 1965, GEEAYK declared that the historic building was at risk and prioritized its restoration as a mosque.[157] GEEAYK's decision mainly rested on the Ottoman past of the building and its association with Mesih Pasha. Yet, in the decision, GEEAYK also acknowledged the Byzantine identity of the building. Tamer emphasized that due to Mesih Pasha's endowment of a mosque the historic Byzantine building could be conserved.[158] Tamer added

---

[154] Altınyıldız, "The Architectural Heritage of Istanbul," 296.

[155] Tamer, "Laleli'de Mesih Paşa Camii (Mireleon Kilisesi) İmalat" (Manuscript, Koç University, Suna Kıraç Library Special Collections and Archives, Cahide Tamer Historic Buildings Restoration Projects Collection, CTA_S106_D01, September 2 1953). https://libdigitalcollections.ku.edu.tr/digital/collection/CTA/id/862/rec/43 (accessed March 29, 2022).

[156] Tamer, "[Projected Repairs for 1955]" (Inventory, Koç University, Suna Kıraç Library Special Collections and Archives, Cahide Tamer Historic Buildings Restoration Projects Collection, CTA_S103_D01_doc_16_02, 1955). https://libdigitalcollections.ku.edu.tr/digital/collection/CTA/id/649/rec/4 (accessed March 29, 2022).

[157] Öz, "Karar," (Memorandum, Koç University, Suna Kıraç Library Special Collections and Archives, Cahide Tamer Historic Buildings Restoration Projects Collection, CTA_S106_D01_doc_03, December 16 & 18 1966). https://libdigitalcollections.ku.edu.tr/digital/collection/CTA/id/854/rec/43 (accessed March 29, 2022).

[158] Tamer, "Bodrum Camii Minaresi Restorasyonu Hakkında Rapor," (Report, Koç University, Suna Kıraç Library Special Collections and Archives, Cahide Tamer Historic Buildings Restoration Projects Collection, CTA_S106_D01_doc_01, November 15 1966). https://libdigitalcollections.ku.edu.tr/digital/collection/CTA/id/854/rec/43 (accessed March 29, 2022).

that the dilapidated monument was being used as a museum at the time. The ruins, however more resembled an archaeological site.[159] In 1966, GEEAYK approved its restitution project prepared by the General Directorate of Endowments, with the construction to be supervised by Tamer.[160] Thirty years after the 1935-dated request of the directorate to discard the Bodrum Mosque, ironically, the same institution oversaw the restoration project to safeguard the historic building for future generations, which still serves as a mosque.

The case of the Bodrum Mosque exhibits that an academic focus prevailed among the preservation circles to protect the Byzantine architectural heritage. Professionals openly identified the Byzantine legacy of the Bodrum Mosque and strove to secure its protection. To exhibit its significance, scholars, carefully, highlighted both its Byzantine and Ottoman legacy and catalogued its architectural elements on the basis of a chronological matrix. Strikingly, the burials of the Byzantine emperor and his family in the monument instilled a further sense of recognition in the architectural records.

Much of this positive review derived from reading the building as a mosque, however. The multi-layered building itself embodied architectural and historical values, to which the authors concurred. Nevertheless, its relationship with Mesih Pasha and its Turkishness contributed to its salvage from a tumble-down condition to a functioning mosque. Over the years, in the negotiations for repairs and maintenance, preservation professionals continuously prioritized Mesih Pasha's endowment to carve up space in the limited budget of architectural preservation projects.

Reading the built works of the *Beyliks*

The built environment of the *Beyliks* culminated in interesting readings in the process of becoming "other" architecture. In the trinity of Seljuks-*Beyliks*-Ottomans, the term "Seljuk Anatolia" denoted a period of more than two centuries prior to the beginning of the story of the Ottomans around 1300. In reality, between the Battle of Manzikert (1071) and the Kalender Çelebi revolt of (1526), originated during the Ottoman incorporation of the Dulkadirid territory, the last remaining dynasty, numerous *Beyliks* were in control of

---

[159] Ibid.

[160] Öz, "Karar," December 16 & 18 1966.

different regions of Anatolia for several generations.[161] These *Beyliks* were often in rivalry; furthermore, they were in direct confrontation with Seljuks. With the breakup of the Seljuk Sultanate at the turn of the fourteenth-century a new group of *Beyliks* emerged in Anatolia. The *Beylik* of *Osmanoğulları*, is one of these second constellations of *Beyliks*, which was established around Söğüt in 1299, and then famously culminated in the Ottoman Empire.[162] The Ottoman state was in active conflict with the *Beyliks*, until the last remaining ones were annihilated following the Kalender Çelebi revolt during the reign of Sultan Süleyman the Lawgiver (r. 1520–66).

In the rubric of a unified Seljuk architectural style dominating the building traditions of Anatolia for centuries, the historical works of the *Beyliks* were relegated to an introverted perspective. To, M. Oluş Arık (1934-present), art historian, the *Beyliks* were disorderly medieval tribes without the capacity to put forward new design solutions. Arık simply wrote,

> The individual emirates had no particular style of their own. As in the Seljuk and Ottoman periods, when Anatolia was united under a single ruling dynasty, the factors that played a basic role in the emergence of various styles were the regional conditions affecting artists of different origins and the different foreign political units which relations were established. All such developments were based on traditions of the Seljuk period: therefore, the architectural works of the period of the emirates can be studied without distinguishing the emirates, by classifying the works according to their building techniques and by investigating typology and regional distribution. This is the most logical approach to the architecture of the period of the emirates.[163]

Behçet Sabri Ünsal, the author of *Turkish Islamic Architecture in Seljuk and Ottoman Times, 1071-1923,* addressed the nine-centuries-long architectural production of the lands through a clear-cut chronological separation, of Seljuk-*Beylik*-Ottoman periods. Retaining the neat periodization, Ünsal read

---

161 Kafadar, "A Rome of One's Own," 8.

162 Oya Pancaroğlu, "Formalism and the Academic Foundation of Turkish Art in the Early Twentieth Century," "History and Ideology: Architectural Heritage of the 'Lands of Rum,'" ed. Bozdoğan and Necipoğlu, special issue, *Muqarnas* 24 (2007): 67.

163 M. Oluş Arık, "Turkish Architecture in Asia Minor in the Period of the Turkish Emirates," in *The Art and Architecure of Turkey,* ed. Ekrem Akurgal, (New York: Rizzoli International Publications, 1980), 112.

the *Beyliks* as a subset of the Seljuk architectural culture.[164] To Ünsal, the individual dynasties in Anatolia maintained the earlier Seljuk building traditions; overall, they did not craft new forms of architecture. The most notable architectural patronage coincided with the rule of *Beylik* of *Karamanoğulları* (the Karamanid dynasty), since the lords replicated the architectural products of the Seljuks, as exemplified in the forms of the tomb of Aladdin Bey, madrasa of Nefise Hatun (Figure 3.23), and the hospice of Ibrahim II.[165]

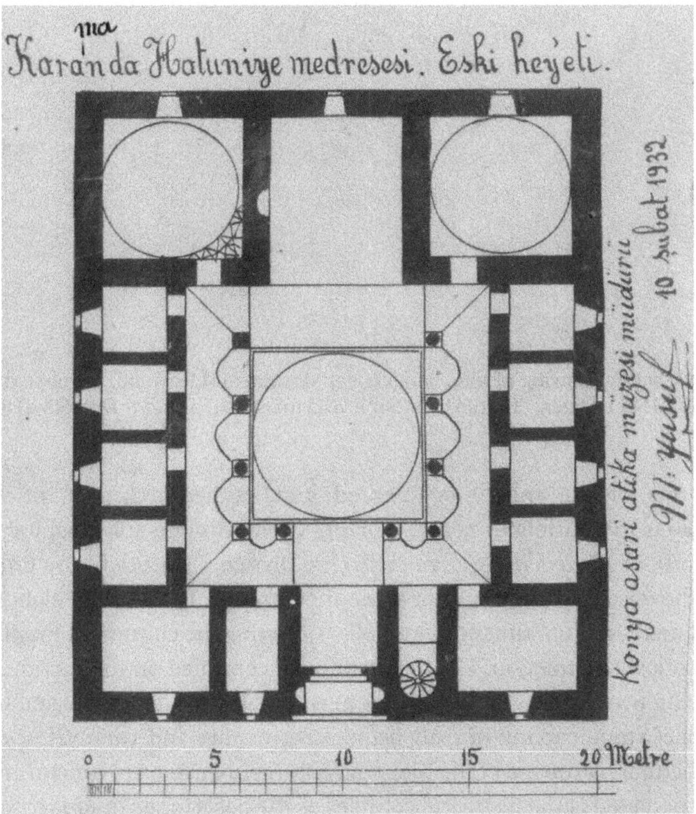

Figure 3.23. Measured drawing of Karaman's Nefise Hatun (Hatuniye) Madrasa, delineated by Yusuf Akyurt, 1932. SALT Research, Ali Saim Ülgen Archive, TASUDOC0246032.

---

[164] Ünsal, *Turkish Islamic Architecture in Seljuk and Ottoman Times*, 14.
[165] Ibid., 5.

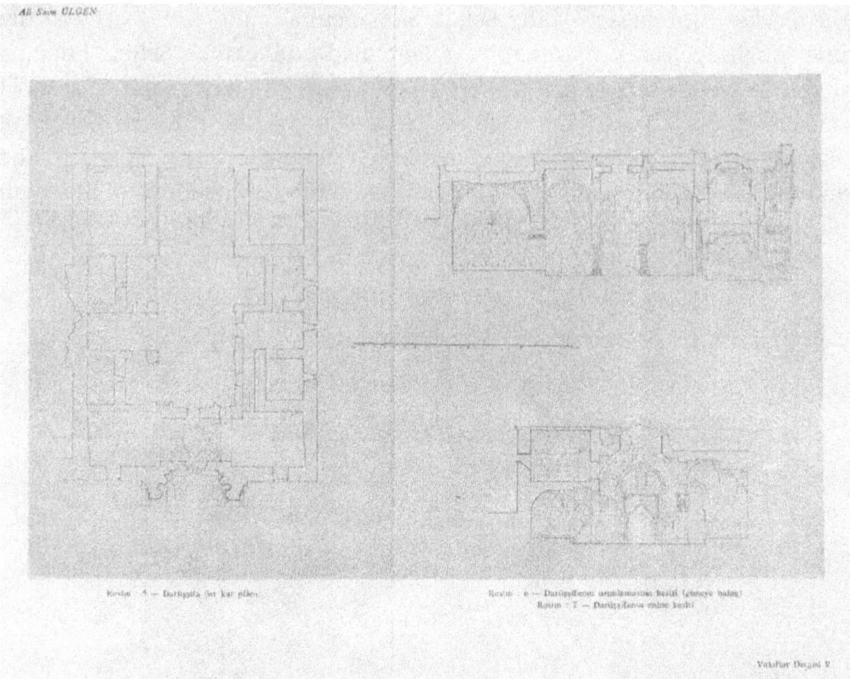

Figure 3.24. Section drawing of the Divriği Great Mosque and Hospital, delineated by Ali Saim Ülgen. Ali Saim Ülgen, "Divriği Ulu Camii ve Darüşşifası," *Vakıflar Dergisi* V, (1962).

Perhaps, one of the most documented and studied examples of *Beylik* architecture is the thirteenth-century Divriği Great Mosque and Hospital, built by the *Beylik* of *Mengüçlü* (Mengujekids), in Divriği, Sivas. Radically different from all known contemporary examples, the complex is the most elaborately decorated medieval monument in Anatolia, reflecting the cultural encounters of its geohistorical conjunction. The decoration concentrated on the monumental portals of the two buildings and consists most notably of stylized vegetal motifs in high-relief stone carving of truly astounding quality and variety.[166] Despite the architectural patronage of the Mengujekids, republican texts concurred with the Seljuk pedigree of the historical complex as the basis for its unique assembly of decoration. For Ünsal, the mosque is "the richest and most impressive" of the

[166] Pancaroğlu, "The Mosque-Hospital Complex in Divriği: A History of Relations and Transitions," *Anadolu ve Çevresinde Ortaçağ* (3), Ankara: AKVAD Anadolu Kültür Varlıklarının Araştırma Derneği (2009), 169-170.

Seljuk monuments in Divriği with its sixteen pillars and ribbed vaulting. The adjoining hospital consists of minimum pillars, which transitioned to the type of the Ottoman Great Mosque.[167] Yetkin stated that the notable feature of the architecture includes its unique decoration.[168] Ülgen's text on the Divriği Great Mosque and Hospital, constituted an academic response to counter the Orientalist art historical reading pronouncing some of the stylistic and structural ingredients were non-Turkish. Although Ülgen found the plastic decoration embodied in the portal of the hospital somewhat excessive, the volumetric progression of spaces inside the structure revealed the purity of Turkish architecture.[169] Attesting to the measured drawings of the complex, Ülgen illustrated the cut through of the monumental portals, vaulted halls, and the conical domes as the material evidence for the Turkishness of architecture (Figure 3.24).

In stark contrast to the academic obliviousness to the identification of *Beylik* architecture, preservation authorities, often the same personalities who contributed to the scholarship on Turkish architecture, orchestrated intense efforts to safeguard the built heritage of the dynasties. Enlisted in official inventories, publications, and reports, a corpus of *Beylik* monuments were highlighted as masterworks of Turkish creativity to be protected.[170] For instance, when Arseven heard that the fifteenth-century Grand Mosque of Aksaray (also known as Karamanoğlu Mosque) near Konya was going to be repaired, he fervently wrote a letter to the General Directorate of Endowments in 1940 to petition for a high-caliber of restoration work that the Turkish monument would rightfully deserve. Arseven cautioned about the shortage of architects in the country who could artistically repair (*sanatça tamir*) the Turkish architectural works. He was concerned that a lay contractor without the capacity to conduct an artistic repair to maintain the authentic form and style, would destroy the monument. Therefore, Arseven recommended the

---

[167] Ünsal, *Turkish Islamic Architecture in Seljuk and Ottoman Times,* 18.

[168] Yetkin, *Türk Mimarisi,* 44.

[169] Ülgen, "Divriği Ulu Camii ve Darüşşifası," *Vakıflar Dergisi* V, (1962), 97.

[170] For example, see, Ülgen, "Türk Mimari Eserleri Listesi," (Manuscript, SALT Research, Ali Saim Ülgen Archive, TASUDOC0530040, date unknown)https://archives.saltresearch.org/handle/123456789/86642 (accessed September 20, 2021)

General Directorate of Endowments to work with Ülgen, his former student who had already written a book on the repair of monuments.[171]

Compartmentalizing built heritage of the Late Ottoman Era

One of the most conspicuous ramifications of the Muslim-Turkish lens constituted the divisions of the Ottoman built environment on the basis of architectural style. Transferred from the rather schematic formulation of a complex Ottoman history as consecutive periods of rise, classical age, stagnation, and decline, an established standard of measures became the lens to read the collective history of imperial architecture. The rise of the imperial building traditions (1299-1453) spanned between the early beginnings of the *Beylik* of *Osmanoğulları* with the associated architectural patronage at the capital of Bursa and the conquest of Constantinople. The classical age corresponded to the aftermath of conquest and amplified the zenith of imperial glory under Sultan Süleyman the Lawgiver. Also coined as the "Golden Age of Sinan," the classical period was attributed to the artistic creativity and testimony of the political power of the Sultan Süleyman's rule. Canonized as the greatest master of Turkish architecture, Sinan became a national hero who perfected the pure building forms of Turks without foreign input. The purified classical forms were seen as a result of Sinan's autonomous pursuit of a rational, structural, and universally applicable system of building, subject to continuous change and innovation.

By the same token, the architectural production from eighteenth-century onward was labeled as "artistic decline," a consequence of the weakening power of the Ottoman Empire. The travels of Yirmisekiz Mehmed Çelebi Efendi (d. 1732, also known as Mehmed Efendi) to Europe was seen as the beginning of the degeneration of Turkish architecture. Yirmisekiz Mehmed Çelebi Efendi, an Ottoman statesman, was delegated as ambassador by Sultan Ahmed III (r. 1703-1730) to Louis XV's France in 1720. The Ottoman ambassador brought architects from Paris, who erected pavilions and palaces in Istanbul in the Baroque style, the then-popular trend in France. Subsequent sultans commissioned royal buildings with Europe-originated architectural styles, for example, Istanbul's Pertevniyal Valide Sultan Mosque

---

[171] Arseven, "Vakıflar Umum Müdürlüğü, yüksek huzuruna" (Reference letter, SALT Research, Ali Saim Ülgen Archive, TASUDOC0534010, 1940) https://archives.saltresearch.org/handle/123456789/83487 (accessed September 20, 2021)

(Figure 3.1), Public Debts Building, and Sirkeci Railway Station.[172] In this context, republican authors openly disregarded the late imperial buildings and labeled them as derivative, of dubious authenticity, inferior in material quality, and "worthless" due to their style, which was "utterly alien to Turkish taste."[173] For many scholars, these buildings with their Western-inspired architectural styles (especially Baroque, Gothic, Neoclassical, and French Empire), were much departure from the Turkish building tradition's purity and authenticity, which betrayed the "rational feeling and realist notion" of classical built environment.[174]

On the basis of architectural style, some of the Late Ottoman Era buildings attested to the vocabulary of the classical age, which brought them under the republican scholars' intellectual radar. For Altan, the seventeenth-century Yeni Mosque in Eminönü, Istanbul remained the last classical example that represented the school of Sinan, for example. Altan emphasized that the Turkish architects of the Yeni Mosque[175] designed a dome structure in pursuit of Sinan's earlier work, the sixteenth-century Şehzade Mosque, in Istanbul (Figure 3.25). Altan also noted that Istanbul's eighteenth-century Zeynep Sultan Mosque (Figure 3.26) was a noteworthy example of Turkish architecture. Despite its Baroque-inspired style, its architect, Mehmet Tahir Ağa, managed to present "the graceful skills of the Turkish spirit."[176] The facilities in the mosque complex, however, were in a dilapidated condition and were bound to disappear if no provisions were made for protection, Altan added.

---

[172] Çetintaş, "Sedat Çetintaş'la Mülakat," in *İstanbul ve Mimari Yazıları*, ed. Dervişoğlu (Ankara: Türk Tarih Kurumu Basımevi, 2011), 163-164.

[173] Aslanapa, *Turkish Art and Architecture*, 237.

[174] Ülgen, "1958-1959 Türk Mimarisi Ders Programı" (Class notes, SALT Research, Ali Saim Ülgen Archive, TASUDOCA0077, 1958-1959) https://archives.saltresearch.org/handle/123456789/79823 (accessed September 20, 2021).

[175] Royal architects who worked on the construction of Yeni Mosque included Davut Ağa, Dalgıç Ahmed Çavuş, and Mustafa Ağa.

[176] Altan," Zeyneb Sultan Camii," *Akşam*, 1937, June 26, 8.

Figure 3.25. Şehzade Mosque, Istanbul, street view, undated. Koç University, Suna Kıraç Library Special Collections and Archives, Mehmet Nihat Nigizberk Collection of Architectural Drawings and Photographs, MNN_ALB18_phg_026.

Figure 3.26. Zeynep Sultan Mosque, Istanbul, street view, undated. SALT Research, Ali Saim Ülgen Archive, TASUH8099001.

Not surprisingly, in strong association with the search for the origins of Ottoman classical architecture, archival building documentation mainly focused on the early period and Sinan's architectural legacy; scholars assigned the lowest priority to record historic properties from the Late Ottoman Era. Ülgen's monograph on the Yeni Mosque (1942), is an exception to this academic oblivion; Ülgen compiled measured drawings for the mosque and its *hünkâr kasrı* (imperial pavilion) (Figure 3.27).[177] Ülgen confirmed that the weakening of the classical order was evident in the form of the mosque. Its unproportionally elevated dome failed to reach the perfection of harmonious volumes manifested in the nearby Süleymaniye Mosque. Yet, the Yeni Mosque embodied "a worldly royal face, who is longing for the epic, dazzling, and powerful ages," heralded Ülgen.[178]

---

[177] Ülgen, *Yenicami* (Ankara: Vakıflar Umum Müdürlüğü Neşriyatı, 1942).
[178] Ibid., 387.

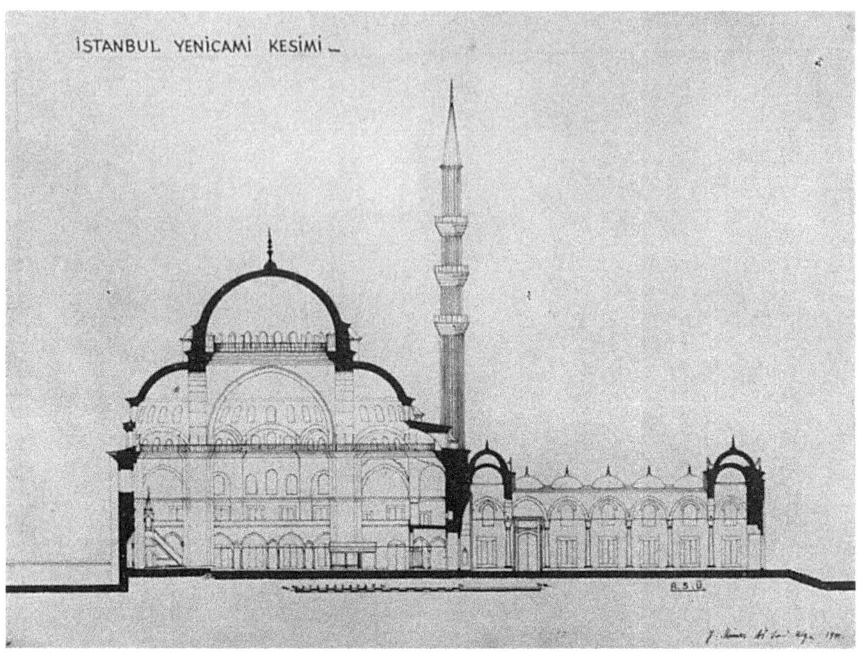

Figure 3.27. Section drawing of the Yeni Mosque, 1941, delineated by Ali Saim Ülgen. Ali Saim Ülgen, *Yenicami*. Ankara: Vakıflar Umum Müdürlüğü Neşriyatı, 1942.

Chapter 4

Formal delineation of Turkish architecture

> This pitiful Ottoman architecture… Neither its absolute greatness and merit have been appreciated; nor its superior architectural styles have been understood.
>
> Ekrem Hakkı Ayverdi [1]

Republican architects and scholars had all been in a position to advise on archival building documentation as the scientific basis to protect the built environment and to ensure its continuity for future generations. The question remained, however: how did the mission of creating measured drawings of historic properties met their goal of protecting the monuments? Was the goal to encourage broader historical understanding of architecture, denoting less need for detailed drawings, or to assist building reconstruction, entailing drawings with more information? Reflecting on the collection of field notes and formalized measured drawings as a whole, the architects did intend to represent architectural heritage on paper. Either for buildings that the drafters were already conducting restoration work, or for ones that they thought significant for the historiography of Turkish architecture, they were active participants in a documentation culture that highly valued the appraisal of architectural forms through drafted lines. Nevertheless, the extent of these measured drawings to meet the needs of all the goals, historical understanding and restoring properties, remained ambivalent.

Perhaps, Ali Saim Ülgen's 1956 memo to the General Directorate of Antiquities and Museums when been officially asked to complete the documentation and restoration project of the thirteenth-century Sultan Han in Aksaray, Niğde in two months,[2] aptly explains the dilemma between

---

[1] Ayverdi, "Bursa Orhan Gazi Camii," 69.

[2] T.C. Maarif Vekaleti, Eski Eserler ve Müzeler Umum Müdürlüğü, "Aksaray Sultanhanı Rölövesinin ve Restorasyon Projesinin Hazırlanması Hakkında," (Memorandum, SALT Research, Ali Saim Ülgen Archive, TASUDOC0438041, April 5 1956) https://archives.saltresearch.org/handle/123456789/78739 (accessed September 20, 2021).

making measured drawings of historic architecture for formal analysis or physical interventions. Ülgen simply put that he would supervise the project but the expectation to complete all the measuring and drawing tasks in two months was physically impossible. Ülgen carefully distinguished between the contents of field notes for the purpose of making measured drawings as a historical record and of calculating costs for repairs and consolidation.[3] The level of information in the 1:100 scaled archival drawings would not suffice to guide physical interventions. The surveying records for the stabilization work should include detailed information and measurements enough to analyze the condition of the foundation and to coordinate the adequate provisions, including anything from minor stabilization to major additions of a retaining wall. Concurrently, the restoration project would consist of technical drawings and itemized costs for the reinforced concrete supplements. Therefore, the 1:50 scaled drawings accompanied with detailed illustrations had to be prepared for the restoration tasks, which inevitably would take a longer time to delineate (Figure 4.1 and Figure 4.2). Besides, the half-buried structure would not allow gathering field measurements either for documentation or restoration until the area was fully excavated.

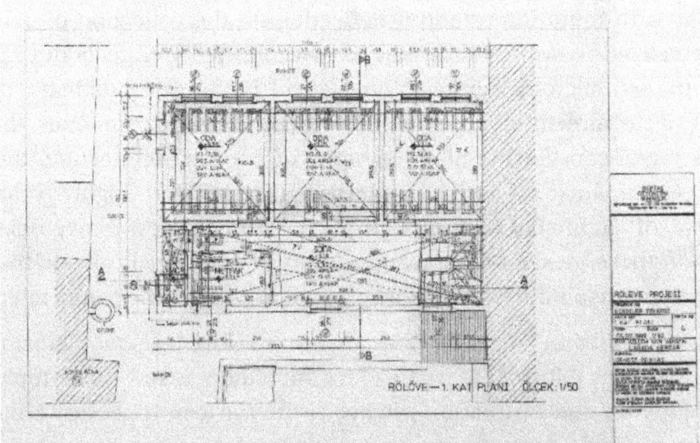

Figure 4.1. Example of a measured drawing drawn to 1:50 to guide the construction work for the Hindiler Dervish Lodge, July 7 1999, delineated by Willem van Winsen and Çağada Serdar. SALT Research, Cengiz Bektaş Archive, TCBPHTD001004.

[3] Ülgen, "Maarif Vekaletine," (Memorandum, SALT Research, Ali Saim Ülgen Archive, TASUDOC0438042-3, 1956) https://archives.saltresearch.org/handle/123456789/78739 (accessed September 20, 2021)

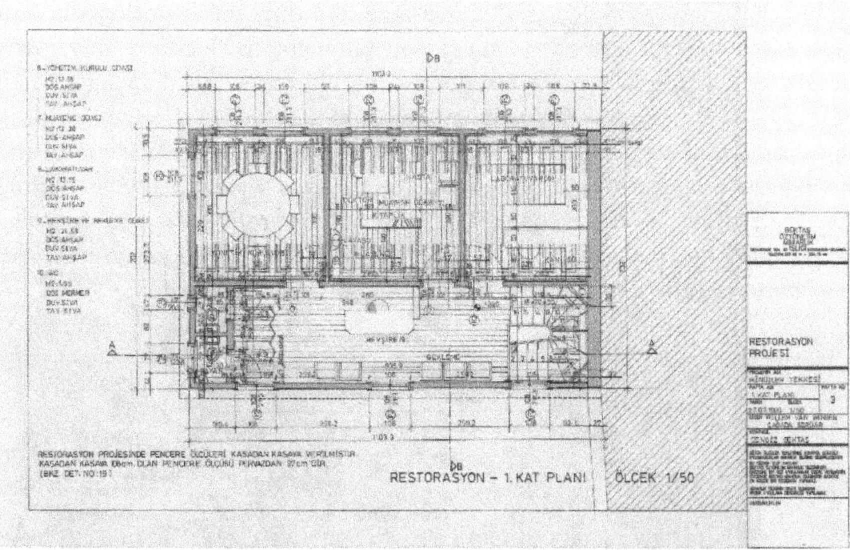

Figure 4.2. A working drawing of 1:50 scale for the application of the restoration project for the Hindiler Dervish Lodge, July 27, 1999, delineated by Willem van Winsen and Çağada Serdar. SALT Research, Cengiz Bektaş Archive, TCBPHTD003003.

The General Directorate's request for a bundle of measured drawings and restoration plans indicates that there was no significant agreement about whether documentation records ought to be about creating a historical record easily understandable to the public or stipulating technical renderings to be used by experts for reconstruction. In tightly circumscribed budgets, the republican government's interest in architectural documentation had been epic, which in fact set the stage for the modern preservation movement. Clearly, the state agencies believed in preservation through documentation since they allocated significant funds to build an architectural historiography on the basis of measured drawings. However, not all the documentation work was directly linked to the goal of preserving the physical building. By contrast, most published texts were examples of archival documentation typically compiled for the sake of the historical record, education, and research.

For instance, the French scholar Albert Louis Gabriel's pioneering documentation work on medieval Anatolia, *Monuments Turcs d'Anatolie* (1931-1934), hardly qualifies as a technical guide to preserve the physical aspects of buildings. Commissioned by the Ministry of Education and Culture, between 1926-1930 Gabriel surveyed the built environment across the country. Gabriel's work stands out as the first comprehensive survey of the architecture of the Seljuk and *Beylik* periods Anatolia. The culminating volumes include his beautifully rendered drawings of historic buildings accompanied with descriptive notes and photographs (Figure 4.3). Yet, the renderings in the volumes were not technically measured drawings. When Gabriel was entrusted with documentation and the study of the built heritage, most of the properties were either in ruins or half-buried in their urban and topographic landscapes. Therefore, his depictions were themselves virtual reconstructions of what he had thought on paper. For the measured drawings that Gabriel depicted, the as-is condition of the building surfaces, the illustrations were not detailed enough to allow the reconstruction.

Figure 4.3. Perspective drawing of the Seljuk Sungurbey Mosque in Niğde, rendering its condition in the past, delineated by Albert Gabriel. Albert Gabriel, *Monuments Turcs D'Anatolie: Kayseri-Nigde.* Paris: Paris Libraire des écoles françaises d'Athènes et de Rome, 1931. Reprinted in idem, İstanbul: Arkeoloji ve Sanat Yayınları, 2014.

Through the 1936 decree of the parliament, the establishment of the Surveying Bureau, the first state-agency dedicated to architectural documentation, specified the republican government's official involvement in the act of measuring and drawing as a provision of historic preservation.[4] Institutionalized in the structure of the General Directorate of the Antiquities and Museums, Sedat Çetintaş was assigned as the chief of the bureau. During his tenure, Çetintaş and his team directly contributed to the surveying projects across the country and became influential in the codification of the practice of architectural documentation. Besides the founding chief Çetintaş, over the years many prominent preservation professionals such as Adil Denktaş, Cahide Aksel Tamer, Emine Mualla Eyüboğlu Anhegger, Hüsrev Tayla, Macit Rüştü Kural, Mehmet İlban Öz, Mustafa Ayaşlıoğlu, and Süreyya Aşkın worked at the Surveying Bureau and implemented the core of the historic preservation practice through the trinity of measured surveys-restitution-restoration. In fact, the bureau began to build an archive on the completed historic preservation projects, including the before-and-after records of the repaired structures.[5]

The founding mission of the Surveying Bureau was not precisely in line with informing the act of restoration, however. In 1932, when Çetintaş presented his measured drawing set of the Sokollu Mehmet Pasha Mosque in Kadırga to Atatürk, the progressive leader took an acute interest in recording and representing Turkish monuments. In the following year, when Atatürk supported the establishment of the Conservation Council of Monuments, Çetintaş was assigned as a member of the council along with the restoration-architect Kural, Professor Miltner from Vienna Archaeological Institute, and Schüller, an expert working at Istanbul museums. In the bylaw of the council, measuring and drawing historic architecture was outlined as a mission that had to be achieved promptly. The reasons for documentation included conducting analysis and study of history of architecture, building scientific records of architecture for new generations of republican youth, aiding the classification of monuments, informing repairs and restoration, building an architectural survey museum, and publicizing Turkish architecture in the international arena.[6]

---

[4] With the decree of 2/5326, June 15 1936. See, Madran, *Tanzimattan Cumhuriyete.*

[5] Nur Akın, "Koruma Alanının Büyük Kaybı: Cahide Tamer," *Mimarlık* 328, March-April 2006. http://www.mimarlikdergisi.com/index.cfm?sayfa=mimarlik&DergiSayi=46&RecID=1091 (accessed September 20, 2021)

[6] Madran, "Koruma Alanının Örgütlenmesi-I," 71-72.

Figure 4.4. Photograph of the measured drawing folio of Bursa's Alaeddin Mosque, delineated by Sedat Çetintaş, January 1 1934. SALT Research, Ali Saim Ülgen Archive, TASUH0756002.

Tasked by the Conservation Council of Monuments, Çetintaş set off to Bursa and Edirne to document the Turkish monuments (Figure 4.4). When addressing the nature of his work, Çetintaş noted: to reconstruct historic monuments if needed, to compile the historiography of the national architecture of Turks, and to exhibit the attributes of Turkish art and architecture to the world.[7] It is not far-fetched to reflect that the Surveying Bureau was actually established to meet Çetintaş' professional pursuit of archival documentation. Until his retirement from the bureau in 1954, Çetintaş dedicated his time to producing folios of measured drawings of Turkish monuments across the country.

In terms of contents and presentation techniques, the drawings of Bursa and Edirne maintained the high caliber of craftsmanship embodied in the renderings of the Sokollu Mehmet Pasha Mosque, which in fact had paved the way for Çetintaş' recruitment in the first place. His extremely elegant Beaux-Arts-styled drawings became the centerpiece of numerous catalogues, exhibitions, and publications in the following years. Yet, these salon drawings without dimensions, notes, and structural details lacked the technical prescriptions to conduct repairs, let alone reconstruction. In terms of its overall ideological framing of Turkish nationalism, his depictions of impeccable monuments became artifactual objects in themselves, rather than procedural demonstrations of architecture.

In fact, Ülgen, during his tenure as the director of the Office of Monuments,[8] another division operating under the General Directorate of the Antiquities and Museums, criticized that their associate the Surveying Bureau was not contributing to the actual building preservation tasks. Ülgen noted that the staff of the Office of Monuments had dutifully shouldered the surveying and construction work across the country and they were zealously traveling to meet the project needs. In respect, Ülgen petitioned to the General Directorate, to authorize Çetintaş and his bureau to actively help the Office of Monuments with the swelling workload.[9]

---

[7] Anonymous, "Edirnedeki bütün Tarihi Abideler Tetkik Ediliyor," 5.

[8] In 1940, Office of Monuments was established under the umbrella of General Directorate of the Antiquities and Museums.

[9] Ülgen, "Sayın Genel Müdür'den," (Report, SALT Research, Ali Saim Ülgen Archive, TASUDOC1311125, date unknown) https://archives.saltresearch.org/handle/123456789/75853 (accessed September 20, 2021); see, also, Ülgen, "Kontrol İşleri," (Report, SALT Research, Ali Saim Ülgen Archive, TASUDOC1311025, date unknown) https://archives.saltresearch.org/handle/123456789/75853 (accessed September 20, 2021).

Ülgen, an influential figure in the implementation of a documentation culture, vehemently advocated for the elevation of professional standards. During his tenure at the Office of Monuments, then at the Office of Monuments and Construction Works,[10] he continuously stressed that the caliber of the restoration work was directly related to architectural surveying as the scientific basis of physical interventions. The shrinking budgets were culminating in field contingencies pertaining to the measured surveys, which was threatening the integrity of physical interventions.

Typically, the restoration architects who were tasked with the historic preservation treatments, themselves created the measured drawings in situ. To meet the procedural needs of growing historic preservation projects, however, separate surveying offices were established within the General Directorate of Endowments: an Istanbul agency in 1952 along with a central branch in Ankara in 1961 (Figure 4.5 and Figure 4.6).[11] Historically, these offices along with Çetintaş' Surveying Bureau[12] became critical to provide the methodological records. As a matter of fact, a job opening for the Istanbul surveying office reveals the intensifying supply and demand for measured surveys. When the office was set to hire seven surveyors in 1959, the candidates were expected to be experienced draftsmen, to be equipped with knowledge in recording monuments, and to be able to operate surveying tools.[13]

---

[10] Office of Monuments and Construction Works was operating at the General Directorate of Endowments.

[11] Akar, "Vakıflar Genel Müdürlüğü ve Vakıf Kültür Varlıklarının Korunması," *Erdem* 59 (2011): 26. Akar, "The Role of Vakıf Institution in the Conservation of Vakıf based Cultural Heritage," (PhD diss., Middle East Technical University, 2009), 83.

[12] Later in 1976, Istanbul's Surveying Bureau was renamed as Directorate Surveying and Monuments and an Ankara branch was opened at the General Directorate of the Antiquities and Museums. See, İffet Billur, "Türkiye'de Kültürel Mirası Koruma Çalışmaları Bağlamında İstanbul Rölöve ve Anıtlar Müdürlüğü'nün Rolü," (PhD diss., Mimar Sinan Fine Arts University, 2020), 26.

[13] Ülgen, "Sultan Selim Camii 1959 Yılı Onarımı Hakkında;" Tamer, "Abide ve Yapı İşleri Şubesine," TASUDOC0481112; Ülgen, "Topkapı Ahmed Paşa Camii 1959 Yılı Onarımı Hakkında;" Tamer, "Abide ve Yapı İşleri Şubesine," TASUDOC0481114; Ülgen, "Rölöve Yapılmak İstenilen Onarımlar Hakkında," Özden, "Rapor, 11. Gurup Şefliğine."

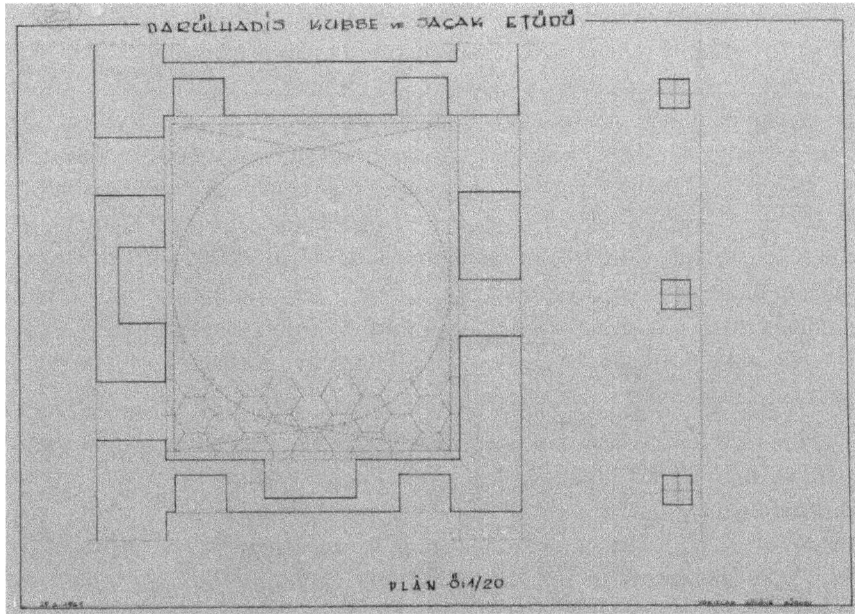

Figure 4.5. 1: 20 scaled plan drawing of the dome of the Darülhadis, June 29, 1961, delineated by Vakıflar Rölöve Bürosu (Surveying Office of General Directorate of Endowments). SALT Research, Ali Saim Ülgen Archive, TASUPAMS190.

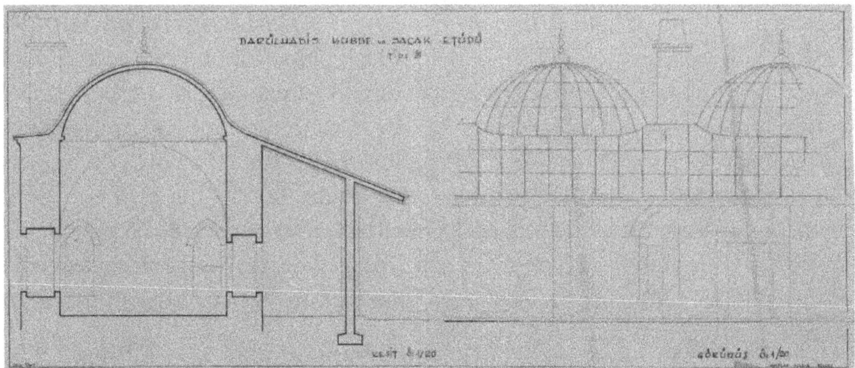

Figure 4.6. 1: 20 scaled elevation and section drawing of the dome of the Darülhadis, June 29, 1961, delineated by Vakıflar Rölöve Bürosu (Surveying Office of General Directorate of Endowments). SALT Research, Ali Saim Ülgen Archive, TASUPAMS191.

In this context, the documentation work of Sedad Hakkı Eldem and his students at the Academy, is founded on another theory of image construction: tracing the universal lines belonging to vernacular Turkish architecture.

Eldem's teaching career at the Academy coincided with the appointment of Ernst A. Egli as the head of the architecture program between 1926-1940. A proponent of modern design, Egli stressed to have a balanced composition; the technically and scientifically superior forms had to be complemented with regional elements of design.[14] Given this, Egli considered the Anatolian houses as the inspirational source to bring forward the new architecture of Turks. To investigate the anatomy of the Turkish house, in 1933, Egli initiated the National Architecture Seminar with his assistants Eldem and Arif Hikmet Holtay. When Egli left the Academy, Eldem took over the course. Eldem's students made measured drawings of traditional houses and mansions across the country and translated these illustrations to rationalize the rudiments of modern design.

The search for intelligible universals in vernacular examples was not meant to replicate the exact qualities of the architectural patrimony in the service of restoration, however. In contrast, the essence of Eldem and his students' work was to provide a critical approach to architectural research that is a product of the study of vernacular architecture. True, Eldem continuously noted the dizzying pace of urban development as the major cause of the destruction of the Turkish house and lamented the introduction of foreign elements of residential design as a substitute.[15] In response, he built a research agenda that was founded on revealing the rational category of Turkish vernacular forms and commemorating those qualities in new design. In this mental vocabulary, the ontological dimensions of the Turkish house were left out. Eldem clarified that the essence of the Turkish house had been the floor plan centered around the hall, regardless of the chronological or topographical background of individual buildings.[16] Derived from the National Architecture Seminar surveys, Eldem crafted a typological matrix for house plans, based on the classification of the form and location of the hall as the organizational element, without a hall, central hall, inner hall, and outer hall. In this highly academic transaction, there was no room left for understanding the anthropological roots of the buildings or recording the physical surfaces for architectural restoration.

Intensified with the Kemalist modernization, the measured drawings' undisputed precision had made the preservation professionals' task into

---

[14] Ernst Egli, "Mimari Muhit," *Türk Yurdu* 30, no.224, (1930): 35.

[15] Eldem, *Türk Evi Plan Tipleri*, 12.

[16] Ibid., "Önsöz."

something akin to applied science and their efficiency was deemed to be a proof of quality. Such geometric abstraction, which is still prevalent in the representation of architecture today, has deeply conditioned the knowledge and perception of Turkish architecture.

Turning to European institutions for methodical documentation

The varying degrees of building documentation in republican Turkey indicates the recognition of epistemological grounds and theorizations in Europe. A 1954 memorandum written by Celâl Esad Arseven and Ülgen exemplifies how professionals conditioned the success of the preservation movement through the commitment to the scientific methods utilized in Europe.[17] Tasked by GEEAYK, the duo prepared a report on the classification and registration of historic works of architecture. Arseven and Ülgen warned that the regulations in Turkey already lagged behind the developments in France and Italy. For the last 130 years, the professionals in aforementioned countries had already been tediously working to classify and register the built heritage, and accumulated an extensive collection. Solely in France, prior to WWI, the agencies classified 9000 historic properties. Thus, the duo noted that instead of focusing on the methods utilized by the European colleagues, the Turkish authorities had to target the results achieved abroad. To this end, Arseven and Ülgen suggested to attain mass registration of historic properties across the country rather than the piecemeal procedures in Europe due to the disruption of wars.

Arseven and Ülgen's selection of France as a model of progress was due to the establishment of *Commission des Monuments Historiques* (Commission of the Historical Monuments) in 1837 as a result of the nascent consciousness for the protection of the built environment. [18] By the same token, Arseven and Ülgen's formal interest in Italy stemmed from the well-organized codification of the 1909-Law of Fine Arts and Antiquities and the establishment of the Supreme Council of Immovable Antiquities and Fine Arts. For Ülgen, the centralized administration of the conservation tasks by the supreme council,

---

[17] Arseven and Ülgen, "Gayrimenkul Eski Eserler ve Anıtlar Yüksek Kurulu Başkanlığına," (Memorandum, SALT Research, Ali Saim Ülgen Archive, TASUDOC0070, November 6 1954) https://archives.saltresearch.org/handle/123456789/76552 (accessed April 5, 2022).

[18] *Anıtların Korunması ve Onarılması (Conservation and Restoration of Monuments),* is the first book on historic preservation in the republic, which reflected Ülgen's learning during his post-graduate fellowship in Europe. See, Ülgen, *Anıtların Korunması ve Onarılması-I* (Ankara: Maarif Matbaası, 1943), 8-15.

coupled with the well-articulated working measures of the 1909-law, the Italian authorities achieved monumental success in the protection and restoration of the built heritage.[19] Another reason for Arseven and Ülgen's emphasis on Italy included the formulation of the Italian principles of restoration, *Carta del Restauro* in 1932.[20] The strictly-regulated four principles were consolidation, recomposition (anastylosis, for archeological heritage), liberation, and completion or renovation.[21] Years later, in 1961 Ülgen endorsed the implementation of the Italian principles of restoration in Turkey and requested the preservation authorities to secure these provisions. [22]

In Europe, building documentation emerged as a reaction to the adverse effects of the developments in the industrial age. With a focus on a linear path of progress, popular concern for the past ebbed, damage and destruction of ancient monuments accelerated as roads and other modern improvements were built to accompany the swelling population moving from the rural areas to the cities. Factories multiplied, cities grew at an unexpected rapid pace, and migration to the urban areas brought new socio-economic challenges. In the midst of the industrial and technological revolutions through mechanization, mass-production, improved communication and transportation systems, many historic properties were destroyed.

The buildings salvaged from the ravages of modernization, yet, did not survive the Napoleonic wars. Napoléon Bonaparte (1769 - 1821), the French statesman and military leader rose to prominence during the French Revolution. When his army sacked and occupied other European countries, whole segments of the built environment were destroyed: churches were vandalized, cities were burned, and many of the artworks and monuments were defaced. Likewise, during the French Revolution, many of the religious buildings and those associated with royalty and nobility in France were destroyed.[23] Soon after, the revolutionaries' ill conduct with the architectural

---

[19] Ibid., 17.

[20] Ibid., 17 & 33-34.

[21] Jukka Jokilehto, *A History of Architectural Conservation* (New York: Butterworth-Heinemann, 2011), 199 and 222.

[22] Ülgen, "Restorasyon Kriterleri ve Carte de Restauro Makalesi ile ilgili Rapor," (Memorandum, SALT Research, Ali Saim Ülgen Archive, TASUDOC0077, June 8 1961) https://archives.saltresearch.org/handle/123456789/82527 (accessed April 5, 2022).

[23] John H. Stubbs, *Time Honored: A Global view of architectural conservation, Parameters, Theory, & Evolution of an Ethos* (Hoboken, N.J.: John Wiley & Sons, 2009), 206-211.

heritage created a reaction to protect the built heritage. Aubin-Louis Millin (1759-1818)'s six-volume monograph, *Antiquitiés Nationales ou Recueil de Monuments*, marked the intensifying consciousness of national heritage and its documentation and representation.[24] The revolutionary administration of France embarked on a research and documentation campaign to classify and make an inventory of the nationalized properties formerly owned by the Catholic Church, the crown, and the nobility.[25] These documentation efforts continued intermittently until the establishment of the Commission of the Historical Monuments was tasked with the documentation, classification, registration and protection of monuments.

The destruction of the Napoleonic invasions was not limited to France. In central Europe, the liberation of the German states from Napoleon's army nurtured a formal interest in studying historic buildings that represented the spirit of the nation. One of the contributors to the preservation movement in Germany, Prussian architect Karl Friedrich Schinkel (1781- 1841), was tasked with the documentation of the conditions of the public buildings in the Rheinland in 1815. Disturbed by the war-damaged and dilapidated condition of buildings, his report included a proposal to create an inventory of historic buildings and to develop a preservation plan for each kind of building (e.g. religious, civic, military) in Prussia.[26] Likewise, when Napoleon's army occupied Rome and annexed the Papal States in 1789, many monuments were scattered and destroyed. As a result, the Italian clergy maintained a legal framework to conduct excavations of national antiquities and to exhibit artifacts. By 1820, Pope Pius VII took formal measures to catalog significant historic buildings and to establish standards for their restoration. One noteworthy example included architect Giuseppe Valadier's (1762 - 1839) restoration work for the Temple of Hercules in 1809-1810 and the Arch of Titus in 1821. Both projects were based on careful documentation and excavation to reveal the foundations and verify the exact form of the monuments.[27]

Nineteenth-century nationalist motivation to document the architectural origins of local cultures led to a nuanced interest in the Ottoman Empire,

---

[24] Aubin-Louis Millin, *Antiquités nationales, ou, Recueil de Monumens* 6 volumes, (Paris: Chez M. Drouhin, 1790).

[25] Stubbs, *Time Honored*, 211-212.

[26] Jokilehto, *A History of Architectural Conservation*, 115; Stubbs, *Time Honored*, 227-228-212.

[27] Jokilehto, *A History of Architectural Conservation*, 84.

however. Reigning sultans were cautious when authorizing an architectural survey against the background of political turbulence caused by the emergence of nation-states in the European and Middle Eastern territories of the empire. The published surveys, conveniently, focused on the built heritage in the imperial capital city, Istanbul, along with the former seats of Bursa and Edirne. For instance, commissioned by Sultan Abdülmecid (r. 1839-1861), the Swiss Fossati brothers restored Istanbul's Hagia Sophia. After this restoration work, the Fossati brothers published a series of lithographs in London with the title of *Aya Sofia as Recently Restored by Order of H. M. the Sultan Abdul Medjid* (1852). The cover of the monograph included the Sultan's name and his tughra, which confirms his connection with the project. The subsequent ruler, Sultan Abdülaziz, appointed the French architect Léon Parvillée to restore the historic buildings in Bursa. Parvillée's subsequent publication, *Architecture at Décoration Turques au XVE siècle* (1874), included measured drawings of the fifteenth-century Green Mosque and the tomb of Sultan Mehmed I in Bursa. Commissioned by the same sultan, *Usūl-i Mi'mārī-i Osmānī* (1873) was distinguished in the architectural historiography written in the age of the late Ottoman empire. The authors of the monograph, Victor Marie de Launay, Pietro Montani, and İbrahim Edhem Pasha, included measured drawings of the Ottoman works in Bursa, Edirne, and Istanbul. This catalogue of measured drawings codified the elements of the Ottoman architectural style. Under Sultan Abdülhamid II's patronage, the German architectural historian Cornelius Gurlitt published two volumes of measured drawings and photographs of Istanbuls' Byzantine and Ottoman built heritage, *Die Baukunst Konstantinopels* (1907 and 1912). Among these surveys, the monographs of Alexander Paspates, an Ottoman physician, historian, and teacher of Greek descent, made personal efforts to document Istanbul's Byzantine architecture.

From 1914 until 1918, WWI resulted in catastrophic damage to scores of European architectural patrimonies, including the Ottoman Empire's. The aerial bombing of cities and intense combat annihilated whole regions in a magnitude unseen before. The historic town of Ypres in Belgium, for instance, was completely destroyed. Many peer cities, Antwerp, Gallipoli, Lier, and Louvain, became theaters of warfare. Due to a general outcry, in 1914, the German army dispatched military units to identify and protect cultural properties. Following the 1918 armistice, numerous nations embarked on major documentation campaigns to assess the loss. For example, it took nearly four years for the Commission of the Historical Monuments in France, to document and conduct the first phase of emergency consolidation of damaged buildings.[28]

The theory of historic preservation, largely, was shaped with the post-war Athens Charter of 1931, the first international document outlining the modern policies of preservation when honored the protection of the historic stratification of built heritage and discouraged stylistic restorations. Rather than simply addressing regulations for protection, the charter proclaimed the universality of preservation values and the necessity for international collaboration. As the first attempt to signify an international perspective, the document proposed the formation of a forum through which technical information and best practices could be shared. The value of documentation lay in the effective circulation of official information. Each country or associated institutions should create an inventory of monuments to cultivate collective appreciation of architectural heritage. The best practices of preservation would derive from the "respect and attachment of the peoples themselves," where documentation constituted the formal step to take an active role for protection. Carta del Restauro, in fact, mirrored the doctrines of the Athens Charter. [29]

The Venice Charter, penned ten years after Arseven and Ülgen's plea to GEEAYK became instrumental in the historic preservation movement. The international charter was drafted in 1964 and was accepted by ICOMOS in 1966. The post-war Athens Charter was written in the turbulent political and social epochs of the war. Yet, the damage of WWII and the following world economic depression brought further destruction. Much of the built environment in Europe was left in ruins; numerous cities in eastern China, Japan, and Southeast Asia were damaged or completely destroyed. Most countries, either active allies in the war or nonparticipating nations, faced rapid changes because of mechanization and new economic conditions. Measured with the circumstances of the new world order, the exchange of views and practices between different nations cultivated an increasingly unified perception of architectural documentation.

The Venice Charter provided standard definitions and articulated procedures for physical interventions. To maintain the authenticity of the historic fabric, the

---

[28] Ibid., 282; Stubbs, *Time Honored*, 218.

[29] Jokilehto, *A History of Architectural Conservation*, 199 & 222.

charter encouraged precise documentation, scientific investigation, and rational interventions. Therefore, the document superseded the Athens Charter, with its emphasis on documentation. Article 16 of the Charter distinctly dictated the significance of thorough documentation to safeguard the architectural heritage, (a) recording of "as found" conditions, (b) the history of the asset, and (c) the preservation process:

> In all works of preservation, restoration or excavation, there should always be precise documentation in the form of analytical and critical reports, illustrated with drawings and photographs. Every stage of the work of clearing, consolidation, rearrangement and integration, as well as technical and formal features identified during the course of the work, should be included. This record should be placed in the archives of a public institution and made available to research workers. It is recommended that the report should be published.

Architectural texts and project records clearly show that Turkish preservation circles were actively following the discussions among their European colleagues and the development of the international agreements. For example, Macit Rüştü Kural, a restoration-architect who supervised the work at Bursa's Green Tomb between 1941 and 1943, initiated a restoration archive at the Surveying Bureau of the General Directorate of the Antiquities and Museums. [30] In other words, twenty-years prior to the international recognition of the Venice Charter, the architects at the Surveying Bureau were already assembling an archive documenting the before and after conditions of the restored historic properties. Thus, restoration-architect Cahide Tamer's project correspondence during her tenure at the Surveying Bureau, then at the General Directorate of Endowments, portrays the specialized emphasis on recording the architectural elements. [31] In many cases Tamer ordered the building contractors not to proceed unless there was a measured survey. In this vein, Sedad Hakkı Eldem highly criticized the 1940s restoration work conducted at the Topkapı Palace Museum due to the

---

[30] Akın, "Koruma Alanının Büyük Kaybı," http://www.mimarlikdergisi.com/index.cfm?sayfa=mimarlik&DergiSayi=46&RecID=1091

[31] Ülgen, "Sultan Selim Camii 1959 Yılı Onarımı Hakkında," TASUDOC0481111; Tamer, "Abide ve Yapı İşleri Şubesine," TASUDOC0481112; Ülgen, "Topkapı Ahmed Paşa Camii 1959 Yılı Onarımı Hakkında," TASUDOC0481113; Tamer, "Abide ve Yapı İşleri Şubesine," TASUDOC0481114; Ülgen, "Rölöve Yapılmak İstenilen Onarımlar Hakkında," TASUDOC0481115; Özden, "Rapor, 11. Gurup Şefliğine," TASUDOC0481116.

absence of the documentation records.[32] Tahsin Öz, the founding director of the museum, conducted an extensive restoration project targeting the most dilapidated buildings of the museum. Öz described the essence of the restoration agenda to liberate the buildings from additions that "stuck on during the period of decline" and to revitalize the glorious past. [33] For Eldem, however, the passion for reviving the past culminated in a calamitous situation at the Topkapı Palace Museum. Without thorough documentation, the removal of the later Baroque and rococo-style decorative elements in the *Harem* section resulted in irreversible loss of cultural heritage. The classical elements were also damaged in the process, since they were scraped without documentation of their as-is conditions.

Preservation professionals tried to secure the success of a grass-rooted preservation movement through the execution of a systematic architectural documentation campaign. Ülgen defined the scientific methodology to create an inventory of historic properties, to classify and register monuments, to secure funds for architectural documentation, to establish an archive of documentation and restoration, to institutionalize material research and storage facilities, to launch a state propaganda to prioritize the protection of monuments, and to train architects, contractors, and crafts-people working on preservation projects.[34] The professionals' efforts to establish a nationwide preservation program and its methodical implementation did not materialize regrettably. In a 1962-letter, Ülgen resented the dire conditions surrounding the built heritage, "Unfortunately, nobody regards scientific materials and documentation research and even those concerned do not place importance on achieving this difficult task."

When it came to scientific documentation, the infamous and enigmatic words of the French architectural theorist and architect Eugène Emmanuel Viollet-le-Duc (1814-1879) had a captivating ring for the republican scholars, "To restore an edifice means neither to maintain it, nor to repair it, nor to

---

[32] Eldem and Akozan, *Topkapı Sarayı, Bir Mimarî Araştırma* (Ankara: Kültür Bakanlığı Eski Eserler ve Müzeler Genel Müdürlüğü, 1982): 96.

[33] Shaw, "Museums and Narratives of Display from the Late Ottoman Empire to the Turkish Republic," *Muqarnas* 24, (2007), 270.

[34] Ülgen, "Rapor," (Memorandum, SALT Research, Ali Saim Ülgen Archive, TASUDOC0486-TASUDOC0486021, 1947). https://archives.saltresearch.org/handle/123456789/82564 (accessed September 20, 2021); Ayverdi, "Osmanlı Âbidelerinin Restorasyonları," *Makaleler*, 97-98.

rebuild it; it means to reestablish it in a finished state, which may in fact never have actually existed at any given moment."[35] Viollet-le-Duc professed his arguments through the rigorous restoration of medieval structures based on a unity of style. To be authentic in art required being true to one's national origins. In the case of French art, the medieval Gothic architecture represented the pure state of rational construction. Although a Gothic cathedral had been completed over the centuries and encompassed stratified styles, the modern architect was tasked with retrieving the pure concept of its origins. Accordingly, Viollet-le-Duc's restorations involved rigorous interventions and eliminations "to reestablish" the harmony in a historic property. His contemporaries fervently criticized his work (e.g., Notre-Dame de Paris and Our Lady of Reims Cathedral) for removing successive layers developed in time and adding non-historical additions, which culminated in the loss of authentic elements.

Viollet-le-Duc defined architectural documentation as the rational methodology required to study buildings and to define the elements of physical interventions. He believed that "to arrive at synthesis we must necessarily pass-through analysis" since a thorough documentation would provide the scientific basis for further work.[36] For Viollet-le-Duc, before any repair work began, the architects' duty was to ascertain the exact age and character of each part of the building and to compile written notes, drawings, and illustrations in a documentation report.[37] When the restoration work began, the exact knowledge of the building would allow for informed decisions.

The formative influence of Viollet-le-Duc's philosophy on Ülgen stemmed from his internship in the Bureau of Historical Monuments and Sites at the French General Directorate of Fine Arts. In 1938, after graduation from the Academy, Ülgen was awarded a state-fellowship to pursue post archaeology-architecture studies in Europe,[38] "A priori in the implementation of the

---

[35] Eugène-Emmanuel Viollet-le-Duc, "Restoration," *The Foundations of Architecture: Selections from the Dictionnaire Raisonne,* trans. Kenneth D. Whitehead (New York: George Braziller, Inc., 1990), reprinted in idem, in *Historical and Philosophical Issues in the Conservation of Cultural Heritage,* ed. Nicholas Stanley Price, M. Kirby Talley Jr., and Alessandra Melucco Vaccaro (Los Angeles: The Getty Conservation Institute, 1996), 314.

[36] Ibid.

[37] Ibid.

[38] Türkiye Cumhuriyeti Kültür Bakanlığı, "Seçme Sınavında Muvaffak Olduğunuza Dair," (Memorandum, SALT Research, Ali Saim Ülgen Archive, TASUDOC0534108, November 2 1938) https://archives.saltresearch.org/handle/123456789/83487 (accessed April 5, 2022).

European methods, the Ministry of Education has introduced numerous provisions for the repairs and preservation of the monuments. To this end... to internalize the scientific principles and practices, the Ministry sent me to Europe."[39] Upon his return to Turkey, Ülgen was sent to work at the Ministry of Education to restore Seljuk and Ottoman monuments.[40] While in France, Ülgen read the treaties of Viollet-le-Duc and studied his work first-hand. In particular, he got acquainted with his restoration of Our Lady of Reims Cathedral.[41] Viollet-le-Duc's priority on analytical documentation is evident in Ülgen's words,

> Restoration of the monuments necessitates architectural evidence and historical records of great significance. This evidence has to be searched, either on the surface of the building or on peer monuments formed in the same era. Records such as historical works, miniatures, engravings, archival, maps, plans, and pictures, specifications and deeds of buildings can be utilized.[42]

Viollet-le-Duc's focus on stylistic unity in restoration was characterized by an unprecedented scholarship and became an academic concern of archeologically accurate composition, however. Arseven defined restoration as artistic repair, the act of repairing and improving the deteriorated and demolished elements of historic architecture without compromising its artistic value and authentic form.[43] Arseven celebrated Viollet-le-Duc's theory of restoration as "artistic repairs of medieval monuments of France that did not damage the old form and nature."[44] Arseven, however, was well aware of the critique against Viollet-le-

---

[39] Ülgen, *Anıtların Korunması ve Onarılması-I*, XXVIII.

[40] Hasan Âli Yücel, T.C. Maarif Vekilliği, "Avrupa'da mimarlık tahsil edecek talebe hak.," (Memorandum, SALT Research, Ali Saim Ülgen Archive, TASUDOC0534114, April 19 1939). https://archives.saltresearch.org/handle/123456789/83487 (accessed April 7, 2022); T.C. Kültür Bakanlığı, "Saim Ülgen (C. 268 Mf), (Memorandum, SALT Research, Ali Saim Ülgen Archive, TASUDOC0534105, November 30 1938).
https://archives.saltresearch.org/handle/123456789/83487 (accessed April 5, 2022).

[41] T.C. Kültür Bakanlığı, Güzel Sanatlar Akademisi, "Bay Saim Ülgen, Yüksek Mimar," (Memorandum, SALT Research, Ali Saim Ülgen Archive, TASUDOC0534117, June 21 1939). https://archives.saltresearch.org/handle/123456789/83487 (accessed April 5, 2022).

[42] Ülgen, *Anıtların Korunması ve Onarılması-I*, 76.

[43] Arseven, *Sanat Ansiklopedisi*, IV/21 (İstanbul: Milli Eğitim Basımevi), 1758.

[44] Ibid., 1759.

Duc's practice of enforced stylistic unity. Arseven cautioned that the excessive additions and the introduction of non-authentic elements, would entail the loss of the historical value.

French architect and historian, Albert Gabriel, who documented the medieval architecture of Anatolia with the assistance of Ülgen, noted "The era, when the reconstruction of a slightly damaged stone or a ruined decorative [piece] was essential, no longer exists. Previously, a historical monument would lose all its character along with its grace, and would appear new despite its old age."[45] Gabriel confirmed "the most diligent and recognized architect of the nineteenth-century, Viollet-le-Duc and his unprecedented knowledge" on historic architecture.[46] Nevertheless, Gabriel stated that Viollet-le-Duc's "oversight of style" created a ground for false architecture, an approach that should not be pursued in the act of restoration.

Ülgen reiterated Gabriel's narrative and disapproved of European restaurateurs' audacity to fabricate an architectural setting; these "imaginative" hierarchies haunted historical buildings and turned them into a "catastrophic witness of the erroneous" restoration applications.[47] A genuine architect, on the other hand, would be obligated "to search for the truth, to be meticulous and patient," and to avoid immature "conclusions from weak and vague terms." Significantly, Ülgen defined restoration as a scientific discipline to probe informed decisions about the future of the building, "The creation of new motifs and the assembly of new compositions are loose acts that a scientist, hence an architect, should avoid." [48]

Projecting the formal order of descriptive drawings

The conceptual elaboration of elements of architecture on paper were highly susceptible to the tools of representation available.[49] With the introduction of Euclidean geometry in the eighteenth- century, architectural representation was equated to algebraic analysis of flat-surface geometry.[50] Hence, drawings

---

[45] Gabriel, "Tarihî Âbidelerin Tasnif ve Muhafazası," *Anıtların Korunması ve Onarılması-I*, XXI-XXII.

[46] Ibid., XXIII.

[47] Ülgen, *Anıtların Korunması ve Onarılması-I*, 76.

[48] Ibid., 80.

[49] Akboy-İlk, "Crafting the Architectural Measured Drawings," *The Plan Journal* 2, no. 1 (2017): 39–61.

[50] Around 300 BC, Euclid wrote The Elements, a major treatise on the geometry of the time, and what would be considered 'geometry' for many years after. In his book, Euclid

came to be seen as a precise mathematical description of reality.[51] When the École Polytechnique was established in 1795 in France, the conception of the school was to establish radically reformed technical education for architects and engineers. Therefore, the school focused on descriptive geometry that articulated the physical description of objects in space with a set of coordinates in line with X, Y, Z axes (Figure 4.7). Henceforth, the dose of algebraic analysis in architectural education increased considerably. While scientific methods and descriptive geometry were considered integral to advancements in technology, architects along with engineers came to be educated in order to make production more efficient.[52]

The nineteenth-century witnessed the development of another strategy in architectural thinking. The French architect, Jean Nicolas Louis Durand (1760-1834), pushed the boundaries of the reductionist approach to architectural discourse by introducing the representation of a building with a descriptive set of projections on different scales (Figure 4.8). Durand's design method "rejected both personal expression and the appeal to any transcendent authorities such as nature, divine proportions, ideal prototypes, or absolute standards of beauty to which virtually all previous architecture in the western tradition referred."[53] This design method condensed architectural production to the selection and combination of building forms and elements.[54] In

---

states five postulates of geometry which he uses as the foundation for all his proofs. It is from these postulates we get the term Euclidean geometry, for in these Euclid strove to define what constitutes 'flat-surface' geometry.

These postulates are:

1. [It is possible] to draw a straight line from any point to any other.
2. [It is possible] to produce a finite straight line continuously in a straight line.
3. [It is possible] to describe a circle with any centre and distance [radius].
4. That all right angles are equal to each other.
5. That, if a straight line falling on two straight lines makes the interior angles on the same side less than two right angles, the two lines, if produced indefinitely, meet on that side on which the angles are less than the two right angles Daniel Marshall and Paul Scott, "A Brief History of Non-Euclidean Geometry," *Australian Mathematics Teacher* 60, no. 3 (2004): 1.

[51] Alberto Pérez Gómez, *Architecture and the Crisis of Modern Science* (Cambridge, Mass.: MIT Press, 1983), 279.

[52] Akboy-İlk, "The Nature of Drawing in the Changing Culture of Architectural Documentation," *Journal of Architectural and Planning Research* 33, no.1 (2016): 29-44.

[53] Sam Ridgway, "The Representation of Construction," *Architectural Theory Review* 14, no. 3 (2009): 274-75.

[54] Robert Bruegmann, "The Pencil and Electronic Sketchboard: Architectural Representation and the Computer," in *Architecture and Its Image: Four Centuries of*

contemporary practice, architects still use this geometrized set of projections of a building to represent real space.

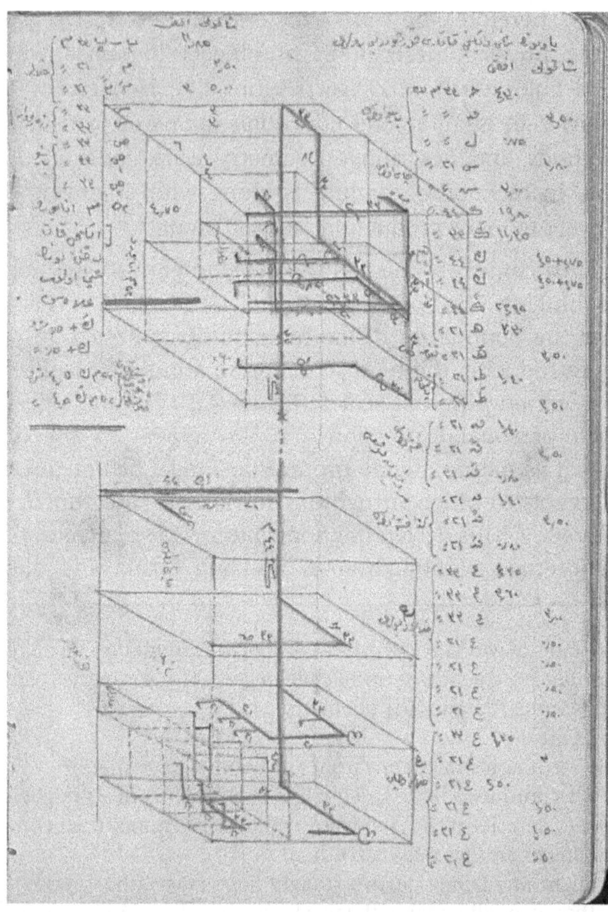

Figure 4.7. The three-dimensional model of Bezmialem Valide Sultan Hospital, drawn by Mehmet Nihat Nigizberk, undated. Koç University, Suna Kıraç Library Special Collections and Archives, Mehmet Nihat Nigizberk Collection of Architectural Drawings and Photographs MNN_NB_01, 539.

Architectural Representation: Works from the Collection of the Canadian Centre for Architecture, ed. Eve Blau, Edward Kaufman, and Robin Evans (Montreal Cambridge, Mass.: Centre Canadien d'Architecture/Canadian Centre for Architecture, Distributed by the MIT Press, 1989), 141.

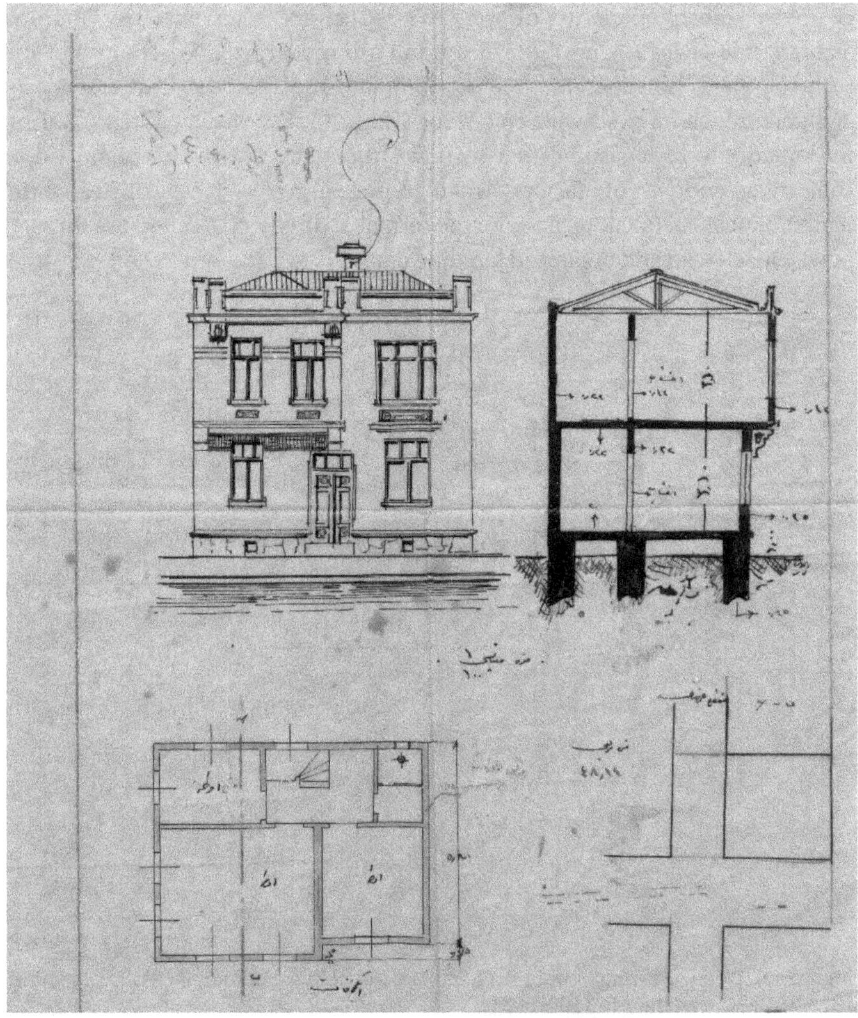

Figure 4.8. The descriptive projection of two-dimensional plan, section, and elevation of a house, ca. early twentieth century, Ottoman Empire, delineated by Architect Şemsettin. SALT Research, TMSSD049.

It is fair to say, since the mid-1900s architectural thought has been preoccupied with the elimination of the irrational and the personal in favor of a universally applicable system of principles and rules based on absolute certainties. The intellectual seeds of the mathematical representation of architecture reverberated with the modern construction of archival building documentation in the Late Ottoman Empire. Authors of *Usūl* looked no further than Durand's geometric abstraction to dissect the structural elements of Ottoman architectural styles (Figure 4.9). In the intense modernization schemes of the early republic, however, the will to dominate the mathematical essence of architecture was viewed with epic favor. Motivated by the same determinism, the exactitude of measured drawings was thought to eliminate imprecise or subjective entities of factors when representing surfaces. Instead, the mathematical abstractions became the formal anatomy of architecture through precisely selected and organized building data.

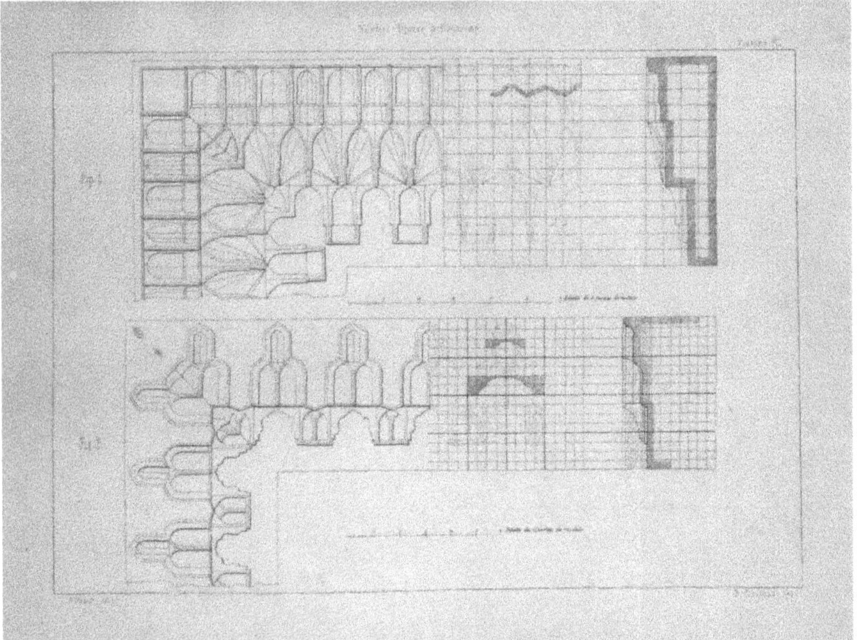

Figure 4.9. Detail drawing of Bursa's Green Mosque. *Usūl-i Mi'mārī-i Osmānī*, Istanbul, 1873. SALT Research, AMN1100200211.

Constructing images through drawing styles

Along with the mathematical description of a flat system of architectural drawing, the construction of measured drawings has been susceptible to the design trends present at ateliers and schools. Individual professionals had a different level of involvement with the programs of architecture and engineering; through their education they learned how to operate in the descriptive system of drawing and to hone their drafting skills. In the changes at the end of the Ottoman Empire and the birth of the Republic of Turkey, the academic transition between the Beaux-Arts tradition and the Modern Movement at the prestigious institutions of higher education, dominated the visual hierarchy of the drawings.

Figure 4.10. Façade of a library, watercolor on paper, school project, drawn by Şemsettin then a student at the Academy, ca. 1912, SALT Research, TMSSD121.

Figure 4.11. Detail drawing of a capital and its column, school project, drawn by Şemsettin then a student at the Academy, ca. 1912, SALT Research, TMSSD111.

Established in 1882, the only art and architecture school in the Ottoman Empire, *Sanayi-i Nefise Mekteb-i Âlisi,* followed the tenets of the French École des Beaux Arts curriculum. The teaching heavily emphasized the classical composition, with an academic emphasis on façade design along with the domination of axiality and symmetry in architectural forms. Drawing and rendering exercises instituted the core of the architectural curriculum at the prestigious imperial school where students prepared project drawings with ink and watercolors (Figure 4.10). In these drawings, students would prioritize façades and individual building details (for example, a capital or an entablature), enhanced with meticulous shadowing techniques and the use of color (Figure 4.11). The architectural courses in the imperial engineering school, *Mühendis Mekteb-i Âlîsi,* followed a similar curriculum based on the study of classical orders and their inherent rendering techniques.[55]

Figure 4.12. A mosque façade designed in the Greek order, delineated by Sedad Hakkı Eldem. SALT Research, Sedad Hakkı Eldem Archive, AEXSHE0010830.

The first generation of republican professionals graduated from these institutions with the Beaux Arts tradition; their draftsmanship with intense

[55] Bozdoğan, Modernism and Nation Building, 31.

shading and coloring techniques became a badge of distinction. Graduated from the Academy in 1917, Çetintaş' elevations and sections of immaculate Ottoman architecture against the serene patterning of sky and foliage, themselves became artifactual objects. In fact, his highly elegant Beaux-Arts style measured drawings secured him post-graduation positions in the practice of architecture, including the establishment of the Surveying Bureau. A graduate of the Academy in 1928, Eldem also had a classical education, which was rooted in the documentation and examination of the Ottoman and Greco-Roman orders. His sketchbooks crafted while a student-architect at the Academy would include building skins that embodied revivalist elements mirrored along horizontal and vertical axes (Figure 4.12). Similarly, a graduate of the imperial engineering school in 1920, Ayverdi had a formal education in the École des Beaux Arts tradition. One of his school projects, a proposed mosque against the cloudy sky, clearly exemplified the artistic rendering of Euclidian figures for its beauty and stability (Figure 4.13 and Figure 4.14).

Figure 4.13. Façade of a proposed mosque, school project, drawn by Ekrem Hakkı Ayverdi then a student at the *Mühendis Mekteb-i Âlîsi,* March 1920. Ekrem Hakkı Ayverdi Institute Archive, Kubbealtı Waqf Collection, Istanbul.

Figure 4.14. Section and plan drawing of the proposed mosque, school project, drawn by Ekrem Hakkı Ayverdi then a student at the *Mühendis Mekteb-i Âlîsi*, March 1920. Ekrem Hakkı Ayverdi Institute Archive, Kubbealtı Waqf Collection, Istanbul.

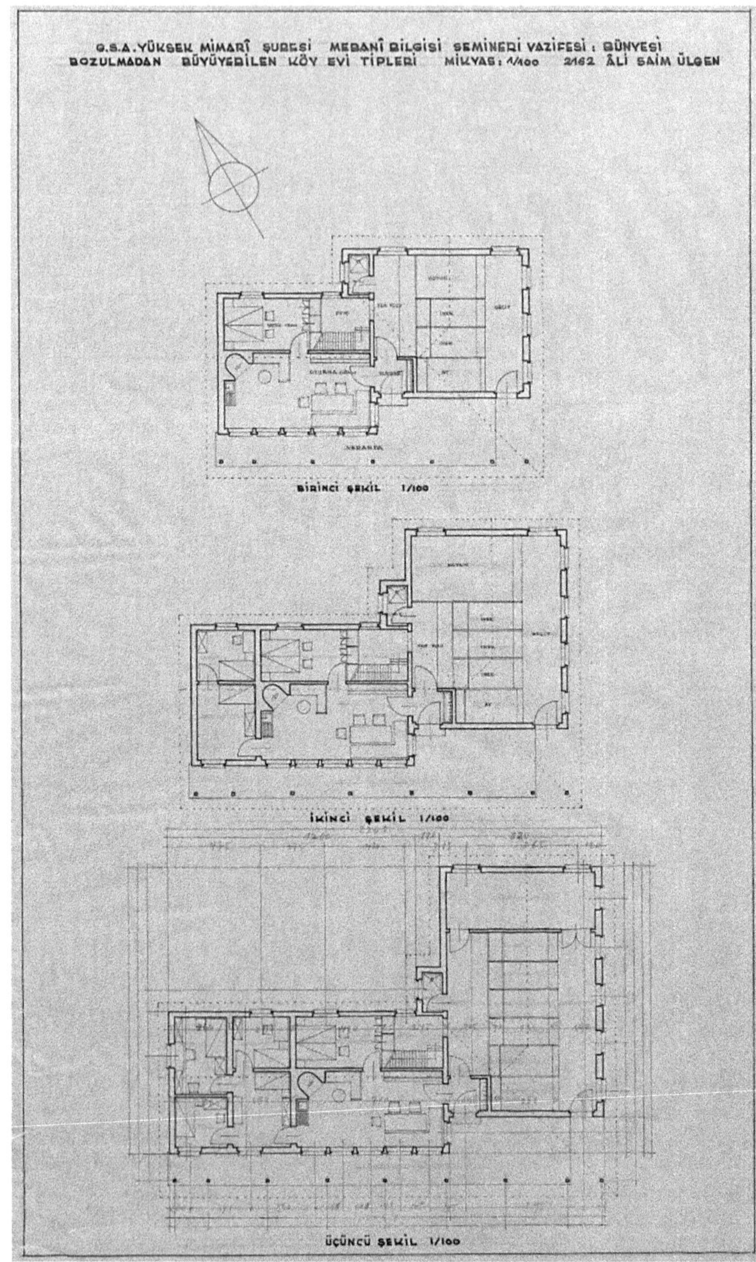

Figure 4.15. Concept drawing of an expandable village house, school project, drawn by Ali Saim Ülgen then a student at the Academy. SALT Research, Ali Saim Ülgen Archive, TASUPA0043.

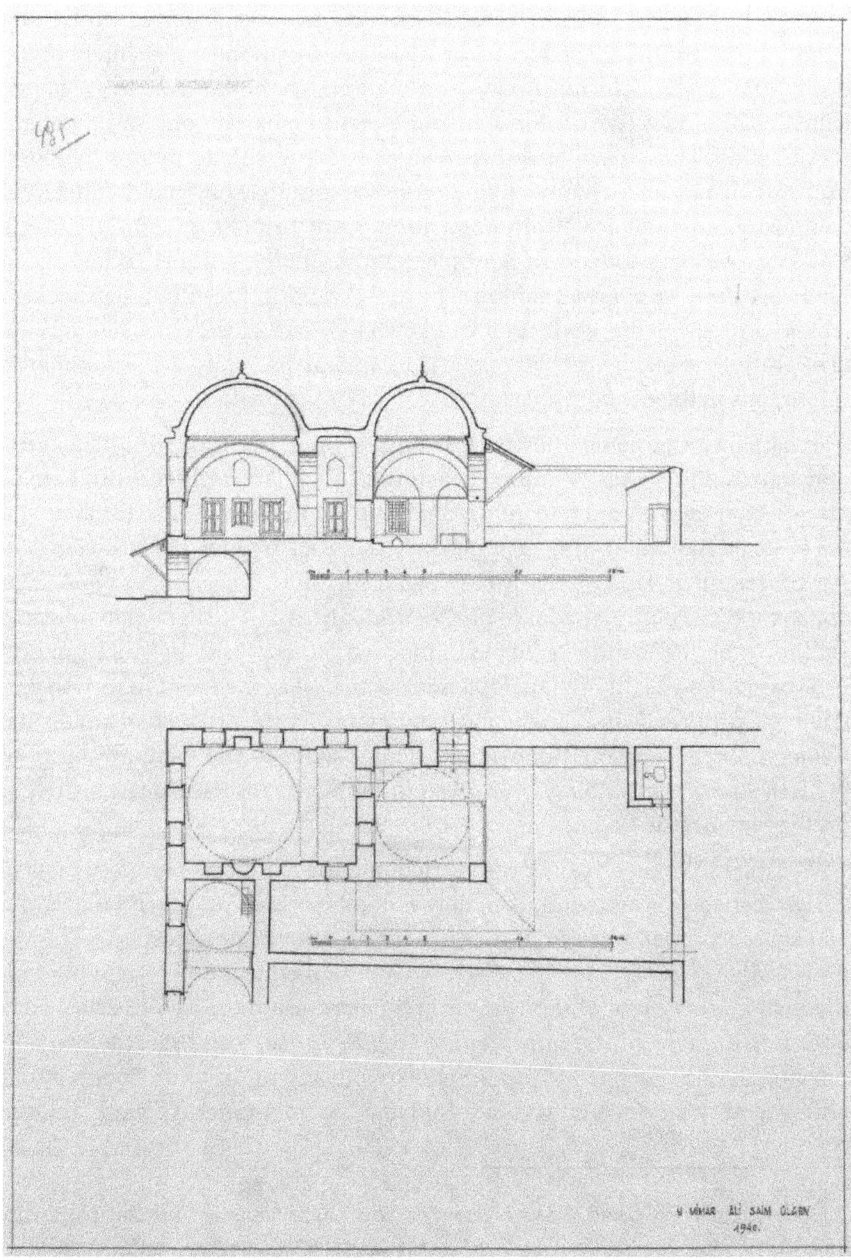

Figure 4.16. Elementary school of Süleymaniye Mosque Complex, delineated by Ali Saim Ülgen, 1940. SALT Research, Ali Saim Ülgen Archive, TASUPAMS213.

In 1928, the name of *Sanayi-i Nefise Mekteb-i Âlisi* was changed into the *Güzel Sanatlar Akademisi* (Academy of Fine Arts), along with the replacement of the Beaux-Arts model with a German-central European modernism. In 1930, Egli launched a new curriculum of architecture based on the Modern Movement.[56] The teaching advocated that form should follow function (functionalism), architecture should embrace minimalism, and architectural composition should reject ornamentation. Concurrently, student architects worked to develop functional floor plans rather than monumental façades of the École des Beaux Arts tradition. The aesthetic priorities of modern design (cubic form, flat roofs, horizontal window bands, structural consoles, and the like) prescribed an abstract order of a geometrical discipline to the volumetric resolutions in the overall appearances.

Remarkably, the meticulous neo-classical style of the École des Beaux Arts drawing tradition was abruptly substituted with an aesthetic of "Less is more." New and simplified representation of building forms became the norm of architectural drawings. Against the backdrop of plain sheets, the unadorned plastered walls were depicted with fewer lines and less application of color. A graduate of the Academy in 1938, Ülgen had a formal architectural education reflected modern lines. His school projects showcased the weight of plan depictions in the refinement of proportion and scale of proposed building concepts (Figure 4.15). His later published monographs of measured drawings strictly adhere to the extreme clarity of modern lines, transcribing centuries-old architectural paragons as straight profiles against the skyline (Figure 4.16).

With the radical overhaul of the curriculum, the triumph of modern lines in design concepts was complete: domes, arches, and tile decoration were banished from architectural production as reactionary nostalgia.[57] Even professionals who initially had acquired a design education concentrated on the Beaux Arts school of thought, promptly cast aside the neo-classical style drawings in favor of modern drafting trends. In this context, Eldem's later drawings heavily attested to modern lines, with an emphasis on floor plans to understand historic architecture. In fact, his monumental work on the

---

[56] Neslinur Hızlı and Nezih R. Aysel, "Ernst Egli'nin Güzel Sanatlar Akademisi Mimarlık Eğitimi Reformu Çalışmaları," in *Ernst A. Egli: Türkiye'ye Katkılar*, ed. Ali Cengizkan, Selda Bancı, and N. Müge Cengizkan (İstanbul: TMMOB Mimarlar Odası Yayınları, 2017), 75.

[57] Bozdoğan and Akcan, *Turkey: Modern Architectures in History*, 25.

typological analysis of the Turkish house was none other than applying the lines, squares, and rectangles as the basis of a modern building (Figure 4.17). Outlining his ideas in a strict hierarchy of plan types, Eldem drew what he felt was essential on the horizontal projections and omitted unnecessary components of geometric abstraction. Ayverdi's drawings during his tenure as a restoration engineer also reflect the tenets of modern lines. His spare and precise delineation of historic architecture anchored with an academic interest in floor plans. Coupled with his copious use of white space to focus attention on the actual building, his depiction of form heavily resides in the "less-is-more" inspired drafting techniques of modern design (Figure 4.18).

Figure 4.17. Drawing of a modernist *yalı* (waterfront mansion), drawn by Sedad Hakkı Eldem, 1927-1928. SALT Research, Sedad Hakkı Eldem Archive, AEXSHE0010292.

Figure 4.18. Section drawing of the Orhan Gazi Mosque, delineated by Ekrem Hakkı Ayverdi, 1962. Ekrem Hakkı Ayverdi, "Bursa Orhan Gazi Camii ve Osmanlı Mimarisinin Menşei Meselesi," *Vakıflar Dergisi* VI, 1965.

Streamlining the processes of documentation and restoration

Gleaned from the rich collection of measured drawings, there were four major operational routes for architectural documentation. First, architects compiled measured drawings to depict the as-is conditions of the building surfaces prior to the repairs. Given this, the information annotated in the graphic illustrations informed the direction of the historic preservation treatment. Second, state agencies directly commissioned scholars to compile monographs on certain topics. Although useful to guide physical interventions, to a certain degree, these archival drawings embodied theoretical images of architectural heritage. Third, architects intended to use the measured drawings later in their professional work; therefore, they recorded what they thought was important. Regardless of an academic pursuit to publish the field findings, their illustrations perceptually merged in the sense that the professionals were acutely aware of a vanishing architectural legacy. Through recording, they aimed to capture the historic properties on paper before they were lost; but also, they hoped to bring formal attention to the preservation of these resources. Fourth, during the course of a building preservation job, architects compiled monographs as a by-product of the ongoing work.

The weaving thread in all these endeavors of architectural documentation, however, was the tendency to monopolize a certain representation of the building surface and leave out the so-called non-essential layers of architecture. The modern drafting apparatus acted entirely in the service of the architects. In selecting floor plans and structural elements to be drawn from the buildings and selecting the lines and planes to record them on paper, the architects were testing the fit of geometric patterns and seeking the forms that define architecture.[58] The abstracted plans, columns, friezes, and walls through horizontal and vertical projections of plans, sections, and elevations defined the institutions of historic architecture. The "left-out" profiles, in other words, the elements of space that geometrically fall behind the cut-line of a plan or a section, were not thought to be in contradiction to the order of representation on paper. In this vein, the methodological path of descriptive drawing required drafters to peel away individual qualities while omitting the rest of the building features that they felt irrelevant to the architectural form.

---

[58] Akboy-İlk, "The Mediated Environment of Heritage Recording and Documentation," 14-15.

Furthermore, the modern emphasis on plans as the essence of architectural design heightened the significance of horizontal projections. It is no surprise, for the most part, deconstructing that the built environment through floor plans became a systemized method of historical analysis. Measured and drawn floor plans of historic architecture attested to the scientific roots of building information, and these two-dimensional renderings were ranked and weighed in the stylistic evolution of Turkish architecture. The prioritization of plans as the geometric blueprint of a structure, however, took its toll as a partial representation of the building surface. This descriptive transposition involved inevitable processes of selection, where the drafters only focused on the horizontal associations and left out the vertical progression of elements and spaces.

The curatorial tracings created ambivalent measures in the generative procedure to restore. When looking closely at the contents of the archival surveys, the sequence of drawings, from documentation to restoration, had been interrupted. Surprisingly, the same preservation professionals who advocated the scientific methodology to compile (1) measured surveys to show the existing condition of the building, (2) restitution proposals based on documentation findings and archival research, and (3) restoration drawings to apply the informed decisions, did not entirely distinguish between existing features and new construction in the representations.

Concurrently, Gabriel understood measured drawing, at best, as a major part of the work of restoration. Yet, the theoretical distance between measured and restitution drawings remained opaque and ambiguous in his *Monuments Turcs d'Anatolie.* Indeed, much of the confusion is directly linked to the level of reduction in his illustrations. Tasked by the government, Gabriel embarked on the didactic project of formulating points of reference for the restoration of the material culture of the Turks. For this ambitious volume, Gabriel prepared graphically restored depictions of not only the historic buildings, often half-ruined at the time, but also their projected setting in the past. For Gabriel, the role of drawing was to appoint the historic property and its setting to a proper place in its history. His resulting images entailed proportion and beautiful order, confirming an intellectual manifestation of the École des Beaux Arts. His drawings illustrated the imagined condition of the structure at the time of documentation and communicated unambiguous heritage information (Figure 4.19 and Figure 4.20). In these idealized images, what Gabriel was referring to in the present or past, and how he reconciled field findings and archival research with the drawings remained elusive.

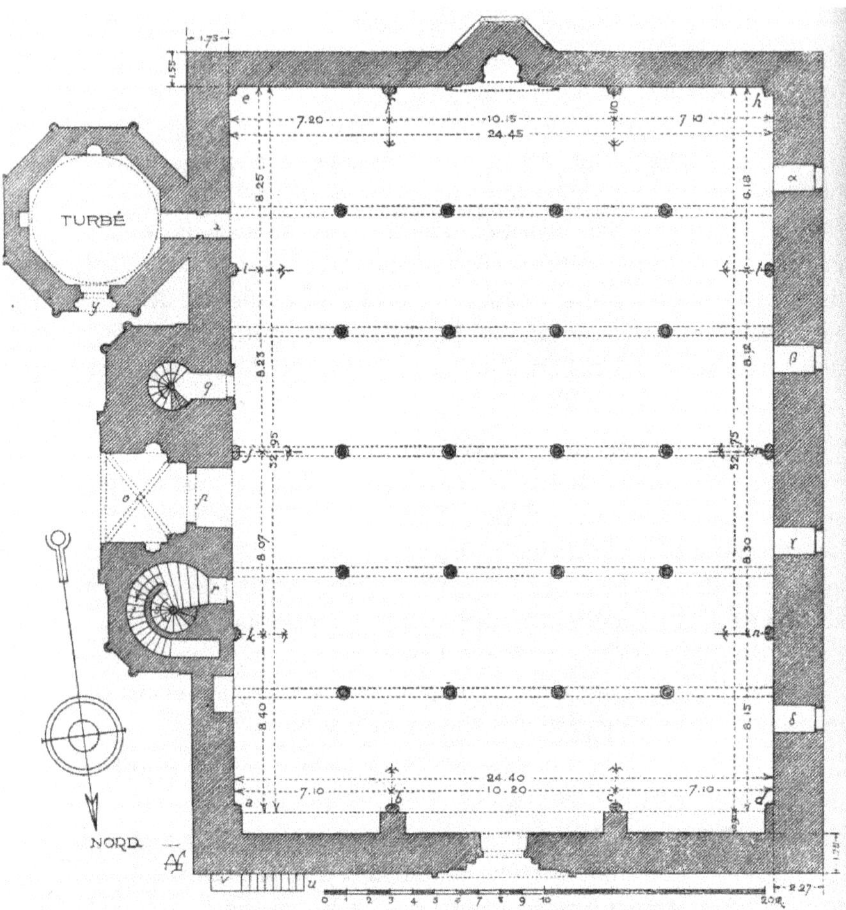

Figure 4.19. The measured drawing of the existing condition of the Seljuk Sungurbey Mosque in Niğde, delineated by Albert Gabriel. Albert Gabriel, *Monuments Turcs D'Anatolie: Kayseri-Nigde.* Paris: Paris Libraire des écoles françaises d'Athènes et de Rome, 1931. Reprinted in idem, Istanbul: Arkeoloji ve Sanat Yayınları, 2014.

The architectural intention to restore was also evident in Ülgen's archival documentation work; he assisted Gabriel during the surveying campaign in Anatolia and later collaborated on many projects. Ülgen promoted a primary and instrumental presence for measured drawings for the protection of architectural resources. In terms of its referentiality, however, his published monographs embodied a fluctuating translation between archival documentation and physical building preservation. In his epic work, *Mimar Sinan Yapıları*, for example, the organizing perception entailed the production of measured drawings pertaining to Sinan's architectural legacy. In the volume, however, Ülgen often alternated the meaning of measured drawing, by synthetizing the already lost elements from Sinan's authentic design with period-appropriate contemporary additions. Sometimes stating "restitution," but often omitting such explanation on the drawing sheet, Ülgen materialized a graphically restored version of the ailing monuments. Ülgen was well aware that a building would change in the course of time and a measured drawing, regardless of how many alterations and subtractions had occurred, had to be loyal to the architectural appearances at the time of documentation. Therefore, his tendency to introduce restitution drawings in a monograph of measured surveys could only be explained with his prioritization of measured drawings as a generative procedure in the service of physical interventions. Perhaps his reconciliation between existing form and proposed elements in one sheet of drawing became the pragmatic function for Ülgen (Figure 4.21), who had been tasked with the conservation of the entire building stock across the country during his highly respected career.

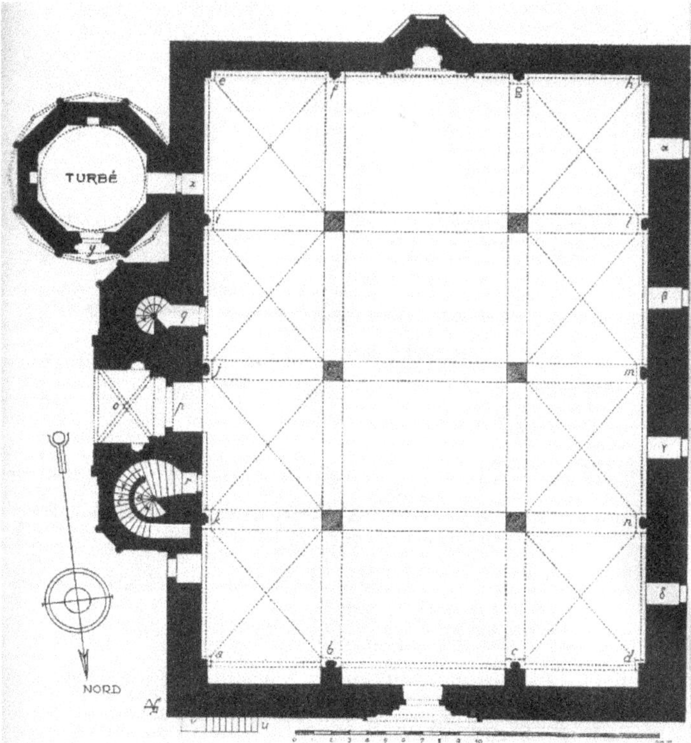

Figure 4.20. The graphically restored depiction of the Seljuk Sungurbey Mosque in Niğde, delineated by Albert Gabriel. Albert Gabriel, *Monuments Turcs D'Anatolie: Kayseri-Nigde*. Paris: Paris Libraire des écoles françaises d'Athènes et de Rome, 1931. Reprinted in idem, Istanbul: Arkeoloji ve Sanat Yayınları, 2014.

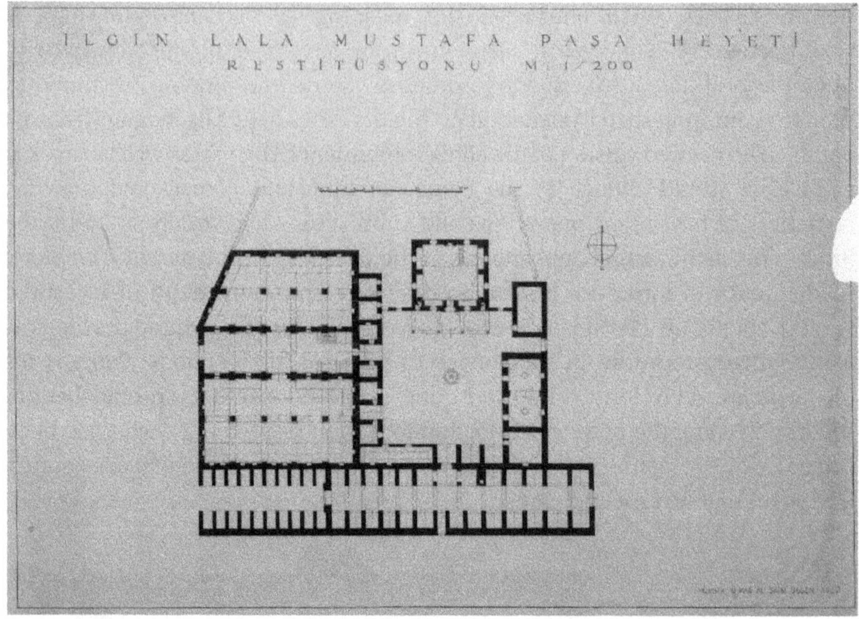

Figure 4.21. Restitution drawing for Ilgın Lala Mustafa Paşa Mosque, delineated by Ali Saim Ülgen, 1952. SALT Research, Ali Saim Ülgen Archive, TASUPA0346.

Ülgen's drawing style in *Mimar Sinan Yapıları* presents the other side of the coin. Ülgen's modernist drawings with plain sheets, devoid of the clutter of details, dimensions, and notes align with the "less-is-more" apparatus of the Modern Movement. Then the measured drawings barely attested to a technical template, but became analogous to archival building documentation with their power to connect separate and diverse elements embodied in the historical surfaces.

In the non-linear application of archival building documentation, Ülgen and Hikmet Turhan Dağlıoğlu's monograph on Ankara's sixteenth-century Cenabî Ahmed Pasha Mosque Complex confirms the mission of restoration. As the only work of Sinan's in Ankara, the Ottoman mosque complex became a national beacon in the early preservation efforts. Signed by Atatürk and deputies of the Grand National Assembly, decrees of 1936, 1937, and 1938 allocated public funds to maintain and restore the historic property.[59] In 1940,

---

59 Mustafa Kemal Atatürk, "Ankara'da tarihi kıymeti bulunan Cenabî Ahmed Paşa Camii'nin emaneten tamir ettirilmesi," (Decision, Türkiye Cumhuriyeti Cumhurbaşkanlığı

the General Directorate of Endowments completed the restoration project, which included the mosque, two tombs, and the fountain. The preservation work focused on restoring the grandeur of the sixteenth-century classical configuration of Sinan's buildings. Subsequently, later additions of the buildings (for example hipped roofs of the porticos and colonnades) were removed and replaced with replicas of classical elements. Furthermore, non-contributing structures on the premises were demolished to create an open space around the mosque.[60]

Subsequent to the restoration work, Ülgen published *Ankara'da Cenabî Ahmed Paşa Camii ve Türbesi* (*Cenabî Ahmed Pasha Mosque and Tomb in Ankara,* 1942) coauthored with Dağlıoğlu. The monograph consisted of two sections; Dağlıoğlu wrote the historical context while Ülgen provided the architectural description. Dağlıoğlu's analysis mainly included the translation of the calligraphy to modern Turkish and the biographical information on Cenabî Pasha. [61] Ülgen focused on the mosque and tomb of Cenabî Pasha and provided two sheets of measured drawings (Figure 4.22 and 4.23), which interestingly, included only the restored version of the structures. Ülgen barely noted the recent occupation of the military barracks in the courtyard and the poor quality of the repairs conducted in the past. Instead, he celebrated the General Directorate's pursuit of stylistic unity, which included removing features from other periods in history and reconstructing of missing features from Sinan's era.[62] In this context, Ülgen's measured drawings of the mosque and the tomb were not part of a preservation plan since the complex

---

Devlet Arşivleri, Başkanlık Cumhuriyet Arşivi, 68-78-19, October 1 1936); Atatürk, "Ankara Cebeci'deki Cenabî Ahmed Paşa Camii'nin tamiri" (Decision, Türkiye Cumhuriyeti Cumhurbaşkanlığı Devlet Arşivleri, Başkanlık Cumhuriyet Arşivi, 80-96-8, November 23 1937); Atatürk, "Ankara'nin Cebeci civarindaki Cenabî Ahmed Paşa Camii'nin emaneten tamir ettirilmesi," (Decision, Türkiye Cumhuriyeti Cumhurbaşkanlığı Devlet Arşivleri, Başkanlık Cumhuriyet Arşivi, 83-52-8, June 10 1938); İnönü, "Ankara'da Cebeci'deki Cenabî Ahmetpaşa Camii'ne ait Yeniden Yapılacak bazı İşlerinin Emaneten Yapılması," (Decision, Türkiye Cumhuriyeti Cumhurbaşkanlığı Devlet Arşivleri, Başkanlık Cumhuriyet Arşivi, 87-47-4, May 5 1939).

[60] *Belediye Yapı ve Yollar Kanunu* of 10 June 1933 (The Building and Roads Law) required that an open space with a radius of ten meters be left around each monument. See, anonymous, "Belediye Yapı ve Yollar Kanunu," *Arkitekt* 6, no. 30 (1933), 192.

[61] Hikmet Turhan Dağlıoğlu, *Ankara'da Cenabî Ahmed Paşa Camii ve Cenabî Ahmed Paşa* (Ankara: Vakıflar Umum Müdürlüğü Neşriyatı, 1942), 48-49 and 121.

[62] Ülgen, *Ankara'da Cenabî Ahmed Paşa Camii ve Türbesi* (Ankara: Vakıflar Umum Müdürlüğü Neşriyatı, 1942), 221.

had just been restored two years prior. By contrast, the illustrative depiction of the post-restoration condition attested to a subjective view of building documentation in the sense that Ülgen took the historic elements apart and drew what he felt was important as an archival record.

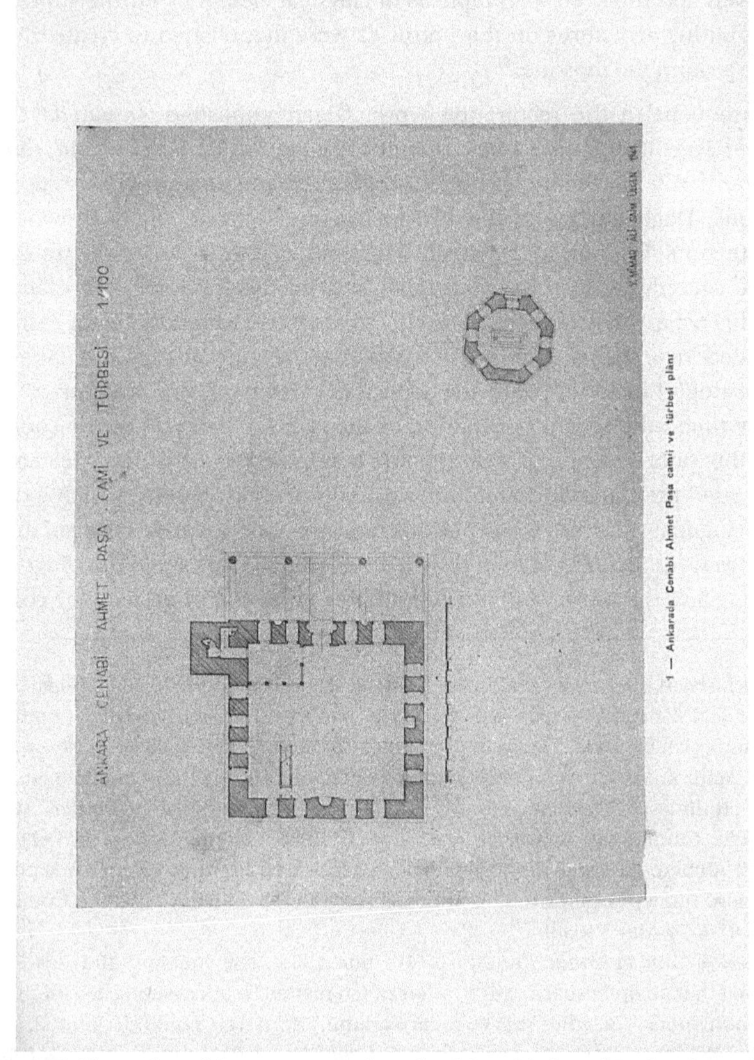

Figure 4.22. Floor plan of the mosque and tomb of Cenabî Ahmed Pasha, drawn by Ali Saim Ülgen. Ali Saim Ülgen, *Ankara'da Cenabî Ahmed Paşa Camii ve Türbesi.* Ankara: Vakıflar Umum Müdürlüğü Neşriyatı, 1942. SALT Research, Ali Saim Ülgen Archive, TASUDOCA0101010.

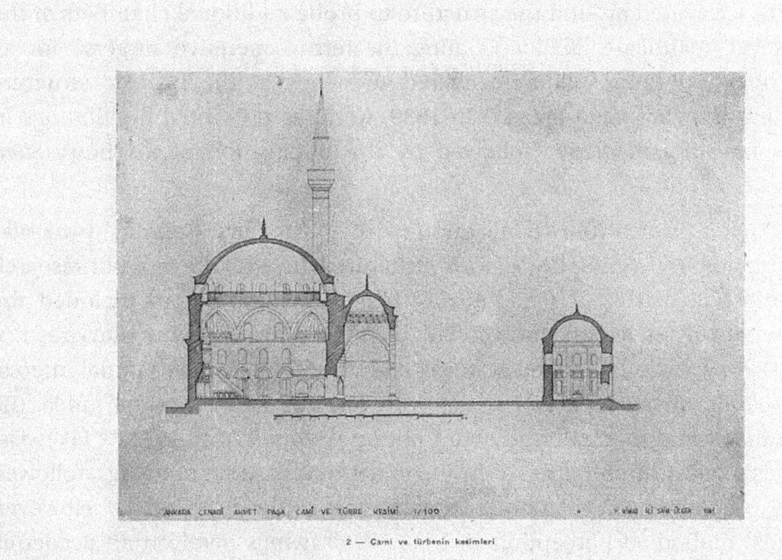

Figure 4.23. Section of the mosque and tomb of Cenabî Ahmed Pasha, drawn by Ali Saim Ülgen. Ali Saim Ülgen, *Ankara'da Cenabî Ahmed Paşa Camii ve Türbesi.* Ankara: Vakıflar Umum Müdürlüğü Neşriyatı, 1942. SALT Research, Ali Saim Ülgen Archive, TASUDOCA0101011.

Çetintaş' work on the thirteenth-century Sivas Şifaiye Hospital/Madrasa, for instance, posits an order of reality to understand the true potential of mediaeval architecture. Çetintaş's professional interest in the Seljuk structure commenced when he investigated its erroneously depicted floor plan in Gabriel's *Monuments Turcs d'Anatolie.* To Çetintaş' surprise, Gabriel did not delineate any windows in the patient rooms, which was not realistic in a hospital building. Once Çetintaş set off to Sivas in 1937 to examine the structure in-situ, he determined that the medieval structure in fact had windows in every room which would let natural light into the prestigious healthcare facility.

Tasked by the Conservation Council of Monuments and TTK, Çetintaş conducted an excavation campaign at the Seljuk structure between 1937-1938. Çetintaş' task, as the chief of the Surveying Bureau, was to study, analyze, document, and plan for its protection. Çetintaş perceived the documentation fieldwork as an opportunity to bring the Seljuk monument back to its authentic grandeur of the thirteenth century. During the course of this work, Çetintaş cleaned the structure of the later additions and removed the debris. The authentic tilework, arches, vaults, and walls were revealed.

Çetintaş excavated around the structure to probe additional chambers of the mediaeval healthcare facility. Coining the term "operative surgery" for all these tasks, Çetintaş made measured drawings of the historic structure including the excavated areas.[63] In 1939, Çetintaş presented his findings in TTK's *Journal of Belleten,* followed by the publication of his book *Sivas Darüşşifası,* 1953.

Conducted prior to the stabilization work and repairs, Çetintaş' work was monumental in defining the historic structure where no drawings or research accounts had existed. Then the only known historic record included the endowment of its benefactor, the Sultan I. İzzeddin Keykâvus (Kaykaus I, r. 1211-1220), which in fact had culminated in the state agencies initial interest in the study of the medieval structure.[64] Yet, due to the limited funds, the excavation came to a halt and could not be resumed until 1973. [65] Likewise, Çetintaş's quest of preparing a thorough set of measured drawings, followed by the preparation of restoration documents, came to no avail.[66] However, Çetintaş' embodied perception in his field drawings involved an academic preference for the mediaeval configuration of the structure at the cost of omitting the stratified architectural elements. Resulting measured drawings did not include enough measurements and details to guide the physical treatments either. In this sense, his illustrations became an example of archival building documentation in terms of their limited contents, while ignoring the delineations of working drawings needed for restoration.

At the intersection of documentation and restoration, Ayverdi's graphic treatment of the fifteenth-century *Ağalar Camii* (Mosque of the Aghas) in the Topkapı Palace Museum confirms the primacy of dictating a set of restitution instructions in measured drawings. Ayverdi, a practicing civil engineer with an honorary degree in architecture, restored numerous structures including the Hagia Sofia Museum, Selimiye Mosque, Edirne Üç Serefeli Mosque, Bozdoğan Su Kemeri (Aqueduct of Valens) and many buildings at the Topkapı Palace Museum. In *Fatih Devri Mimarisi,* Ayverdi included drawings of the Mosque of the Aghas, which was built after the conquest of Constantinople and served as the central mosque of the Topkapı Palace. In the late Ottoman

[63] Çetintaş, "Türk Tarih Kurumu Tarafından Sivas Darüşşifasında Yaptırılan Mimari Hafriyat," *TTK Belleten* 3 no. 9 (1939): 63.

[64] Gönül Cantay, "Sivas I. İzzeddin Keykavus Darüşşifası," *Erdem* 9, no. 27 (1997): 976.

[65] Ibid., 978.

[66] Çetintaş, *Sivas Darüşşifası,* 127.

Empire, the facility had undergone major repairs: the walls were elevated, the authentic windows were replaced with larger ones, and the original roof cover was substituted with a barrel vault. Furthermore, a masjid was built as an annex to the building. To capture the current configuration, Ayverdi created two measured drawings of the cluster with annotations on the structural changes (Figure 4.24 and Figure 4.25). Besides, Ayverdi included a restitution plan (Figure 4.26), where he suggested to demolish the masjid, remove later structural elements, and introduce a dome instead of the barrel vault to the main building. Given this, Ayverdi posited that the mosque would return to its authentic fifteenth-century setting and retain its integrity.[67]

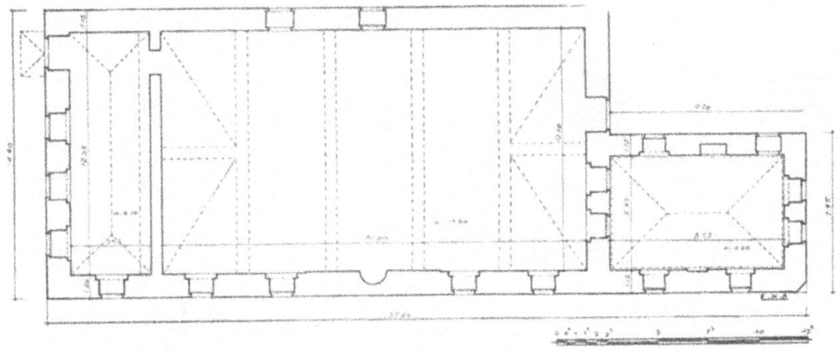

Figure 4.24. Measured plan drawing of the Mosque of the Aghas, Topkapı Palace Museum, drawn by Ekrem Hakkı Ayverdi. Ekrem Hakkı Ayverdi, *Fatih Devri Mimarisi*, İstanbul: İstanbul Fetih Cemiyeti Neşriyatı, 1953.

Ayverdi's proposal of restitution did not take place, but his appraisal of the Mosque of the Aghas reveals the curatorial selection of architectural restoration in the early republic. As a restoration engineer, Ayverdi was acutely aware that two measured drawings and a couple of photographs were not sufficient to constitute a restoration project.[68] Given this, he commented that based on what he could observe on the actual building surface, he

---

[67] Ibid., 106-107.

[68] In fact, for the restoration of Ankara's Mahmud Pasha Bedesteni, Ayverdi criticized the lack of detailed measured drawings. Ayverdi, "Ankara Çarşısı ve Bedesteni," in *Osmanlı Mimarisinde Fatih Devri 855-886 (1451-1481)* 3 (İstanbul: Baha Matbaası, 1973), 35.

fashioned his "attempted restitution plan drawing."[69] Later, in 1973, Ayverdi, himself, abandoned the idea of introducing a dome structure as a substitute for the barrel vault.[70] Yet, his delivery of a restitution concept in a monograph meant for measured surveys, clearly shows his professional proclivity to construct the compositional guides for a prospective restoration task. Perhaps, due to his rigorous preservation work at the Topkapı Palace Museum, Ayverdi was anticipating the possibility of restoring the Mosque of the Aghas.

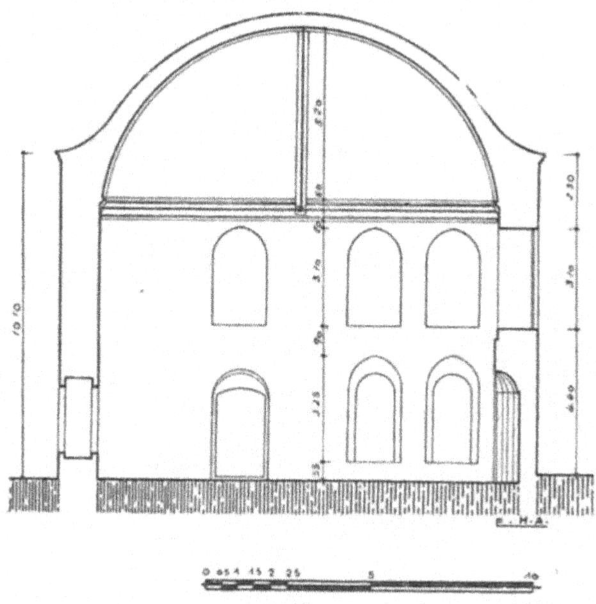

(Resim 21) Topkapı Sarayında Ağalar camii makta rölevesi

Figure 4.25. Measured section drawing of the Mosque of the Aghas, Topkapı Palace Museum, drawn by Ekrem Hakkı Ayverdi. Ekrem Hakkı Ayverdi, *Fatih Devri Mimarisi,* İstanbul: İstanbul Fetih Cemiyeti Neşriyatı, 1953.

---

[69] Çetintaş, *Sivas Darüşşifası,* 106.

[70] Ayverdi, *Osmanlı Mimarisinde Fatih Devri,* 310-312.

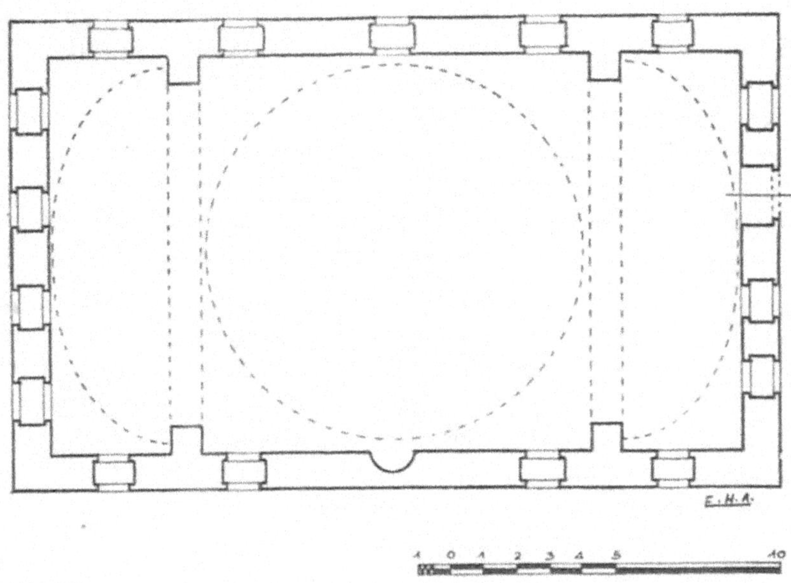

(Resim 23) Topkapı Sarayında Ağalar Camii restütasyon plânı

Figure 4.26. Restitution drawing for the Mosque of the Aghas, Topkapı Palace Museum, drawn by Ekrem Hakkı Ayverdi. Ekrem Hakkı Ayverdi, *Fatih Devri Mimarisi,* İstanbul: İstanbul Fetih Cemiyeti Neşriyatı, 1953.

Illustrating the priorities of Turkish nationalism

For the purpose of archival building documentation, the early republican projections clearly indicate that these records were meant to act as the repository of a complete idea of Turkish architecture. First, the functional motivations of recording and studying historic architecture would have helped the republican intelligentsia to translate the architectural paragons into a history of Turks. Second, these graphic descriptions were seen as a necessary surrogate of the built work and an integral tool for safeguarding the architectural resources for future generations. In 1938, when Çetintaş requested a grant from the TTK for the Sivas Şifaiye Hospital/Madrasa, he had two priorities: to bring the already demolished annex of the medieval healthcare facility to light and to secure provisions for repairs and restorations of the compound.[71] A member of the TTK board, historian and politician, İsmail Hakkı Uzunçarşılı's (1888-1977) reply to Çetintaş' request confirms the unequivocal trust in architectural documentation.[72] "Calling the proposed study a tempting subject, Uzunçarşılı celebrated Çetintaş' line of pursuit to investigate a mysterious thread in the endowment of Sultan I. İzzeddin Keykâvus and to unearth an isolated building in the history of the Anatolian Turks.[73] Although Çetintaş' proposal of a twin-building on the premises came to no avail years later, his measured drawings prevailed as a significant record to prioritize Turkish architecture.[74]

In terms of the representation of the history of Turks from Central Asia to Anatolia, the work went through a diligent process of rationalization. Advocating for an autonomous development of Turkish architecture, the codification of architectural history into types and styles, the use of grids and axes, and the formulation of precise measurements eliminated all the cultural and personal in favor of universal absolutes. To this end, the descriptive documentation records relied on syntactic connections between images, with each building only a part of a dissected whole.

Projecting architectural concepts through descriptive plans, sections, and elevations became a technological measure to insure consistency in the representation of architecture. Especially in understanding the translation that occurs between an existing building and a representative measured drawing, the status of archival building documentation has equated measured drawings with the ability to capture the unique qualities of built forms. Although two-dimensional measured drawings belong to a certain system of representation, the illustrations themselves became the mediums that represented the Turkish soul. In this interpretive projection, the instrumental and symbolic representation, automatically, were unified in the historic building. In the republican reality, this union led to the intellectual presentation of a building. The transmutation conspicuously took place in the graphic arrangement of building elements, of scholars adding or subtracting elements that did not fit with the prescribed Turkish history.

Analogous to the construction of modern design, measured and drawn plans of historic buildings gained prominence as a point of negotiation. In return, the

---

[71] Çetintaş, *Sivas Darüşşifası*, 73.

[72] Ibid., 74.

[73] Ibid.

[74] Cantay, "Sivas I. İzzeddin Keykavus Darüşşifası," 976.

horizontal profiles entailed the anatomical representation of a historic edifice, building the formalist construct of architectural coordinates. The academic focus on descriptive measured plans as an entity in their own right, shifted the emphasis to the singularity of plan types devised by Turkish architects, particularly Sinan, as works of art, while overlooking other building elements. This formalist architectural outlook catapulted built works into structural units with the belief that Turkish architects developed their designs along a linear path of creative progress and replicated their schemes for all populations and situations from the Asian to Anatolian frontiers.

In the published volumes, a sequence of section and elevation drawings revealed the magnitude of plan depictions. The vertical projections sanctioned the official presentation of the dome structure and its proportion with other elements such as columns, portals, and windows. Typically consisting of a single drawing view, extensive white space, and few if any details, dimensions, or notes, these vertical projections were made for the attentive concentration of the viewers' gaze and to gain broader interest in the qualities of architectural heritage.

Overall, folios of archival drawings may have lacked details to guide technical procedures; nevertheless, these graphic depictions were widely regarded as very useful for illustrations in publications. For instance, a floor plan of a madrasa, for years, would be heavily circulated in articles, brochures, monographs, and tabloids to the point that the architectural image would be more recognizable than the actual building. The viewers may have vaguely discerned the specific historic events and dates associated with the built work, but these drafted lines would bring the historic properties to the collective mind. A point of reference, the measured drawings became art objects themselves possessing immutable characteristics of architectural heritage that communicated across space and time.

Chapter 5

Conclusion

> The existence of every nation in the world, the right of freedom and independence, is in proportion to their civilized works of the past and the future.
>
> Mustafa Kemal Atatürk[1]

The path of archival building documentation from the Late Ottoman Era to Republican Turkey convincingly displays that the intellectuals truly believed that the everlasting qualities of a culture could be transferred through architectural forms. Replicating the cultural products on paper, measured drawings served as self-referential scientific documents for purposes of education, historic preservation, and research; but most importantly, these descriptive projections essentialized the basis for a collective memory in the defined borders of a country. Yet, the dominant obsession with ethnic purity and linear narratives of ancestry entailed a limited definition of architectural heritage. The historicist consciousness perpetuated ideological tendencies to modify, amplify, and even disregard historical elements on paper, and remained within the orbit of the rising Turkish state.

Miscellaneous texts written by the agents of archival building documentation however, appear to be a notable exception to the monolithic understanding of nationalism. Nationalist claims inherently have sought to combine the state, in our case either Ottoman or Turkish, with an overriding culture, in which the building documentation records were used to reflect the perceived roots of the country. With the official realization of a nationalist claim, certain building eras and styles came to the fore, such as Seljuks and Ottomans, while the rest of the architectural examples were omitted from the published monographs.

Within the political climate, scholars concurrently sought a single past of the nation and its corroborating architectural evidence; the same individuals

[1] İnan, *Mimar Koca Sinan* (Ankara: Türkiye Emlak Kredi Bankası Neşriyatı, Ayyıldız Matbaası A.Ş., 1968), 63; Mardin, *Türk Modernleşmesi* (İstanbul: İletişim Yayınları, 1992).

held different positions, that gave rise to nuances in the definition of national built heritage. Just how much of an exception is difficult to quantify with any certainty because our present reading is limited to the availability of archival records. Taken as a whole however, it is clear that in spite of the uniform sanctions of the nationalist movement, there was complexity and fluidity involved in the curatorial management of historic properties, their documentation, and their representation in the sweeping definition of Turkish architecture.

Many scholars' divergent paths responded to the ambiguities embedded in their efforts to merge Turkishness with modernity. For the Turkish revolutionaries who were instrumental in the establishment of the modern-state, modernity was both a source of inspiration and a threat. Bitterness toward the West originated from the perceived unfairness of the Orientalist discourse, which relegated Turks to the category of unable to modernize or to create a civilization. This ambivalence led to the quest for modernity in local and genuine ways. Early republican scholars' goal was to insert modernity into Turkishness while presenting Turkish contributions to the very modernity that relegated Turks as non-modern. The ambivalence implanted in this monumental task led to the search for an undefined and timeless Turkish essence in the elements of historic architecture. Seen as a scientific record, measured drawings of historic properties played a vital role in the republican authors' encounters with western modernity and its variable associations. To clear away the Orientalist doubts about the Turkish civilization, scholars formulated measured drawings in a descriptive manner, which directly spoke to the disputed building elements. Annotations on drawing sheets with supplementary dimensions or comparisons of certain building elements with morphological and typological peers were recognized ways of eliciting the characteristics of Turkish architecture.

Archival building documentation became one of the key disciplines in proving the essential propensity of Turks to modernize in republican Turkey. In fact, it is significant to note that initially the intelligentsia in the Late Ottoman Era embraced western science and modernity as they sought a national future. Supported by the reigning sultans, the published monographs of measured drawings clearly aimed to uncover an immutable identity in the particularity of a timeless Ottoman past. Commissioned by Sultan Abdülaziz, the authors of *Usūl-i Mi'mārī-i Osmānī* (1873) presented the Ottoman architectural style as a rational, fluid, and universally applicable building system that was subject to continuous change and innovation. The measured drawings of Ottoman monuments in the monograph served as the scientific evidence of authentic building traditions that had evolved in the modern multi-cultural empire.

To locate a place in the wider community of the Western world, the Ottoman sultans authorized work permits for foreign scholars for the documentation of historic architecture. Despite the fact that these were sporadic acts of documentation, the resulting monographs strove to introduce the built environment of the modern empire to Western audiences. Ultimately, it was the republican government's direct involvement in the production of knowledge and the reformers' scholarly mobilization that led the way to the increasing weight of measured surveys. Given this, republican scholars, via an immense emphasis on measured drawings as a scientific record, strove to create a niche for Turkish architecture in modern history. Thus, early republican Turkey allotted some of its meager resources to documentation, excavation, publications, and scholarly activities; by doing so this propelled the late Ottoman enterprise of building documentation into becoming a systemized discipline. Although the republican government initially invited foreign experts for critical positions of architectural production, documentation, research, and teaching, the state agencies deemed it necessary to cultivate native professionals for the progress of the country. The foreign professionals working at universities and state agencies were charged with introducing the Western-style scientific methods and helping with its systemized implementation. Nevertheless, it was the young generation of the republic who would embrace the modern future.

Although the Ottoman Empire was never formally colonized, in many ways, the construction of the modern state approximated the difficulties faced by colonized modernizers. Rooted in the Late Ottoman Empire and magnified in the early republic, the reformers leaned heavily on concepts and notions of Western modernity, but in order to count as a modern nation-state, they keenly utilized the apparatuses and processes that had shaped the new world order. A Western-style scientific method, two-dimensional drawings and archival building documentation became instrumental in arriving at a carefully constructed, distinctly constrained, and autonomous self of the nation. The measured and drawn Seljuk and Ottoman monuments then befitted a scientific inquiry of constructing a national historical narrative based on the typological and morphological evidence embodied in the built environment.

In a historical period in which political elites were busy carving nation-states out of outdated empires, the nineteenth-century rhetoric of Ottomanness embodied in *Usūl* was replaced with Turkish nationalism. With the 1908 Second Constitutional Era, the Young Turks came to power, forming the CUP. To counter the nationalist sentiments nibbling away the territories in the Balkans, Middle East, and North Africa, the CUP leaders publicly promoted Turkish civilization as the collective identity of the empire. The ideology of the Young Turks began to transform the Islamic monuments into an unconcealed means of nationalist manifestation and intellectual opposition at the height of Western colonial ambitions in the Ottoman Empire, especially during the disintegration of the imperial polity. Prominent Turkish architects, mostly sympathizers with the Young Turks movement, turned to Seljuk and Ottoman-built heritage, as a timeless source of the national identity of Turks. These architects and scholars read the monuments as tangible evidence in the long trajectory of Turks, which originated in Central Asia and expanded to the Ottoman Empire. Taking an equally scientific approach, they made measured drawings of the architectural works to access their anatomy, which regrettably did not translate to formulated publications. [2] Kemalettin Bey, together with other prominent architects such as Vedat Bey, Arif Hikmet Koyunoğlu, and Vasfi Egeli, codified the First National Style, which was based on reviving Seljuk and Ottoman stylistic elements in new constructions.

It is in this context, the immutable characteristics of nationalism gained significant status among the eyes of different communities, and to define their historic architecture in the Ottoman lands. The nineteenth-century publications of the Greek Ottoman cognoscenti Patriarch Konstatinias, Skarlatos Byzantios, and Alexander Paspates introduced the Byzantine built heritage of Istanbul to a wider audience. The underlying pattern of these monographs is the authors' passion for tracing the Greek material remains in modern Istanbul. To this end, the authors drew upon existing literature and their own observations of the Byzantine built environment. Paspates' work, however, was distinguished with his prioritization of architectural documentation. In fervent response to a vanishing Byzantine heritage, Paspates saw documentation as integral to cultivating public interest in the built environment and its protection. Along with rising Greek nationalism in the Ottoman state, all these nineteenth-century monographs on Byzantine Istanbul, ultimately, contributed to a national historiography that gave more significance to the Greek heritage of Istanbulites.

We should not quickly take archival building documentation solely as an ideological cause within the challenges presented in the nineteenth-century

---

[2] Kemalettin Bey, "Bulgarların Ahval-i Medeniye-i Hazırası," in *Mimar Kemalettin'in Yazdıkları*, 79.

nationalist sentiments in the Ottoman Empire. Even a cursory look at the popular newspapers and periodicals reveals a deep protest against the loss of built heritage. In the midst of modernization efforts, Istanbul became a stage on which to experiment with European urban regulations. Coupled with the major fires in the traditional city, the burned-down areas along with dilapidated properties became pilot areas for massive urban transformation projects which introduced large avenues, modern arteries, public squares, and state-of-the-art buildings. In this sea of urban changes, Ottoman authors such as Paspates turned to measured surveys to raise awareness of heritage at risk. Interestingly enough, the public debates between the Commission for the Preservation of Monuments, the Mayor of Istanbul, and the Ministry of Endowments at this time disclose that the destruction was not limited to the architecture associated with the non-Muslim communities. Many properties symbolizing the culture of the Muslim-Turks such as elementary schools, madrasas, masjids, public kitchens, and tombs were also pulled down to build anew.

Careful attention to the conditions and motivations behind knowledge production of the nineteenth-century Ottoman world, however, uncovers the links between nationalism and the founding ideology of the republic, as evidenced in the Turkish History Thesis. The ethnic essence of the Thesis was the intensification of the Young Turks' appropriation of the "national monuments of Turks" through an academic development of archeology and history. In retrospect, early republican agencies supported documentation and research of architectural heritage to define the binding identity of the nation that originated in the archaic Turkic people and tribes in Central Asia, which then advanced West carrying the civilization of Turks. The Turkish History Thesis postulated a Turco-centric view of world history, claiming that Turks had their homeland in Central Asia where the origins of all human civilizations were found; thus, Turks were the first people to develop both language and civilization before they migrated to the West. The early republican studies re-formulated Anatolia as the true homeland of Turks and as their link to the West. Finding the proof of the existence of Turks in Anatolia since prehistoric times became the slogan of these official studies. In stark contrast to the Ottoman conceptualization of the national roots embodied in the recent past, the republican propaganda stretched this timeframe noticeably further, to appropriate the pre-Ottoman past as the national history of Turks.

In this equilibrium, the dynastic, periodic, and stylistic classification of the historical patrimony was condensed into a sweeping national label. Stripped from their Islamic milieu, Seljuks, *Beyliks*, and Ottomans were merely charged with transmitting the Turkish spirit to the modern state. In particular, the chronicle of the Ottoman past entailed a conspicuous de-emphasis on the civilization of Turks. The only intimate link to the "stagnant and decadent empire" in the long history of Turks included the decline of the Ottoman state and the rise of Atatürk and the Turkish nation. The attempts to link the great variety of built heritage to a single cultural nexus became itself an intriguing loop. Entangled with the nationalist sentiments, preservation professionals, including Kemal Altan and Ali Saim Ülgen asserted the Turkishness of Anatolia's multiple architectural pasts. Considering the Byzantine architecture in terms of the repairs and maintenance conducted under the Ottoman rule, these professionals championed the Turkish character of these architectural works and wrote detailed reports to secure their protection.

Archival building documentation's contribution to national state formation is not an exceptional phenomenon. On the contrary, the rise of the ethnic essence put measured surveys into the political center of the republican nationalist projects. Architectural documentation, from its inception by Ottomans to pursue a model of Western scientific inquiry, to its intensified implementation by republican reformers, was by definition implicated in the attempts to discover architectural heritage that exclusively belonged to the Turkish nation and gave the nation-state sole propriety. The nation-state and archival documentation strengthened each other in such a way that, on the one hand, building records contributed to the legitimacy of the Turkishness of the built heritage, while on the other hand, the rise of the Turkish state supported the institutionalization of archival building documentation as an independent discipline. All "native" scholars, including Altan, Ülgen, Ekrem Hakkı Ayverdi, Sedad Çetintaş, and Sedad Hakkı Eldem, confined their professional inquiry of archival building documentation within the rhetorical circles of Turkish architecture.

In the transition from the empire to the nation-state, the state-supported architectural documentation campaigns mainly focused on the built works "created by the hands, labor, and taste of Turks."[3] State-agencies became the exclusive patron of these architectural studies since they directly

[3] Öz, "Atatürk'ün Topkapı Sarayını Ziyareti," (Newspaper column, SALT Research, FFT068004, May 15 1951) https://archives.saltresearch.org/handle/123456789/18209 (accessed September 20, 2021)

commissioned scholars to record built heritage and to write monographs on the examples that attested to Turkish art and architecture. From Istanbul to provincial towns in Anatolia, scholars canvassed the entire country to make measured drawings. The pragmatic overlap between measured surveys and building preservation work, furthermore, culminated in a considerable number of publications. Many preservation professionals published measured drawings of the buildings they were tasked to repair and restore. In conjunction, professionals also focused on architectural heritage at risk and they documented properties in danger of destruction or demolition. They frequently shared their documentation dossiers in journals, newspapers, and tabloids to garner interest for the protection of the built works. In all these efforts of documentation, measured drawings became a point of reference for elements of Turkish architecture. The descriptive breakdown of plans, sections, and elevations allowed these scholars to discuss a wide collection of structural elements from Central Asia to Anatolia.

One needs to consider the early republican emphasis on the proto-Turkishness of the built environment in this context. For the nation-state, documentation and research into the Anatolian past to counter territorial claims demonstrated a strategy with no limits to its inclusive zeal. Once the origins of the Turkish race were pushed to Central Asia, the sense of self-confidence in the establishment of an earliest civilization by Turks opened the road to a more territorial, rather than ethnic, approach. The Ministry of Education's circulars in the mid-1930s reflected this territorial interest; that all the cultural heritage in the country exhibit the building traditions of the Turkish race and culture, even though they have been named Hittite, Phrygian, Lydian, Roman, Byzantine, Seljuk, or Ottoman over the centuries. In establishing a Turkish past in the modern borders, scholars set out to establish links between a previous civilization (for example Hittites, Greeks, or Seljuks) and the modern Turks. Various culture zones and ethnic groups in Anatolia were quickly subsumed under a timeless Turkish essence, often through across-the-board generalizations. Eldem's highly appraised documentation project of the vernacular architecture derived from this unity of a proto-Turkish perspective. Yet, Eldem was not acutely interested in the formal rediscovery of the Turkish past in the ancient building elements. Instead, he presented the centuries-long, building traditions of the multi-ethnic Ottoman Empire in a blanket category: Turkish.

The high-level interest in the creative power of Turks did not translate to a transparent understanding of cultural heritage at the state level, however. The ambivalence toward Greek, Roman, and Byzantine heritages manifested itself in different ways. Miscellaneous circulars published by Ministry of Education and other agencies did not fully embrace the all-inclusive stewardship of the state. To this end, the Anatolian past was classified into ethnically recognizable and essentialist units, where Turks, an ethnic group that had an immense capacity to blend with others and to improve their material culture, contributed to these other societies while maintaining their Turkish essence. In other words, classical antiquity or Byzantine culture owed their artistic achievements to the Turkish civilization. The confusion embodied in the pedigree of architecture was evident in early republican professionals' rhetoric of built heritage. The same figures such as Altan and Ülgen who played a central role in promoting the Turkishness of Byzantine architecture, also emphasized that the pure ethnic ancestry of Turks culminated in national forms without foreign input. For them, from Central Asia to Anatolia and the Balkans, Turks maintained their pure lines of national architecture although they co-habited in these regions with different societies.

Despite the almost universal appeal of documenting Turkish works of architecture, the scholars' inspirational roots for national architecture remained divergent. For example, Ayverdi ridiculed the scholarly attempts of depicting the cultural production of ancient Anatolia as Turkish. Ayverdi consistently referred to connections to Central Asian roots, and ultimately an Ottoman civilization as the sources of architectural achievements in Anatolia, the Balkans, and the Middle East. Following this logic, Ayverdi's documentation campaigns revolved around the Ottoman architecture in Turkey along with former provinces of the Ottoman Empire. Çetintaş also distanced himself from the documentation of the non-Turkish built heritage of Anatolia and focused on the works of Ottoman architecture. Çetintaş, particularly, turned to measured surveys of medieval Anatolian and classical Ottoman structures, by seizing the opportunities they offered for exalting the assimilative and creative powers of Turks.

Almost immediately upon Atatürk's passing in 1938, the multi-faceted ethnic ideology came to an end with the rise of Islamic background. The Turkish History Thesis provided the citizens of the modern nation-state with an ancestry that circumvented the Ottoman centuries. The Thesis reformulated a past which was Turkish first and Islamic only second, even for the Seljuk and Ottoman periods, which were profoundly associated with the culture of Islam. The 1930's secular tendencies of the Thesis were substituted with a number of movements that nurtured ethnic nationalisms and Islam. The rise of the DP along with the establishment of religious doctrines at schools and state-facilities coincided with the rise of Turkish nationalism in the context of Islam. These movements paved the way for the Turkish-Islamic Synthesis, which subsequent governments have extensively exploited. Inevitably, the focus of archival building documentation shifted to the architectural heritage created by Muslim-Turks. The Ottoman past was still observed as a historical epoch in the civilization of Turks. Nevertheless, the once distant memories of an imperial and Islamic past became integrated with the nationalist present.

The passing of Atatürk and the changing concept for the history of Turks, deprived the state agencies sponsorship for documentation studies and scholarship at the highest level. Yet, on a scale reminiscent of the archival building documentation conducted in the early republic, the 500th-anniversary celebrations of the Ottoman conquest of Constantinople in 1953 brought the weight of measured surveys to the forefront. A supplement to the celebrations, measured surveys and published volumes highlighted the architectural production of the era, which was labeled as the glorious centuries of the Ottoman Empire. Given this, the residual authority of the Turkish History Thesis nibbled away, yielding an ideological focus on Ottoman and Islamic building traditions.

Concurrently, the academic focus on Muslim-Turks became the critical quest for the appraisal of Ottoman architecture. The Battle of Manzikert of 1071 defined the cut-off date to assign the pedigree of historic architecture. Populations of Anatolia that were not Turkish or Muslim did not become the subject of dedicated volumes of archival building documentation. If they qualified to be included in a compilation, then their architectural descriptions could not escape from the orbit of the rising Ottoman-Turkish state. Few publications of measured surveys of Byzantine architecture accompanied the quincentenary celebrations of the conquest. To a large extent the repurposed Byzantine monuments under Turkish rule became the subject of the preservation efforts and drafted lines. Significantly, these measured drawings of Byzantine architecture mediated academic transactions in order to exhibit the autonomous development of the Turkish building forms, free from foreign influence.

With this linear perspective of Turkish architecture, the documentation findings did not negotiate the transformations in architecture and patronage in medieval Anatolia when new political actors were rising and cultural institutions shifting. In fact that mediaeval Anatolia was a fluid frontier for Mongols, Ilkhanids, Seljuks, and *Beyliks* against the background of Byzantines and other local cultures, from west to east; the entire region became a vibrant space for architectural patronage. Unlike the perceived Turkified Anatolia, no unified imperial patronage was available to standardize regional styles and use of materials, a phenomenon that continued into the late fifteenth century. In fact, only when the Ottomans conquered large parts of central and eastern Anatolia, subsequent to the conquest of Constantinople in 1453, the patronage and style began to change. In stark contrast to the proliferation of regional forms in medieval Anatolia, the architectural production of Seljuks and *Beyliks* were seen as a direct predecessor of the Ottoman forms due to their common Turkish ancestry. Once the non-Turkish elements of Anatolia were excluded from the nationalist narrative of Turks, the prevailing focus then became the Seljuk continuity in architectural patronage and style.

Under the rubric of Seljuk forms, diverse architectural programs of the individual *Beyliks* were also marginalized in the published volumes of building documentation. The fact that the Ottoman polity was in active conflict with the *Beyliks* until the execution of the last remaining lords in the sixteenth century, culminated in an academic vacuum for the identification of the *Beylik* architecture. Many remaining built works of individual *Beyliks* were either overlooked in the monographs or they were simply considered as an artistic production as part of a unified Seljuk imperial culture. For the rest, catalogues of measured drawings exhibited a strictly hierarchical and categorical framework of historical facilities, clearly distinguishing between Seljuk, *Beylik*, and Ottoman works of architecture, although such a clear-cut classification did not exist in the vibrant climate of medieval Anatolia.

The nationalist emphasis on the purity of Ottoman architectural forms, created further academic gaps in the monographs of building documentation. By shifting the focus to the conquest of Constantinople and the flourishing classical Ottoman period, the architectural production of the Late Ottoman Era did not garner sufficient academic interest. A consequence of the weakening power of the Ottoman Empire, the architectural production of the Late Ottoman Empire was labeled as artistic decline. Coupled with the obsession with purity of architectural lines, the domination of the Western-inspired architectural forms and elements from the eighteenth century was read as artistic degeneration, hence the buildings created in this era did not quite meet the formal interest to be measured and drawn as an archival record. Besides Ülgen's monograph on Istanbul's Yeni Mosque, late imperial architectural heritage did not become the subject of the dedicated documentation publications. For the late Ottoman buildings that somewhat embodied details reminiscent of the classical order, scholars including Altan and Ülgen raised awareness for their protection and strove to document them. Overall, these isolated and sporadic efforts could not rescue Late Ottoman properties from academic neglect.

In this vein, the architectural examples in the former Ottoman provinces were close to absent in the monographs, with the exception of the academic quests of Ayverdi and Eldem. The de-emphasis on the Ottoman built environment in the Balkans, Middle East, or North Africa was partly due to the geographical and political difficulties to claim national architecture of Turks in places then had already established their own nation-states. In many of these newly created states Ottoman architecture was already regarded as a foreign entity among their national forms. Accordingly, historic properties associated with their Ottoman past were neglected and even demolished in many places. Thus, Ayverdi's projection of the Ottoman Empire through the lens of the civilization of Anatolia and Rumelia motivated his building documentation campaigns in the Balkans. Fueled by the systematic destruction of the Ottoman architectural heritage abroad, Ayverdi towed the Balkan countries and continuously published his documentation records. Eldem, on the other hand, did not actively pursue building documentation outside the modern borders of Turkey. His research however focused on the diffusion of the elements of the Turkish house using the scale of the geographical borders of the Ottoman Empire. Given this, Eldem persistently conducted a comparative analysis of the Anatolian Turkish house and the dwellings in former Ottoman provinces, although his later findings did not culminate in dedicated publications.

Another reason for the absence of the analysis and documentation of the architectural works in the former Ottoman provinces included the republican authors' teleological lens through which they linked the progress of national architecture with the migration routes embodied in the Turkish History Thesis, and with the final stage of the modern-day home of Turks: Anatolia. Although demonstrating diverse motivations when it came to conducting architectural documentation, the republican authors concurred in the Central Asian roots of Turks and Anatolia as their motherland. In this manner, the authors symbolically appropriated a common architectural heritage transcending the national borders from archaic Central Asian tribes to modern Turks, along with connecting the layered archeological and architectural heritage of Anatolia to the Turkish culture. A fundamental thesis shared by many authors was the assumption that formal research methodologies, namely morphological and typological analysis of forms and structural elements, were vital to elaborate reconstructions of historical continuity.

One should not hastily isolate archival building documentation from the historic preservation movement and the challenges of saving architectural heritage at risk, however. Historic properties salvaged from the decades-long armed conflicts were in imminent danger of destruction or material alteration due to neglect, urban development, and vandalism. One of the primary concerns of the professionals was the creation of a record of endangered buildings that could not be preserved through other means. Altan continuously wrote that an unstoppable tide of destruction was destined to wipe out the great majority of the buildings which defined the Turkish civilization. Although monuments were occasionally rescued, historic properties of minor scale were disturbingly lost to the forces of progress. Altan stressed that it was the responsibility of the architects if a great number of historic properties were disappearing, as they should not pass into unrecorded oblivion. Altan, himself, went to neighborhoods of Istanbul to make measured drawings of architectural heritage at risk and to publish his drawings.

Ülgen, due to his administrative role at diverse state agencies had to juggle the growing lists of priority buildings and the increasingly complex bureaucratic procedures, which created an almost overwhelming task. Coupled with the difficulties of pooling stewardship, expertise, and resources, the historic properties were diminishing at an alarming rate. Ülgen, ultimately, focused on archival documentation of buildings scheduled to be demolished, their materials to be sold for new construction, or were already in ruins. Some parts of the country simply lacked documentation due to inadequate staffing or travel difficulties. Seen in his administrative records and fieldnotes, however, Ülgen and his staff consistently made measured drawings of historic properties that he came across in his business trips across the country. Then, he shared his findings with his colleagues at state agencies, members of the GEEAYK, students enrolled in his classes, and attendees of his public lectures to garner attention for their protection.

Çetintaş, also, defended preservation through documentation through his continued conviction that measured drawings preserve irreplaceable material evidence for future generations. During his tenure at the Surveying Bureau, Çetintaş enjoyed a life-long career dedicated to making measured drawings of built heritage across the country. Çetintaş regretted that there was far more danger from indifference to buildings than vandalism and urban development. With his writings in popular newspapers and tabloids along with his public lectures, Çetintaş became instrumental in saving numerous historic properties from destruction. Likewise, Ayverdi and Eldem relished a unique continuity with the Turkish past through their professional dedication to building documentation. Many of the properties being catalogued in their drawing collections, unfortunately, have shared the same dramatic fates as their peers, and have vanished in the path to progress.

Archival building documentation became the sort of initiative that should be followed in order to keep a very significant part of the past from being completely obliterated. Architects, either through formal procedures or personal quests, prioritized building documentation. Resulting publications, however, entailed the overwhelming task of portraying floor plans as a uniform signifier. The decision to prioritize plan depictions without consideration of other viewpoints or historical context, conflicted with the sincere interest in creating a tangible record of historic properties. With the alarming rate of destruction of the built environment, the opportunity to articulate the regional themes and unique motifs of individual properties was lost. The decision to prioritize the floor plans without supplementary input impacted studies with a broader scope, by analyzing the building stock spanning a larger geography or a longer timeframe. Although many authors had extensive knowledge of regional histories and building forms through their own experiences, professional practices and scholarship, not all were able to compile a thick descriptive analysis of architecture. The publications would be illustrated with measured drawings and photographs, and would primarily underscore broad historical narratives.

Prioritization of floor plans grew out of the popular enthusiasm for the scientific representation of architecture. Rooted in the eighteenth-century rational thinking, the mathematical descriptive of a two-dimensional system of drawings dominated architectural education, representation and production. The projective tool of descriptive geometry, a product grounded in the industrial progress of the Western world, was integral to the modern world-view that the late Ottoman intelligentsia, then the early republican scholars, could not simply reject. In this sense, the transition from the Beaux-Arts representational system to the Modern Movement did not alter the visual hierarchy of the geometric two-dimensional drawings. Measured drawings of architectural heritage still entailed the status of efficient neutral tools for analysis and comparison. Borrowed from the Modern Movement however, the design emphasis on the neo-classical facades of the Beaux- Arts model, was substituted with floor plans as the cement of modern design. Republican professionals had different levels of involvement with the programs of architecture and engineering; they all operated in the modern vocabulary of architecture. The descriptive plans of historic buildings then became integral to unveil the essence of architecture. Merely weighing their floor plans against each other, authors strove to explain the creative process and the evolution of structural elements embodied in Turkish architecture.[4]

In the height of Kemalist modernization, the codification of measured drawings had grown into a highly esteemed scientific manifestation of

[4] Bozdoğan, "Reading Ottoman Architecture Through Modernist Lenses," 199-201.

education, research, and historic preservation. The revolutionary spirit of the early republic, coupled with sizeable state support of measured surveys, solidified a documentation culture which analyzed, studied and recorded the built heritage. Although diminishing state funds in the aftermath of Atatürk hindered the materialization of a grandiose scale of archival building documentation similar to the earlier years, the establishment of inhouse surveying offices at diverse state agencies showcased the central role of building documentation in the theory and practice of historic preservation, and the dissemination of information. Overall, the printed volumes of measured drawings along with the unpublished fieldnotes and manuscripts demonstrate the care and effort that went into producing measured drawings. Obliging a national duty, a highly mobile circle of architects and scholars reached the remotest parts of the country to record and protect the architecture of the nation. Despite the fact that they attempted an unmanageable synthesis of the development of Turkish architecture spanning several ages and geographical terrains, their drafted lines have guided generations of architects and scholars who strive to gain a deeper understanding of the built environment.

With the systematized destruction of architectural heritage in contemporary Turkish culture, the early republican interest in archival building documentation is a timely reminder of the values we have lost along the way. Clearly, preservation professionals got entangled with the politics of Turkish nationalism; monuments of Turks served a rhetoric that would solidify the nationalist ends of self-legitimacy and ethnic identification. The resulting monographs convincingly showed that the authors were not referring to a linear perspective of documenting the present-day architectural appearances but rather to a limited projection of the building's totality, a view which reconciled the architectural orders of Turkish nationalism. However, we should not forget the republican professionals' zealous commitment and passion to the progress of their own country. The drafted lines became a manifestation of an idealistic future for their own society to which republican professionals had unconditionally projected their knowledge and experience. Their measured drawings have long prevailed as the sole evidence of once-extant national treasures; and became objects of nostalgic yearning for the already lost.

Bibliography

Primary sources

Anonymous. "Rapor." Rapor, Eski Eserleri Koruma Encümeni Arşivi, İstanbul, GN 115, June 24 1935.

Anonymous. "Sivas Divriği Ulu Cami 1959 Yılı Onarımına ait Rölöve Şartnamesi." Memorandum, SALT Research, Ali Saim Ülgen Archive, TASUDOC0709054, TASUDOC0437, and TASUDOC1407, March 7 1963. https://archives.saltresearch.org/handle/123456789/70246 (accessed September 20, 2021).

Arseven, Celâl Esad. "Vakıflar Umum Müdürlüğü, yüksek huzuruna." Reference letter, SALT Research, Ali Saim Ülgen Archive, TASUDOC0534010, 1940. https://archives.saltresearch.org/handle/123456789/83487 (accessed September 20, 2021).

Arseven, Celâl Esad and Ali Saim Ülgen. "Gayrimenkul Eski Eserler ve Anıtlar Yüksek Kurulu Başkanlığına." Memorandum, SALT Research, Ali Saim Ülgen Archive, TASUDOC0070, November 6 1954. https://archives.saltresearch.org/handle/123456789/76552 (accessed April 5, 2022).

Atatürk, Mustafa Kemal. "Ankara Cebeci'deki Cenabî Ahmed Paşa Camii'nin tamiri." Decision, Türkiye Cumhuriyeti Cumhurbaşkanlığı Devlet Arşivleri, Başkanlık Cumhuriyet Arşivi, 80-96-8, November 23 1937.

Atatürk, Mustafa Kemal. "Ankara'da tarihi kıymeti bulunan Cenabî Ahmed Paşa Camii'nin emaneten tamir ettirilmesi." Decision, Türkiye Cumhuriyeti Cumhurbaşkanlığı Devlet Arşivleri, Başkanlık Cumhuriyet Arşivi, 68-78-19, October 1 1936.

Atatürk, Mustafa Kemal. "Ankara'nın Cebeci civarindaki Cenabî Ahmed Paşa Camii'nin emaneten tamir ettirilmesi." Decision, Türkiye Cumhuriyeti Cumhurbaşkanlığı Devlet Arşivleri, Başkanlık Cumhuriyet Arşivi, 83-52-8, June 10 1938.

Dahiliye Nezareti. Letter, Türkiye Cumhuriyeti Cumhurbaşkanlığı Devlet Arşivleri, Başkanlık Osmanlı Arşivi, BEO 126/9382, 30 Cemaziyülevvel 1310 [20 December 1892].

GEEAYK. "Karar." Memorandum, SALT Research, Ali Saim Ülgen Archive, TASUDOC0437040-41, August 3 1956. https://archives.saltresearch.org/handle/123456789/70246 (accessed September 20, 2021).

İnönü, İsmet. "Ankara'da Cebeci'deki Cenabî Ahmetpaşa Camii'ne ait Yeniden Yapılacak bazı İşlerinin Emaneten Yapılması." Decision, Türkiye Cumhuriyeti Cumhurbaşkanlığı Devlet Arşivleri, Başkanlık Cumhuriyet Arşivi, 87-47-4, May 5 1939.

Kiper, Fahri. "T.C. Vakıflar Genel Müdürlüğü Hususi." Letter, SALT Research, Ali Saim Ülgen Archive, TASUDOC0534009, November 28 1939. https://archives.saltresearch.org/handle/123456789/83487 (accessed September 20, 2021).

Koşay, Hamit Zübeyir. "Yüksek Mimar Saim Ülgen, Bursa Müzesi Müdürlüğü Vasıtasıyla, Bursa." Letter, SALT Research, Ali Saim Ülgen Archive, TASUDOC0534063, October 21 1939. https://archives.saltresearch.org/handle/123456789/83487 (accessed September 20, 2021).

Kunter, Halim Baki. "[Letter about the Turkish Architecture Exhibition in London, April 1960]." Letter, SALT Research, Ali Saim Ülgen Archive, TASUDOC0484, May 9 1959. https://archives.saltresearch.org/handle/123456789/86640 (accessed September 20, 2021).

Nigizberk, Mehmet Nihat. "Çok Muhterem Meslektaşım." Letter, SALT Research, Ali Saim Ülgen Archive, TASUDOC0534043, April 5 1941. https://archives.saltresearch.org/handle/123456789/83487 (accessed September 20, 2021).

Ogan Aziz. "Eminönü Kaymakamlığına." Letter, Eski Eserleri Koruma Encümeni Arşivi, İstanbul, GN 115, September 14 1946.

Öz, Tahsin. "Karar." Memorandum, Koç University, Suna Kıraç Library Special Collections and Archives, Cahide Tamer Historic Buildings Restoration Projects Collection, CTA_S106_D01_doc_03, December 16 & 18 1966. https://libdigitalcollections.ku.edu.tr/digital/collection/CTA/id/854/rec/43 (accessed March 29, 2022).

Özden, Şevket. "Rapor, 11. Gurup Şefliğine." Memorandum, SALT Research, Ali Saim Ülgen Archive, TASUDOC0481116, October 7 1959. https://archives.saltresearch.org/handle/123456789/85567 (accessed September 20, 2021).

Sadaret. Letter, Türkiye Cumhuriyeti Cumhurbaşkanlığı Devlet Arşivleri, Başkanlık Osmanlı Arşivi, DH.MKT 1940/18, 12 Ramazan 1309 [April 10 1892].

Söylemezoğlu, Hamit Kemali. "Sevgili Kardeşim." Postcard, SALT Research, Ali Saim Ülgen Archive, TASUDOC0281045, April 2 1944. https://archives.saltresearch.org/handle/123456789/77682 (accessed September 20, 2021).

Tamer, Cahide Aksel. "Abide ve Yapı İşleri Şubesine." Memorandum, SALT Research, Ali Saim Ülgen Archive, TASUDOC0481112, October 1 1959. https://archives.saltresearch.org/handle/123456789/85567 (accessed September 20, 2021).

Tamer, Cahide Aksel. "Abide ve Yapı İşleri Şubesine." Memorandum, SALT Research, Ali Saim Ülgen Archive, TASUDOC0481114, October 1 1959. https://archives.saltresearch.org/handle/123456789/85567 (accessed September 20, 2021).

Tamer, Cahide Aksel. "Bizans anıtlarında bakım ve onarım." Photograph and document, Koç University, Suna Kıraç Library Special Collections and Archives, Cahide Tamer Historic Buildings Restoration Projects Collection, S108 _A01_doc_01 and S108_A01_doc_02, 1955. https://libdigitalcollections.ku.edu.tr/digital/collection/CTA/id/928/rec/3 (accessed September 20, 2021).

Tamer, Cahide Aksel. "Bodrum Camii Minaresi Restorasyonu Hakkında Rapor." Report, Koç University, Suna Kıraç Library Special Collections and Archives, Cahide Tamer Historic Buildings Restoration Projects Collection, CTA_S106_D01_doc_01, November 15 1966. https://libdigitalcollections.ku.edu.tr/digital/collection/CTA/id/854/rec/43 (accessed March 29, 2022).

Tamer, Cahide Aksel. "Laleli'de Mesih Paşa Camii (Mireleon Kilisesi) İmalat." Manuscript, Koç University, Suna Kıraç Library Special Collections and Archives, Cahide Tamer Historic Buildings Restoration Projects Collection, CTA_S106_D01, September 2 1953. https://libdigitalcollections.ku.edu.tr/digital/collection/CTA/id/862/rec/43 (accessed March 29, 2022).

Tamer, Cahide Aksel. "[Projected Repairs for 1955]." Inventory, Koç University, Suna Kıraç Library Special Collections and Archives, Cahide Tamer Historic Buildings Restoration Projects Collection, CTA_S103_D01_doc_16_02, 1955. https://libdigitalcollections.ku.edu.tr/digital/collection/CTA/id/649/rec4 (accessed March 29, 2022).

T.C. Kültür Bakanlığı. "Saim Ülgen (C. 268 Mf). Memorandum, SALT Research, Ali Saim Ülgen Archive, TASUDOC0534105, November 30 1938. https://archives.saltresearch.org/handle/123456789/83487 (accessed April 5, 2022).

T.C. Kültür Bakanlığı, Güzel Sanatlar Akademisi. "Bay Saim Ülgen, Yüksek Mimar." Memorandum, SALT Research, Ali Saim Ülgen Archive, TASUDOC0534117, June 21 1939. https://archives.saltresearch.org/handle/123456789/83487 (accessed April 5, 2022).

T.C. Maarif Vekaleti, Eski Eserler ve Müzeler Umum Müdürlüğü. "Aksaray Sultanhanı Rölövesinin ve Restorasyon Projesinin Hazırlanması Hakkında." Memorandum, SALT Research, Ali Saim Ülgen Archive, TASUDOC0438041, April 5 1956. https://archives.saltresearch.org/handle/123456789/78739 (accessed September 20, 2021).

T.C. Milli Eğitim Vekaleti, Eski Eserler ve Müzeler Genel Müdürlüğü. "Yusuf Akyurt'un Dairemize Alınmasında Fayda Umulan Eserlerinin Tetkiki için bir Komisyon Kurulması Hakkında." Letter, SALT Research, Ali Saim Ülgen Archive, TASUDOC0438, July 24 1953. https://archives.saltresearch.org/handle/123456789/78739 (accessed September 20, 2021).

T.C. Milli Eğitim Vekaleti, Eski Eserler ve Müzeler Genel Müdürlüğü. "Yusuf Akyurt'un Eserlerinin Tetkiki ve Kıymetlendırılmesi Hakkında." Letter, SALT Research, Ali Saim Ülgen Archive, TASUDOC0438001, August 1 1953. https://archives.saltresearch.org/handle/123456789/78739 (accessed September 20, 2021).

Tülbentçi, Feridun Fazıl. "Anadolu'nun Fethi." Manuscript, SALT Research, FFTDOC00382, date unknown. https://archives.saltresearch.org/handle/123456789/19096 (accessed September 20, 2021).

Türkiye Cumhuriyeti Kültür Bakanlığı. "Seçme Sınavında Muvaffak Olduğunuza Dair." Memorandum, SALT Research, Ali Saim Ülgen Archive, TASUDOC0534108, November 2 1938. https://archives.saltresearch.org/handle/123456789/83487 (accessed April 5, 2022).

Ülgen, Ali Saim. "[Ali Saim Ülgen to Refi Cevat Ulunay]." Letter, SALT Research, Ali Saim Ülgen Archive, December 1961. https://archives.saltresearch.org (accessed September 20, 2021).

Ülgen, Ali Saim. "Ekrem Hakkı Ayverdi Bibliografya Taslağı." Manuscript, SALT Research, Ali Saim Ülgen Archive, TASUDOCA0113, 1953. https://archives.saltresearch.org/handle/123456789/69129 (accessed September 20, 2021).

Ülgen, Ali Saim. "Fatih Devri Mimarisi." Manuscript, SALT Research, Ali Saim Ülgen Archive, TASUDOCA0155003, 1953. https://archives.saltresearch.org/handle/123456789/89737 (accessed September 20, 2021).

Ülgen, Ali Saim. "İstanbul'daki Bizans Eserleri Hakkında Rapor." Report, SALT Research, Ali Saim Ülgen Archive, TASUDOC1323, September 5 1953. https://archives.saltresearch.org/handle/123456789/75855 (accessed September 20, 2021).

Ülgen, Ali Saim. "Kontrol İşleri." Report, SALT Research, Ali Saim Ülgen Archive, TASUDOC1311025, date unknown. https://archives.saltresearch.org/handle/123456789/75853 (accessed September 20, 2021).

Ülgen, Ali Saim. "Maarif Vekaletine." (Memorandum, SALT Research, Ali Saim Ülgen Archive, TASUDOC0438040, July 9 1956. https://archives.saltresearch.org/handle/123456789/78739 (accessed September 20, 2021).

Ülgen, Ali Saim. "Maarif Vekaletine." Memorandum, SALT Research, Ali Saim Ülgen Archive, TASUDOC0438042-3, 1956. https://archives.saltresearch.org/handle/123456789/78739 (accessed September 20, 2021).

Ülgen, Ali Saim. "Prensiplerimiz." Report, SALT Research, Ali Saim Ülgen Archive, TASUDOC1381004, date unknown. https://archives.saltresearch.org/handle/123456789/80746 (accessed September 20, 2021).

Ülgen, Ali Saim. "Rapor." Memorandum, SALT Research, Ali Saim Ülgen Archive, TASUDOC1311126, 1940. https://archives.saltresearch.org/handle/123456789/75853 (accessed September 20, 2021).

Ülgen, Ali Saim. "Rapor." Memorandum, SALT Research, Ali Saim Ülgen Archive, TASUDOC0486009, 1947. https://archives.saltresearch.org/handle/123456789/82564 (accessed September 20, 2021).

Ülgen, Ali Saim. "Rapor." Memorandum, SALT Research, Ali Saim Ülgen Archive, TASUDOC0486-TASUDOC0486021, 1947. https://archives.saltresearch.org/handle/123456789/82564 (accessed September 20, 2021).

Ülgen, Ali Saim. "Rapor." Memorandum, SALT Research, Ali Saim Ülgen Archive, TASUDOC0437005, unknown date. https://archives.saltresearch.org/handle/123456789/70246 (accessed September 20, 2021).

Ülgen, Ali Saim. "Rapor." Memorandum, SALT Research, Ali Saim Ülgen Archive, TASUDOC0476021, date unknown. https://archives.saltresearch.org/handle/123456789/73533 (accessed September 20, 2021).

Ülgen, Ali Saim. "Rapor." Memorandum, SALT Research, Ali Saim Ülgen Archive, TASUDOC1311042, date unknown. https://archives.saltresearch.org/handle/123456789/75853 (accessed September 20, 2021).

Ülgen, Ali Saim. "Rapor." Paper, SALT Research, Ali Saim Ülgen Archive, TASUDOC0640021-2, undated. https://archives.saltresearch.org/handle/123456789/80622 (accessed September 20, 2021).

Ülgen, Ali Saim. "Restorasyon Kriterleri ve Carte de Restauro Makalesi ile ilgili Rapor." Memorandum, SALT Research, Ali Saim Ülgen Archive, TASUDOC0077, June 8 1961. https://archives.saltresearch.org/handle/123456789/82527 (accessed April 5, 2022).

Ülgen, Ali Saim. "Restorasyon Projesinin İzahı." Paper, SALT Research, Ali Saim Ülgen Archive, TASUDOC0640023-4, undated. https://archives.saltresearch.org/handle/123456789/80622 (accessed September 20, 2021).

Ülgen, Ali Saim. "Rölöve Yapılmak İstenilen Onarımlar Hakkında." Memorandum, SALT Research, Ali Saim Ülgen Archive, TASUDOC0481115, October 27 1959. https://archives.saltresearch.org/handle/123456789/85567 (accessed September 20, 2021).

Ülgen, Ali Saim. "Sayın Genel Müdür'den." Report, SALT Research, Ali Saim Ülgen Archive, TASUDOC1311125, date unknown. https://archives.saltresearch.org/handle/123456789/75853 (accessed September 20, 2021).

Ülgen, Ali Saim. "Sayın Vekilim." Letter, SALT Research, Ali Saim Ülgen Archive, TASUDOC0534040-41, April 18 1944. https://archives.saltresearch.org/handle/123456789/83487 (accessed September 20, 2021).

Ülgen, Ali Saim. "Sultan Selim Camii 1959 Yılı Onarımı Hakkında." Memorandum, SALT Research, Ali Saim Ülgen Archive, TASUDOC0481111, October 27 1959. https://archives.saltresearch.org/handle/123456789/85567 (accessed September 20, 2021).

Ülgen, Ali Saim. "Tarihi Anıtların Korunması ve Onarılmasına ait Prensipler." Manuscript, SALT Research, Ali Saim Ülgen Archive, TASUDOCA0224, date unknown. https://archives.saltresearch.org/handle/123456789/69124 (accessed September 20, 2021).

Ülgen, Ali Saim. "Tescil 165." Manuscript, Koç University, Suna Kıraç Library Special Collections and Archives, Cahide Tamer Historic Buildings Restoration Projects Collection, CTA_S106_D01_doc_06_01, July 17 1936. https://libdigitalcollections.ku.edu.tr/digital/collection/CTA/id/857/rec/43 (accessed March 29, 2022).

Ülgen, Ali Saim. "Topkapı Ahmed Paşa Camii 1959 Yılı Onarımı Hakkında." Memorandum, SALT Research, Ali Saim Ülgen Archive, TASUDOC0481113, November 4 1959. https://archives.saltresearch.org/handle/123456789/85567 (accessed September 20, 2021).

Ülgen, Ali Saim. "Türk Mimari Eserleri Listesi." Manuscript, SALT Research, Ali Saim Ülgen Archive, TASUDOC0530040, date unknown. https://archives.saltresearch.org/handle/123456789/86642 (accessed September 20, 2021).

Ülgen, Ali Saim. "Türkiye Abide Restorasyonlarındaki Doktorein ve Prensipler ve Son Yıllarda Yapılan Tamirlerden bazı Örnekler." Report, SALT Research, Ali Saim Ülgen Archive, TASUDOC0645, date unknown. https://archives.saltresearch.org/handle/123456789/81901 (accessed September 20, 2021).

Ülgen, Ali Saim. "Türkiye Anıtları ve Bugünkü Feci Durumları." Memorandum, SALT Research, Ali Saim Ülgen Archive, TASUDOC0486025, date unknown. https://archives.saltresearch.org/handle/123456789/82564 (accessed September 20, 2021).

Ülgen, Ali Saim. "Türkiye Müzelerinin Geliştirilmesi için Üç Yıllık Program (Müze olarak kullanılan binaların %70'i Tarihi Anıttır." Memorandum, SALT Research, Ali Saim Ülgen Archive, TASUDOC1311080, date unknown. https://archives.saltresearch.org/handle/123456789/75853 (accessed September 20, 2021).

Ülgen, Ali Saim. "Türkiye'de Yapılması Gerekli Haritalar, ve Gerekli Gorulen Arsive, Atölye, ve Müeyyedeler." Manuscript, SALT Research, TASUDOC1311111 and TASUDOC1311112, date unknown. https://archives.saltresearch.org/handle/123456789/75853 (accessed September 20, 2021).

Ülgen, Ali Saim. "Türkleşmis bir Bizans Abidesi, Ayasofya." Manuscript, SALT Research, Ali Saim Ülgen Archive, TASUDOCA0255, date unknown. https://archives.saltresearch.org/handle/123456789/89733 (accessed September 20, 2021).

Ülgen, Ali Saim. "Üçüncü Kısım: Sinan'ın Eserleri; metninin tercümesinin taslağı, Ottoman Turkish." Manuscript, SALT Research, Ali Saim Ülgen Archive, TASUDOCA0071, date unknown. https://archives.saltresearch.org/handle/123456789/74833 (accessed September 20, 2021).

Ülgen, Ali Saim. "Üçüncü Kısım: Sinan'ın Eserleri metninin tercümesinin taslağı, Ottoman Turkish." Manuscript, SALT Research, Ali Saim Ülgen Archive, TASUDOCM0295, date unknown. https://archives.saltresearch.org/handle/123456789/83641 (accessed September 20, 2021).

Ülgen, Ali Saim. "Vakıflar Genel Müdürlüğü Abide ve Yapı İşleri Dairesi Reisliğine." Report, SALT Research, Ali Saim Ülgen Archive, TASUDOC0437035, unknown date. https://archives.saltresearch.org/handle/123456789/70246 (accessed September 20, 2021).

Ülgen, Ali Saim. "Vakıflar İdaresinin Elindeki Anıtlar Hariç Bilcümle Korunması Gerekli Eski Eserlerin Durumu ve Takribi Keşif Tutarları." Memorandum, SALT Research, Ali Saim Ülgen Archive, TASUDOC1311116- TASUDOC1311124, date unknown. https://archives.saltresearch.org/handle/123456789/75853 (accessed September 20, 2021).

Ülgen, Ali Saim. "Vilayetlere ve Kazalara göre Sınıflandırılmış Onarımları veya Kurtarılmaları elzem Başlıca Anıtlarımız." Memorandum, SALT Research, Ali Saim Ülgen Archive, TASUDOC1311133-TASUDOC1311150, date unknown. https://archives.saltresearch.org/handle/123456789/75853 (accessed September 20, 2021).

Ülgen, Ali Saim. "Zabıt." Memorandum, SALT Research, Ali Saim Ülgen Archive, TASUDOC0471007, October 23 1945. https://archives.saltresearch.org/handle/123456789/78741 (accessed September 20, 2021).

Ülgen, Ali Saim. "1950 Yılı Bütçesinden İstanbul Fethinin 500üncü Yıldönümü Dolayısıyla Onarılması Gerekli Anıtlar." Memorandum, SALT Research, Ali Saim Ülgen Archive, TASUDOC1311044, date unknown. https://archives.saltresearch.org/handle/123456789/75853 (accessed September 20, 2021).

Ülgen, Ali Saim. "1958-1959 Türk Mimarisi Ders Programı." Class notes, SALT Research, Ali Saim Ülgen Archive, TASUDOCA0077, 1958-1959. https://archives.saltresearch.org/handle/123456789/79823 (accessed September 20, 2021).

Vakıflar Umum Müdürü. "Vakıflar Baş Müdürlüğüne, İstanbul." Memorandum, SALT Research, Ali Saim Ülgen Archive, TASUDOC0481121, unknown date. https://archives.saltresearch.org/handle/123456789/85567 (accessed September 20, 2021).

Vakıflar Umum Müdürü. "Vakıflar Baş Müdürlüğüne, İstanbul." Memorandum, SALT Research, Ali Saim Ülgen Archive, TASUDOC0481123, October 26 1959.

https://archives.saltresearch.org/handle/123456789/85567 (accessed September 20, 2021).

Vakıflar Umum Müdürü. "Vakıflar Baş Müdürlüğüne, İstanbul." (Memorandum, SALT Research, Ali Saim Ülgen Archive, TASUDOC0481124, unknown date). https://archives.saltresearch.org/handle/123456789/85567 (accessed September 20, 2021).

Vakıflar Umum Müdürü. "Vakıflar Baş Müdürlüğüne, İstanbul." Memorandum, SALT Research, Ali Saim Ülgen Archive, TASUDOC0481125, unknown date, Examination Topics. https://archives.saltresearch.org/handle/123456789/85567 (accessed September 20, 2021).

Vakıflar Umum Müdürü. "(2)." Memorandum, SALT Research, Ali Saim Ülgen Archive, TASUDOC0481122, unknown date. https://archives.saltresearch.org/handle/123456789/85567 (accessed September 20, 2021).

Yücel, Hasan Âli, T.C. Maarif Vekilliği. "Avrupa'da mimarlık tahsil edecek talebe hak." Memorandum, SALT Research, Ali Saim Ülgen Archive, TASUDOC0534114, April 19 1939. https://archives.saltresearch.org/handle/123456789/83487 (accessed April 7, 2022).

Secondary sources

Acciai, Serena. "The Ottoman-Turkish House According to Architect Sedad Hakkı Eldem: A Refined Domestic Culture Suspended Between Europe and Asia." *ABE Journal* 11 (2017): 1-29.

Açıkgöz, Ümit Fırat. "On the Uses and Meanings of Architectural Preservation in Early Republican Istanbul (1923–1950)." *Journal of the Ottoman and Turkish Studies Association* 1, no. 1/2 (2014): 167–185.

Adıvar, A. Adnan. "Fetih Yılı." *Akşam*, 1952, August 24.

Ağaoğlu, Mehmed. "Fatih Camiinin Şekl-i Aslisi ve Türk San'at-i Mimarisindeki Yeri." *Hayat Mecmuası* 45, 1927.

Akar, Tuba. "The Role of Vakıf Institution in the Conservation of Vakıf based Cultural Heritage." PhD diss., Middle East Technical University, 2009.

Akar, Tuba. "Vakıflar Genel Müdürlüğü ve Vakıf Kültür Varlıklarının Korunması." *Erdem* 59 (2011): 11-36.

Akboy-İlk, Serra. "Ali Saim Ülgen: A Dialectical Frame of the Republican Mind." *Tasarım Kuram* 15, no. 28 (2019): 96-110.

Akboy-İlk, Serra. "Ali Saim Ülgen: Building a Historiography of Turkish Architecture." *Turkish Historical Review* 10, no. 1 (2019): 71-97.

Akboy-İlk, Serra, "Architectural Documentation Through Thick Description," Enquiry, *The ARCC Journal* 12 no.1 (2016): 17-29.

Akboy-İlk, Serra. "Building the Architectural Narrative of the Topkapı Kara Ahmed Pasha Mosque Complex in Early Republican Turkey." *YILLIK: Annual of Istanbul Studies* 2 (2020): 81–102.

Akboy-İlk, Serra. "Crafting the Architectural Measured Drawings." *The Plan Journal* 2, no. 1 (2017): 39–61.

Akboy-İlk, Serra. "Drawing to Read Architectural Heritage." *Drawing: Research, Theory, Practice* 2, no.1 (2017): 97-116.

Akboy-İlk, Serra. "Measured Drawing: A Nationalist Reaction in Early Republican Turkey." *Drawing: Research, Theory, Practice* 5, no. 2 (2020): 363-381.

Akboy-İlk, Serra. "The Mediated Environment of Heritage Recording and Documentation." *Preservation Education & Research* 6 (2013): 7-23.

Akboy-İlk, Serra. "The Nature of Drawing in the Changing Culture of Architectural Documentation." *Journal of Architectural and Planning Research* 33, no.1 (2016): 29-44.

Akın, Nur. "Koruma Alanının Büyük Kaybı: Cahide Tamer." *Mimarlık* 328 (March-April 2006). http://www.mimarlikdergisi.com/index.cfm?sayfa=mimarlik&DergiSayi=46&RecID=1091 (accessed September 20, 2021)

Aktur, Hilal. "Ali Saim Ülgen Arşivi üzerinden Erken Cumhuriyet Dönemi'nin Türk Mimarisi'ne Bakışı: Malatya Ulu Camisi Örneği." Master's thesis, Istanbul Technical University, 2010.

Altan, Kemal. "Ayasofya Etrafında Türk San'at Ekleri." *Arkitekt* 9 no. 57 (1935): 264–67.

Altan, Kemal. "Bizans Eserleri Üzerinde Türk Mimarlarının İşleri." *Arkitekt* 8 no. 68 (1936): 224-226.

Altan, Kemal. "Fethiye Camii," *Arkitekt* 10-11 no. 94-95 (1938): 296-299.

Altan, Kemal. "Mimari Kıymeti olan Binalarımız: Sinan'ın Siyavuş Paşaya Yaptığı Kasır." *Zaman*, May 25, 1935.

Altan, Kemal. "Siyaveş Paşa Kasrı." *Arkitekt* 9 no. 57 (1935): 268-269.

Altan, Kemal. "Zeyneb Sultan Camii." *Akşam*, June 26, 1937.

Altınyıldız, Nur. "The Architectural Heritage of Istanbul and the Ideology of Preservation," edited by Sibel Bozdoğan and Gülru Necipoğlu. *Muqarnas* 24 (2007): 281-305.

Anonymous. "Belediye Yapı ve Yollar Kanunu." *Arkitekt* 6, no. 30 (1933), 191-197.

Anonymous. "Beşyüzüncü Fetih Yılı: İstanbulun Fethini Kutlamak için bir Dernek Kuruluyor." *Akşam*, January 21, 1950.

Anonymous. "Bu Sene İstanbul'da 11 İlkmekteb Yapılacak." *Son Posta*, July 18, 1939.

Anonymous. "Edirnedeki bütün Tarihi Abideler Tetkik Ediliyor." *Akşam*, March 24, 1935.

Anonymous. "Eski Eserlerin Tamirine Bundan sonra Müzeler İdaresi Nezaret Edecek," *Son Posta*, May 5, 1937.

Anonymous. "Fetih Kutlama Derneğindeki İstifalar." *Akşam*, May 23, 1951.

Anonymous. "İstanbullular ve Temizlik: Birçok Hamamcılar Ziyan Ettikleri İddiası ile Mallarını Satılığa Çıkarmışlar." *Son Posta*, July 11, 1935.

Anonymous. "İşte Turist Şehri İstanbul: Tarihte yeni bir Devir Açan Fethin 500üncü Yıl Dönümüne Tam 766 Gün Kaldı." *Akşam*, 24 April, 1951.

Anonymous. "İşte Turist Şehri İstanbul: Tarihte yeni bir Devir Açan Fethin 500üncü Yıl Dönümüne Tam 743 Gün Kaldı." *Akşam*, 1951, May 17.

Anonymous. "Satılığa Çıkarılacak Camiler." *Son Posta*, October 23, 1937.

Anonymous. "Süleymaniye: Caminin Manzarasını Bozan Enstitü Binasının Kaldırılması Muhtemel." *Akşam*, January 29, 1951.

Anonymous. "Yeni Bir Komisyon Kuruluyor." *Son Posta*, February 18, 1937.

Anonymous. "500üncü Fetih Yılı: Bir Kutlama Derneğinin Teşkiline Karar Verildi." *Akşam*, December 28, 1949.

Arık, M. Oluş. "Turkish Architecture in Asia Minor in the Period of the Turkish Emirates." In *The Art and Architecure of Turkey*, edited by Ekrem Akurgal, 111-136. New York: Rizzoli International Publications, 1980.

Arseven, Celâl Esad. *Constantinople de Byzance à Stamboul.* Paris, 1909.

Arseven, Celâl Esad. *Sanat Ansiklopedisi*, IV/21. İstanbul: Milli Eğitim Basımevi.

Arseven, Celâl Esad. *Türk San'atı.* İstanbul, 1928.

Aslanapa, Oktay. Güzel Sanatlar Akademisi Türk San'atı Tarihi Enstitüsü Yayınları 1, İstanbul: Berksoy Matbaası, 1963.

Aslanapa, Oktay. *Turkish Art and Architecture.* London: Praeger, 1971.

Atabinen, Reşit Saffet. "Kaybedilen eski Anıtlar Aşığı Y. Mimar A. S. Ülgen." *Dünya Gazetesi*, February 15, 1963.

Atakuman, Çiğdem. "Shifting Discourses of Heritage and Identity in Turkey: Anatolianist Ideologies and Beyond." In *In Search of Pre-Classical Antiquity: Rediscovering Ancient Peoples in Mediterranean Europe (19th and 20th c.)* vol.13, edited by Antonino de Francesco, 166-181. Leiden: Brill, 2017.

Atakuman, Çiğdem. "Value of Heritage in Turkey: History and Politics of Turkey's World Heritage Nominations." *Journal of Mediterranean Archaeology* 112, no. 23.1 (2010): 107-131.

Aykaç, Pınar. "The Commission for the Preservation of Antiquities and Its Role in the Appropriation of Istanbul's Diverse Heritage as National Heritage (1939–1953)." *New Perspectives on Turkey* 62 (2020): 75–99.

Ayverdi, Ekrem Hakkı. "Anadolu Medeniyeti Masalı." In *Makaleler*, 372-398. İstanbul: İstanbul Fetih Cemiyeti, 1985.

Ayverdi, Ekrem Hakkı. "Ankara Çarşısı ve Bedesteni." In *Osmanlı Mimarisinde Fatih Devri 855-886 (1451-1481)* 3. İstanbul: Baha Matbaası, 1973.

Ayverdi, Ekrem Hakkı. "Bursa Orhan Gazi Camii ve Osmanlı Mimarisinin Menşei Meselesi." *Vakıflar Dergisi* 6 (1965): 69-83.

Ayverdi, Ekrem Hakkı. "Büyük Emanet." In *Makaleler*, 399-411. İstanbul: İstanbul Fetih Cemiyeti, 1985.

Ayverdi, Ekrem Hakkı. "Dimetoka'da Çelebi Sultan Mehmed Cami'i." *Vakıflar Dergisi* 3 (1956): 13-16.

Ayverdi, Ekrem Hakkı. *Fatih Devri Mimarisi.* İstanbul: İstanbul Fetih Cemiyeti Neşriyatı, 1953.

Ayverdi, Ekrem Hakkı. "İlimde Millî Basîretin Ehemmiyeti." In *Makaleler*, 361-371. İstanbul: İstanbul Fetih Cemiyeti, 1985.

Ayverdi, Ekrem Hakkı. "İlk Fatih Camii Hakkında yeni bir Vesika." *Vakıflar Dergisi* 6 (1965): 63-68.

Ayverdi, Ekrem Hakkı. "Osmanlı Âbidelerinin Restorasyonları." In *Makaleler*, 76-113. İstanbul: İstanbul Fetih Cemiyeti, 1985.

Ayverdi, Ekrem Hakkı. "Târihimizde Anadolu ve Rumeli Devirleri." In *Makaleler*, 277-309. İstanbul: İstanbul Fetih Cemiyeti, 1985.

Ayverdi, Ekrem Hakkı. "Yugoslavya'da Türk Âbideleri ve Vakıfları." *Vakıflar Dergisi* 3 (1956): 151-224.

Ayverdi, Ekrem Hakkı and Aydın Yüksel. *Avrupa'da Osmanlı Mîmârî Eserleri, Romanya, Macaristan*, vol. I. İstanbul: İstanbul Fetih Cemiyeti, 1977.

Ayverdi, Ekrem Hakkı and Aydın Yüksel, Gürbüz Ertürk, and İbrahim Numan. *Avrupa'da Osmanlı Mîmârî Eserleri, Yugoslavya*, vol. II. İstanbul: İstanbul Fetih Cemiyeti, 1981.

Ayverdi, Ekrem Hakkı and Aydın Yüksel, Gürbüz Ertürk, and İbrahim Numan. *Avrupa'da Osmanlı Mîmârî Eserleri, Yugoslavya*, vol. III. İstanbul: İstanbul Fetih Cemiyeti, 1981.

Ayverdi, Ekrem Hakkı and Aydın Yüksel, Gürbüz Ertürk, and İbrahim Numan. *Avrupa'da Osmanlı Mîmârî Eserleri, Bulgaristan, Yunanistan, Arnavutluk*, vol. IV. İstanbul: İstanbul Fetih Cemiyeti, 1982.

Baydar Nalbantoğlu, Gülsüm. "Between Civilization and Culture: Appropriation of Traditional Dwelling Forms in Early Republican Turkey." *Journal of Architectural Education* 47, no. 2 (1993): 66-74.

Berkes, Niyazi. *Turkish Nationalism and Western Civilization: Selected Essays of Ziya Gökalp*. New York: Columbia University, 1959.

Bertram, Carel. *Imagining the Turkish House: Collective Visions of Home*. Austin: University of Texas Press, 2008.

Beyatlı, Yahya Kemal. "Kör Kazma." In *Aziz İstanbul*, 152-155. İstanbul: Milli Eğitim Basımevi Devlet Kitapları, 1969.

Bildik, Cemaleddin. "Fatih'in Çiniliköşkü eski hale getiriliyor." *Akşam*, October 16, 1949.

Billur, İffet. "Türkiye'de Kültürel Mirası Koruma Çalışmaları Bağlamında İstanbul Rölöve ve Anıtlar Müdürlüğü'nün Rolü." PhD diss., Mimar Sinan Fine Arts University, 2020.

Bilsel, S. M. Can. "Our Anatolia": Organicism and the Making of Humanist Culture in Turkey." Edited by Sibel Bozdoğan and Gülru Necipoğlu. *Muqarnas* 24 (2007): 223-241.

Boyar, Ebru. *Ottomans, Turks and the Balkans: Empires Lost, Relations Altered*. London, New York: Tauris Academic Studies, 2007.

Bozdoğan, Sibel. *Modernism and Nation Building: Turkish Architectural Culture in the Early Republic*. Seattle: University of Washington Press, 2001.

Bozdoğan, Sibel. "Reading Ottoman Architecture Through Modernist Lenses," edited by Sibel Bozdoğan and Gülru Necipoğlu. *Muqarnas* 24 (2007): 199-221.

Bozdoğan, Sibel. "The Legacy of an Istanbul Architect: Type, Context and Urban Identity in the Work of Sedad Eldem." In *Modern Architecture and the Mediterranean: Vernacular Dialogues and Contested Identities*, edited by Jean-François Lejeune and Michelangelo Sabatino, 131-146. London: Routledge, 2010.

Bozdoğan, Sibel. "The Predicament of Modernism in Turkish Architectural Culture." In *Rethinking Modernity and National Identity in Turkey*, edited by Sibel Bozdoğan and Reşat Kasaba, 133-156. Seattle, University of Washington Press: 1997.

Bozdoğan Sibel and Esra Akcan. *Turkey: Modern Architectures in History*. London: Reaktion Books, 2012.

Bozdoğan, Sibel and Gülru Necipoğlu, "Preface: Entangled Discourses," edited by Sibel Bozdoğan and Gülru Necipoğlu, *Muqarnas* 24 (2007): 1-6.

Brockett, Gavin D. "When Ottomans Become Turks: Commemorating the Conquest of Constantinople and Its Contribution to World History." *The American Historical Review* 119, no. 2 (2014): 399-433.

Bruegmann, Robert. "The Pencil and Electronic Sketchboard: Architectural Representation and the Computer." In *Architecture and Its Image: Four Centuries of Architectural Representation: Works from the Collection of the Canadian Centre for Architecture*, edited by Eve Blau, Edward Kaufman, and Robin Evans, 139-157. Montreal Cambridge, Mass.: Centre Canadien d'Architecture/Canadian Centre for Architecture, Distributed by the MIT Press, 1989.

Byzantios, Skarlatos. *Constantinople, A Topographical, Archaeological & Historical Description*. three vols. Athens: Andreo Koromila Publishers, 1851- 1869 [in Greek].

Byzantios, Skarlatos. *Constantinople*. Translated by Haris Theodorelis-Rigas. İstanbul: Istos Yayın, 2019.

Cantay, Gönül. "Sivas I. İzzeddin Keykavus Darüşşifası." *Erdem* 9, no. 27 (1997): 975-980.

Cengizkan, Ali. "Mehmet Nihat Nigizberk Katkıları, Evkaf İdaresi ve Mimar Kemalettin." In *Mimar Kemalettin ve Çağı*, edited by Ali Cengizkan, 177-208. Ankara: TMMOB Mimarlar Odası, 2008.

Copeaux, Etienne. *Tarih Ders Kitaplarında (1931–1993), Türk Tarih Tezinden Türk İslâm Sentezine*. Translated by Ali Berktay. İstanbul: İletişim Yayınları, 2006.

Cunbur, Müjgan. "İstanbul'un 500üncü Fetih Yıldönümü Dolayısiyle Tertiplenen Sergilere, Yapılan Kültür, San'at ve Neşriyat Hareketlerine dair." *Vakıflar Dergisi* 4 (1958): 265-281.

Çambel, Hasan Cemil. "Atatürk ve Tarih." *T.T.K. Belleten Dergisi* 3, no. 10 (1939): 269-272.

Çetintaş, Sedat. "Eski Eserleri nasıl Restore Edebiliriz." In *İstanbul ve Mimari Yazıları*, edited by İsmail Dervişoğlu, 175-178. Ankara: Türk Tarih Kurumu Basımevi, 2011.

Çetintaş, Sedat. "Fatih Evvela Bizi Fethetmeli." In *İstanbul ve Mimari Yazıları*, edited by İsmail Dervişoğlu, 391-392. Ankara: Türk Tarih Kurumu Basımevi, 2011.

Çetintaş, Sedat. "Fatih'i Tahkir mi yoksa Kutlamak mı?: Tavı Geçmiş Demire Çekiç Vurulursa Kırılır." In *İstanbul ve Mimari Yazıları*, edited by İsmail Dervişoğlu, 444-447. Ankara: Türk Tarih Kurumu Basımevi, 2011.

Çetintaş, Sedat. "İstanbul'un Yıldönümü." In *İstanbul ve Mimari Yazıları*, edited by İsmail Dervişoğlu, 377-380. Ankara: Türk Tarih Kurumu Basımevi, 2011.

Çetintaş, Sedat. "Kör Kazma." In *İstanbul ve Mimari Yazıları*, edited by İsmail Dervişoğlu, 13-19. Ankara: Türk Tarih Kurumu Basımevi, 2011.

Çetintaş, Sedat. "Maruz Kaldığımız Müşkilat ve Tek Çare." In *İstanbul ve Mimari Yazıları*, edited by İsmail Dervişoğlu, 35-37. Ankara: Türk Tarih Kurumu Basımevi, 2011.

Çetintaş, Sedat. "Milli Mimariden Ne Anlıyoruz?" In *İstanbul ve Mimari Yazıları*, edited by İsmail Dervişoğlu, 171-174. Ankara: Türk Tarih Kurumu Basımevi, 2011.

Çetintaş, Sedat. "Mimar Sedat Çetintaş'la bir Konuşma." In *İstanbul ve Mimari Yazıları*, edited by İsmail Dervişoğlu, 110-113. Ankara: Türk Tarih Kurumu Basımevi, 2011.

Çetintaş, Sedat. "Sedat Çetintaş'la Mülakat." In *İstanbul ve Mimari Yazıları*, edited by İsmail Dervişoğlu, 162-165. Ankara: Türk Tarih Kurumu Basımevi, 2011.

Çetintaş, Sedat. *Sivas Darüşşifası: 614-1217.* İstanbul: İbrahim Horoz Basımevi, 1953.

Çetintaş Sedat. "Topkapı Sarayını Tehdit eden Binayı Yıkmalıyız." In *İstanbul ve Mimari Yazıları*, edited by İsmail Dervişoğlu 351-354. Ankara: Türk Tarih Kurumu Basımevi, 2011.

Çetintaş, Sedat. "Tulumcu Hüsameddin Kimdir, Tulumu nasıl bir Şeydir?" in *İstanbul ve Mimari Yazıları*, edited by İsmail Dervişoğlu, 298-300. Ankara: Türk Tarih Kurumu Basımevi, 2011.

Çetintaş, Sedat. *Türk Mimari Anıtları: Osmanlı Devri.* İstanbul: Milli Eğitim Basımevi, 1946.

Çetintaş, Sedat. *Türk Mimari Anıtları: Osmanlı Devri, Bursa'da Murad I ve Bayezid I Binaları.* İstanbul: Milli Eğitim Basımevi, 1952.

Çetintaş, Sedat. "Türk Tarih Kurumu Tarafından Sivas Şifaiyesinde Yaptırılan Mimari Hafriyat." *Belleten* 3, no.9 (January 1939): 61-67.

Derman, M. Uğur. "Ekrem Hakkı Ayverdi as a Collector and the Meetings of the 'Privy Council'." In *Ekrem Hakkı Ayverdi 1899-1984: Architectural Historian, Restorator, Collector*, edited by M. Baha Tanman, 27-32. İstanbul: İstanbul Araştırmaları Enstitüsü, 2014.

Dirimtekin, Feridun. *Fetihten önce Haliç Surları.* İstanbul: İstanbul Fetih Derneği, 1956.

Dirimtekin, Feridun. *Fetihten önce Marmara Surları.* Ankara: Kanaat, Feyz ve Güzel Sanatlar Matbaası, 1953.

Egli, Ernst. "Mimari Muhit." *Türk Yurdu* 30, no.224, (1930): 32-36.

Egli, Ernst. *Sinan: Der Baumeister Osmanischer Glanzzeit.* Zurich: Erlenbach, 1954.

Egli, Ernst. *Sinan: Osmanlı Altın Çağının Mimarı.* Translated by İbrahim Ataç. İstanbul: Arkeoloji ve Sanat Yayınları, 2009.

Eldem, Halil Ethem. *Tarihi Abide ve Eserlerimizi Korumağa Mecburuz.* İstanbul: Devlet Matbaası, 1933.

Eldem, Sedad Hakkı. *Türk Evi Plan Tipleri.* İstanbul: İstanbul Teknik Üniversitesi, 1954.

Eldem, Sedad Hakkı. *Türk Evi: Osmanlı Dönemi = Turkish Houses: Ottoman Period,* vol. 1. İstanbul: Türkiye Anıt Çevre Turizm Değerlerini Koruma Vakfı, 1984.

Eldem, Sedad Hakkı. *Türk Evi, Osmanlı Dönemi = Turkish Houses: Ottoman Period,* 3 vols. İstanbul: Türkiye Anıt Çevre Turizm Değerlerini Koruma Vakfı, 1984–1987.

Eldem, Sedad Hakkı. *Türk Mimari Eserleri (Works of Turkish Architecture).* İstanbul: Binbirdirek Matbaacılık Sanayii A.Ş. Yayınları, 1975.

Eldem, Sedad Hakkı and Feridun Akozan. *Topkapı Sarayı, Bir Mimarî Araştırma.* Ankara: Kültür Bakanlığı Eski Eserler ve Müzeler Genel Müdürlüğü, 1982.

Eldem, Sedad. "Önsöz." In *Rölöve I: İstanbul Boğaziçi Köyleri Yerleşmesi, Resmî ve Kültürel Taş Binalar, İstanbul ve Anadolu Evleri, Çeşmeler ve Selsebiller,* edited by Sedad Eldem, Feridun Akozan, and Köksal Anadol, 3-7. İstanbul: Millî Eğitim Basımevi, 1968.

Erbay, Fethiye and Mutlu Erbay. *Cumhuriyet Dönemi (1923-1938): Atatürk'ün Sanat Politikası.* İstanbul: Boğaziçi Üniversitesi Yayınevi, 2006.

Ergin, Osman Nuri. *Mecelle-i Umur-ı Belediye,* 9 vols. İstanbul: İstanbul Büyükşehir Belediyesi, 1995.

Ersanlı, Büşra. *İktidar ve Tarih: Türkiye'de "Resmî Tarih" Tezinin Oluşumu (1929–1937).* İstanbul: İletişim Yayınları, 2018.

Ersanlı, Büşra. *İktidar ve Tarih: Türkiye'de "Resmî Tarih" Tezinin Oluşumu (1929–1937).* İstanbul: İletişim Yayınları, 2003.

Ersoy, Ahmet A. *Architecture and the Late Ottoman Historical Imaginary: Reconfiguring the Architectural Past in a Modernizing Empire.* New York: Routledge, 2016.

Ersoy, Ahmet A. "Architecture and the Search for Ottoman Origins in the Tanzimat Period." *Muqarnas* 24 (2007): 117-139.

Everett, Sally. *Art Theory and Criticism: An Anthology of Formalist, Avant-Garde, Contextualist and Post-Modernist Thought.* Jefferson, NC: McFarland & Company, Inc., 1991.

Eyüboğlu, Sabahattin. *Mavi ve Kara: Denemeler.* İstanbul: Ataç Kitabevi, 1961.

Fergusson, James. *The Illustrated Handbook of Architecture: Being a Concise and Popular Account of the Different Styles of Architecture Prevailing in all Ages and all Countries.* 2 vols. London: J. Murray, 1855.

Gabriel, Albert. *Monuments Turcs D'Anatolie: Kayseri-Nigde*. Paris: Paris Libraire des écoles françaises d'Athènes et de Rome, 1931. Reprinted in idem, İstanbul: Arkeoloji ve Sanat Yayınları, 2014.

Gabriel, Albert. "Tarihî Âbidelerin Tasnif ve Muhafazası." *Anıtların Korunması ve Onarılması-I*, written by Ali Saim Ülgen, XXI- XXIV. Ankara: Maarif Matbaası: 1943.

Gabriel, Albert. "Türk San'ati ve Sa'nat Tarihindeki Yeri." *Hayat* 40 (1927): 35-38.

Gabriel, Albert. "Türkiye'de Türk Mimarisi." Translated by A. Fırtınalı. *Ankara Üniversitesi İlahiyat Fakültesi Dergisi* (1963): 1-3.

Gasco, Giorgio. "Bruno Taut and the Program for the Protection of Monuments in Turkey (1937-38)/Three Case Studies: Ankara, Edirne, Bursa." *METU.JFA* 27 no.2 (2010): 15-36.

Dağlıoğlu, Hikmet Turhan. *Ankara'da Cenabî Ahmed Paşa Camii ve Cenabî Ahmed Paşa*. Ankara: Vakıflar Umum Müdürlüğü Neşriyatı, 1942.

Danforth, Nicholas. "Multi-Purpose Empire: Ottoman History in Republican Turkey." *Middle Eastern Studies* 50, no. 4 (2014): 655–678.

Girardelli, Paolo. "Re-thinking architect Kemalettin." *Abe Journal: Architecture beyond Europe* 2 (2012) (accessed April 1, 2022).

Giray, Kıymet. *1920'li Yıllarda Sanat Politikası ve Yurtdışına Gönderilen Sanatçılar: 80. Yılında Cumhuriyet'in Türkiye Kültürü*. Ankara: TMMOB Mimarlar Odası ve Sanat Estetik ve Görsel Kültür Derneği ortak yayını, 2003.

Govsa, Alaettin. "Mimar Kemalettin." In *Türk Meşhurları Ansiklopedisi*, 1421-22. İstanbul, 1946.

Gurlitt, Cornelius. *Die Baukunst Konstantinopels*. Two vols. Berlin: Verlag Von Ernst Wasmuth:1907 and 1912.

Gurlitt, Cornelius. *İstanbul'un Mimari Sanatı*. Translated by Rezan Kızıltan. Ankara: Enformasyon ve Dokümantasyon Hizmetleri Vakfı, 1999.

Gülekli, Nurettin Can. *Eski Eserler ve Müzelerle ilgili Kanun Nizamname ve Emirler*. Ankara: Milli Eğitim Bakanlığı, 1948.

Günaltay, Şemsettin. "Türklerin Ana Yurdu ve Irkı Meselesi." *Tarih Semineri Dergisi* 13 (1937): 3-13.

Hanioğlu, M. Şükrü. *A Brief History of the Late Ottoman Empire*. Princeton: Princeton University Press, 2008.

Hızlı, Neslinur and Nezih R. Aysel. "Ernst Egli'nin Güzel Sanatlar Akademisi Mimarlık Eğitimi Reformu Çalışmaları." In *Ernst A. Egli: Türkiye'ye Katkılar*, edited by Ali Cengizkan, Selda Bancı, and N. Müge Cengizkan, 75-84. İstanbul: TMMOB Mimarlar Odası Yayınları, 2017.

İnalcık, Halil. "Rumeli." In *The Encyclopedia of Islam*, second edition, vol. VIII, 608-9. Leiden, 1995.

İnan, Afet. *Atatürk Hakkında Hatıralar ve Belgeler*, edited by Arı İnan. İstanbul: Türkiye İş Bankası Kültür Yayınları, 2014.

İnan, Afet. "Büyük Türk Mimarı Sinan'ın 367. Yıldönümü Münasebetiyle Türk Tarih Kurumu'nun Sinan hakkındaki Çalışmaları: Atatürk ve Mimar Koca Sinan I ve II." *Yeni İstanbul*, April 9, 1955.

İnan, Afet. *Mimar Koca Sinan.* Ankara: Türkiye Emlak Kredi Bankası Neşriyatı, Ayyıldız Matbaası A.Ş., 1968.

İnan, Afet. "Türk Tarih Kurumunun Arkeoloji Faaliyeti." *Belleten* 2, no.5-6 (January 1938): 5-12.

İnönü, İsmet. "10/8/1936." In *Anıtların Korunması ve Onarılması I,* written by Ali Saim Ülgen. Ankara: Maarif Matbaası, 1943, IX.

İnönü, İsmet. "31/1/1938." In *Anıtların Korunması ve Onarılması I,* written by Ali Saim Ülgen. Ankara: Maarif Matbaası, 1943, X.

Janin, Raymond. *Constantinople Byzantine: Développement Urbain et Répertoire Topographique.* Paris: Institut Français D'études Byzantines, 1964.

Jokilehto, Jukka. *A History of Architectural Conservation.* New York: Butterworth-Heinemann, 2011.

Kafadar, Cemal. "A Rome of One's Own: Reflections on Cultural Geography and Identity in the Lands of Rum," edited by Sibel Bozdoğan and Gülru Necipoğlu. *Muqarnas* 24 (2007): 7-25.

Karpat, Kemal H. "Historical Continuity and Identity Change or How to be Modern Muslim, Ottoman, and Turk." In *Ottoman Past and Today's Turkey,* edited by Kemal H. Karpat, 1-28, Leiden: Brill, 2000.

Kasaba, Reşat. "Kemalist Certainties and Modern Ambiguities." In *Rethinking Modernity and National Identity in Turkey,* edited by Sibel Bozdoğan and Reşat Kasaba, 15-36. Seattle, University of Washington Press: 1997.

Kemalettin Bey. "Bulgarların Ahval-i Medeniye-i Hazırası." In *Mimar Kemalettin'in Yazdıkları,* edited by İlhan Tekeli and Selim İlkin, 79-83. Ankara: Şevki Vanlı Mimarlık Vakfı Yayınları, 1997.

Kemalettin Bey, "Eski İstanbul ve İmar-ı Belde Belası." In *Mimar Kemalettin'in Yazdıkları,* edited by İlhan Tekeli and Selim İlkin, 113-115. Ankara: Şevki Vanlı Mimarlık Vakfı Yayınları, 1997.

Kemalettin Bey. "Türk Mimarlığı." In *Mimar Kemalettin'in Yazdıkları,* edited by İlhan Tekeli and Selim İlkin, 149-151. Ankara: Şevki Vanlı Mimarlık Vakfı Yayınları, 1997.

Kemalettin Bey. "Türk ve Müslüman Mimarlığı." In *Mimar Kemalettin'in Yazdıkları,* edited by İlhan Tekeli and Selim İlkin, 153-158. Ankara: Şevki Vanlı Mimarlık Vakfı Yayınları, 1997.

Kemalettin Bey. "Yeni Camii'nin Tamiri Münasebetiyle bir iki Söz." In *Mimar Kemalettin'in Yazdıkları,* edited by İlhan Tekeli and Selim İlkin, 108-111. Ankara: Şevki Vanlı Mimarlık Vakfı Yayınları, 1997.

Kezer, Zeynep. *Building Modern Turkey: State, Space, and Ideology in the Early Republic.* Pittsburgh, Pa: University of Pittsburgh Press, 2015.

Kickingereder, F. Dieter. "Celâl Esad Arseven's Memoirs of his Life as an Artist and a Man of Politics: Sanat ve Siyaset Hatıralarım (1993)." In *Many Ways of Speaking About the Self: Middle Eastern Ego-Documents in Arabic, Persian and Turkish (14th-20th century),* edited by Ralf Elger and Yavuz Köse, 37-46. Wiesbaden: Harrassowitz Verlag 2010.

Konstantinias, I., K. *The Ancient and Modern Environment of Constantinople, from the Beginning until Today.* İstanbul: Dimitris Paspallis Publishers, 1844. [in Greek]

Konstatinias, Patriarch. *Constantinople, Old and New.* İstanbul: Dimitris Paspallis Publishers, 1824.

Konyalı, İbrahim Hakkı. *Mimar Koca Sinan'ın Eserleri.* İstanbul: Ülkü Basımevi, 1950.

Koyunoğlu, Arif Hikmet. "Anılar." In *Osmanlı'dan Cumhuriyet'e Bir Mimar Arif Hikmet Koyunoğlu: Anılar, Yazılar, Mektuplar, Belgeler,* edited by Hasan Kuruyazıcı. İstanbul: Yapı Kredi Yayınları, 2008.

Kunter, Halim Baki and Ali Saim Ülgen. *Fatih Camii ve Bizans Sarnıcı.* İstanbul: Cumhuriyet Matbaası, 1939.

Kuran, Aptullah. "Mimarlıkta 'Yeni-Türk' Üslubu ve Osman Hamdi Bey." In *Selçuklular'dan Cumhuriyet'e Türkiye'de Mimarlık/Architecture in Turkey from the Seljuks to the Republic,* edited by Çiğdem Kafescioğlu and Lucienne Thys-Şenocak, 597-603. İstanbul: Türkiye İş Bankası Kültür Yayınları, 2018.

Kültür Bakanlığı, Antikiteler ve Müzeler Dairesi, Anıtları Koruma Komisyonu. *Anıtları Koruma Komisyonunun 1933–1935 Yıllarındaki Çalışmaları.* İstanbul: Devlet Basımevi, 1935.

Madran, Emre. "Cumhuriyet'in ilk Otuz Yılında (1920–1950) Koruma Alanının Örgütlenmesi-I." *ODTU MFD* 16, no. 1-2 (1996): 59-97.

Madran, Emre. "Cumhuriyet'in ilk Otuz Yılında (1920-1950) Koruma Alanının Örgütlenmesi-II." In *ODTU MFD* 17, no.1-2 (1997): 75-97.

Madran, Emre. *Tanzimattan Cumhuriyete Kültür Varlıklarının Korunmasına ilişkin Tutumlar ve Düzenlemeler: 1850-1950.* Ankara: ODTÜ Mimarlık Fakültesi Yayınları, 2002.

Mango, Andrew. *Atatürk.* Woodstock N.Y.: Overlook Press, 2000.

Mardin, Şerif. *Religion and Social Change in Modern Turkey: The Case of Bediüzzaman Said Nursi.* Albany: State University of New York, 1989.

Mardin, Şerif. "Some Thoughts on Modern Turkish Social Science." In *Rethinking Modernity and National Identity in Turkey,* edited by Sibel Bozdoğan and Reşat Kasaba, 64-80. Seattle, University of Washington Press: 1997.

Mardin, Şerif. *Türk Modernleşmesi.* İstanbul: İletişim Yayınları, 1992.

Marinov, Tchavdar. "The 'Balkan House': Interpretations and Symbolic Appropriations of the Ottoman-Era Vernacular Architecture in the Balkans." In *Entangled Histories of the Balkans,* vol. 4, Concepts, Approaches, and (Self-)Representations, edited by Roumen Daskalov, Tchavdar Marinov, Diana Mishkova, and Alexander Vezenkov, 440-593. Leiden & Boston: Brill, 2017.

Marshall, Daniel and Paul Scott. "A Brief History of Non-Euclidean Geometry." *Australian Mathematics Teacher* 60, no. 3 (2004): 2-4.

Millin, Aubin-Louis. *Antiquités nationales, ou, Recueil de Monumens,* 6 volumes. Paris: Chez M. Drouhin, 1790.

Montani, Pietro et. al. *Usūl-i Mi'mārī-i Osmānī.* Istanbul, 1873. Reprinted in idem, *Osmanlı Mimarisi.* İstanbul: Çamlıca, 2015.

M. R. E. "İstanbul 500üncü Fetih Yılı Kutlama Hazırlığı Aksıyor." *Akşam*, May 17, 1951.

Necipoğlu, Gülru. *Architecture, Ceremonial, and Power: the Topkapı Palace in the Fifteenth and Sixteenth Centuries.* New York, NY: Architectural History Foundation, 1991.

Necipoğlu, Gülru. "Creation of a National Genius, Sinan and the Historiography of 'Classical' Ottoman Architecture," edited by Sibel Bozdoğan and Gülru Necipoğlu. *Muqarnas* 24 (2007): 141-183.

Orgun, Zarif and Serap Aykaç. "La fondation du Musée turque et le Musée des Arts turcs et Islamiques." *Travaux et Recherches en Turquie* 1 (1982): 135–4.

Ödekan, Ayla. "Sedat Çetintaş," *Restorasyon Yıllığı Dergisi* 11 (2015): 88-93.

Ödekan, Ayla. *Yazıları ve Rölöveleriyle Sedat Çetintaş.* İstanbul: İTÜ Yayınları, 2004.

Öndin, Nilüfer. *Cumhuriyet'in Kültür Politikası ve Sanat 1923–1950.* İstanbul: İnsancıl Yayınları, 2003.

Öz, Tahsin. "Atatürk'ün Topkapı Sarayını Ziyareti." Newspaper column, SALT Research, FFT068004, May 15 1951. https://archives.saltresearch.org/handle/123456789/18209 (accessed September 20, 2021).

Öz, Tahsin. "Bir Münakaşa ve İki Konferans." In *Sivas Darüşşifası: 614-1217*, written by Sedat Çetintaş, 123-125. İstanbul: İbrahim Horoz Basımevi, 1953.

Öz, Tahsin. "Bizans Sarayları." Circular, FFT273001, SALT Research, November 1947. https://archives.saltresearch.org/handle/123456789/25581 (accessed September 20, 2021).

Özdoğan, Mehmet "Ideology and Archaeology in Turkey." In *Archaeology under Fire: Nationalism, Politics and Heritage in the Eastern Mediterranean and Middle East*, edited by Lynn Meskell. London: Routledge, 2002: 111-123.

Pancaroğlu, Oya. "Formalism and the Academic Foundation of Turkish Art in the Early Twentieth Century." In "History and Ideology: Architectural Heritage of the 'Lands of Rum,'" edited by Sibel Bozdoğan and Gülru Necipoğlu, special issue, *Muqarnas* 24 (2007): 67–78.

Pancaroğlu, Oya. "The Mosque-Hospital Complex in Divriği: A History of Relations and Transitions." *Anadolu ve Çevresinde Ortaçağ* (3). Ankara: AKVAD Anadolu Kültür Varlıklarının Araştırma Derneği 2009: 169-198.

Parvillée, Léon. *Architecture at Décoration Turques au XVE siècle.* Paris: A. Morel, 1874.

Paspates, Alexander. *Byzantine Studies.* İstanbul: Koromilas Publications, 1877. [in Greek]

Paspates, Alexander. "On the Land Walls of Istanbul." *Greek Literary Society of Constantinople Syngramma Periodikon (1863 – 1915)* vol. 2. İstanbul: Bizantidos Publishers, 1865a. [in Greek]

Paspates, Alexander. "The Epigraphy of the Land Walls," *Greek Literary Society of Constantinople Syngramma Periodikon (1863 – 1915)* vol. 2. İstanbul: Bizantidos Publishers, 1865b. [in Greek]

Paspates, Alexander. "The Gates of the Land Walls." *Greek Literary Society of Constantinople Syngramma Periodikon (1863 – 1915)* vol. 2. İstanbul: Bizantidos Publishers, 1865c. [in Greek]

Pérez Gómez, Alberto. *Architecture and the Crisis of Modern Science.* Cambridge, Mass.: MIT Press, 1983.

Pesmazoglou, Stephanos. "Skarlatos Vyzantios's Konstantinoupolis: Difference and Fusion." In *Economy and Society on Both Shores of the Aegean,* edited by L. Tanatar-Baruh and V. Kechriotis, 23-78. Athens: Alpha Bank Historical Archives, 2010.

Rado, Şevket. "Mimar Çetintaş'la bir Konuşma," Akşam, 10 October 1940. *İstanbul ve Mimari Yazıları,* edited by İsmail Dervişoğlu. Ankara: Türk Tarih Kurumu Basımevi, 2011: 110-113.

Redford, Scott. "'What Have You Done for Anatolia Today?': Islamic Archaeology in the Early Years of the Turkish Republic," edited by Sibel Bozdoğan and Gülru Necipoğlu. *Muqarnas* 24 (2007): 243-252.

Ridgway, Sam. "The Representation of Construction." *Architectural Theory Review* 14, no. 3 (2009): 267-83.

Riegl, Alois. "The Modern Cult of Monuments: Its Essence and its Development." In *Historical and Philosophical Issues in the Conservation of Cultural Heritage,* edited by Nicholas Stanley Price., M. Kirby Talley Jr., and Vaccaro, Alessandra Melucco Vaccaro, 69-83. Los Angeles: The Getty Conservation Institute, 1996.

Services, Technical Preservation. *The Secretary of the Interior's Standards for the Treatment of Historic Properties, with Guidelines for Preserving, Rehabilitating, Restoring & Reconstructing Historic Buildings,* edited by National Park Service, revised by Anne E. Grimmer. Washington D.C., U.S., 2017.

Shaw, Wendy M. K. "Islamic Arts in the Ottoman Imperial Museum, 1889-1923." *Ars Orientalis* 30 (2000): 55-68.

Shaw, Wendy M. K. "Museums and Narratives of Display from the Late Ottoman Empire to the Turkish Republic." *Muqarnas* 24, (2007): 253-279.

Striker, Cecil L. *The Myrelaion (Bodrum Camii) in Istanbul.* Princeton NJ: Princeton University Press, 1981.

Stubbs, John H. *Time Honored: A Global View of Architectural Conservation, Parameters, Theory, & Evolution of an Ethos.* Hoboken, N.J.: John Wiley & Sons, 2009.

Sümertaş, Firuzan Melike. "Bizans Uzmanı Doktor Paspatis'ten İstanbul'un öteki yüzü." *Atlas Tarih,* (Aralık 2016-Ocak 2017): 46-53.

Sümertaş, Firuzan Melike. "Dr. Aleksandros G. Paspatis'ten Dersaadet Rum Cemiyet-i Edebiyesi'ne İstanbul'un Kara Surları üzerine bir Çalışma." *Toplumsal Tarih* 272, (Ağustos 2016): 42-49.

Syngramma Periodikon. "Land Walls of Istanbul." Supplement vol. 14. İstanbul: Bizantidos Publishers, 1884). [in Greek]

Şenyurt, Oya. *Osmanlı Mimarisinin Temel İlkeleri.* İstanbul: Doğu Kitabevi, 2015.

Texier, Charles. *Asie Mineure: Description Géographique, Historique et Archéologique des Provinces et des Villes de la Chersonnèse d'Asie.* 1842.

Texier, Charles. *Asia Minor, Geographical, Historical and Archaeological Descriptions of its Provinces and Cities.* 1862.

Thys-Şenocak, Lucienne. *Divided Spaces, Contested Pasts: The Heritage of the Gallipoli Peninsula.* London: Routledge, 2019.

Uluengin, M. Bülent. *Rölöve.* İstanbul: YEM Yayın, 2016.

Ülgen, Ali Saim. *Anıtların Korunması ve Onarılması-I.* Ankara: Maarif Matbaası: 1943.

Ülgen, Ali Saim. *Ankara'da Cenabî Ahmed Paşa Camii ve Türbesi* (Ankara: Vakıflar Umum Müdürlüğü Neşriyatı, 1942.

Ülgen, Ali Saim. "Divriği Ulu Camii ve Darüşşifası." *Vakıflar Dergisi* V, 1962: 93-97.

Ülgen, Ali Saim. "*İznik'te Türk Eserleri.*" *Vakıflar Dergisi* 1. Ankara, 1938: 53-69.

Ülgen, Ali Saim. "Mimar Sinan." *Yeni Adam,* 13 April, 1939.

Ülgen, Ali Saim. "Türk Mimarisi." *Gençlik* 2 no.38, May 19, 1938.

Ülgen, Ali Saim. *Yenicami.* Ankara: Vakıflar Umum Müdürlüğü Neşriyatı, 1942.

Ülgen, Ali Saim, Filiz Yenişehirlioğlu, and Emre Madran. *The Buildings of Mimar Sinan (Mimar Sinan Yapıları.* Ankara: Türk Tarih Kurumu, 1989.

Ülgen, H. Bedir. "İstanbul'da Tarihi Eserler: Bu Ne Tezat?" *Kurun,* May 13, 1936.

Ünsal, Behçet Sabri. *Turkish Islamic Architecture in Seljuk and Ottoman Times, 1071-1923.* London: Alec Tiranti, 1970.

Viollet-le-Duc, Eugène-Emmanuel. "Restoration." *The Foundations of Architecture: Selections from the Dictionnaire Raisonne,* trans. Kenneth D. Whitehead. New York: George Braziller, Inc: 1990. Reprinted in idem, in *Historical and Philosophical Issues in the Conservation of Cultural Heritage,* edited by Nicholas Stanley Price, M. Kirby Talley Jr., and Alessandra Melucco Vaccaro, 314-318. Los Angeles: The Getty Conservation Institute, 1996.

Yavuz, Yıldırım. "The Restoration Project of the Masjid Al-Aqsa by Mimar Kemalettin (1922-26)." *Muqarnas* 13 (1996): 149-164.

Yenal, Engin and Süha Özkan. *Sedad Eldem ile Söyleşiler.* İstanbul: Literatür Yayınları, 2014.

Yerasimos, Stefanos. "Tanzimattan Günümüze Türkiye'de Kültürel Mirası Koruma Söylemi." *İstanbul* 54 (2005).

Yetkin, Suut Kemal. "The Evolution of Architectural Form in Turkish Mosques (1300-1700)." *Studia Islamica* 11 (1959): 73-91.

Yetkin, Suut Kemal. *Türk Mimarisi.* Ankara: Bilgi Basımevi, 1970.

Zelef, Haluk. "A Research on the Representation of Turkish National Identity: Buildings Abroad." PhD diss., Middle East Technical University, 2003.

Index

A

Academy of Fine Arts, 34, 39, 41, 42, 47, 53, 71, 73, 102, 108, 109, 131, 151, 160, 170, 174
Afet İnan, 92, 93
Ağalar Camii. See Mosque of the Aghas
Albert Louis Gabriel, 48, 50, 67, 95, 145, 162, 177, 178
Alexander Paspates, 24
Ali Saim Ülgen, 39, 52, 59, 62, 63, 65, 73, 77, 91, 96, 100, 101, 102, 103, 119, 124, 126, 128, 129, 131, 137, 141, 143, 149, 150, 153, 157, 159, 160, 162, 174, 178, 180, 181, 196, 198, 200, 202, 208
Alois Riegl, 78
Anıtlar Şubesi. See Office of Monuments
Anıtları Koruma Kurulu. See Conservation Council of Monuments
Architect Kemalettin Bey, 31, 37, 39, 82, 83, 85, 86, 87, 89, 112, 113, 114, 194
Architect Reşid Bey, 116
Architect Sinan, 5, 19, 27, 43, 46, 56, 75, 80, 85, 95, 100, 102, 138, 139, 141, 178, 180, 181, 189
Arif Hikmet Holtay, 152
Arif Hikmet Koyunoğlu, 32, 35, 194
Asar-i Atika Encümeni. See Commission for the Preservation of Monuments
Asar-i Atika Encümen-i Daimisi, 86
Asar-i Atika Nizamnamesi, 81
Athens Charter, 157, 158
Azapkapı Saliha Sultan Fountain, 30, 40
Aziz Ogan, 131

B

Battle of *Malazgirt,* 5, *See* Battle of Manzikert
Battle of Manzikert, 120, 133, 199
Behçet Sabri Ünsal, 58, 59, 66, 134, 136
Beylik of *Karamanoğulları,* 135
Beylik of *Mengüçlü,* 136
Beylik of *Osmanoğulları,* 134, 138
Beyliks, 3, 56, 68, 94, 120, 133, 134, 136, 137, 138, 145, 196, 199
Birinci Ulusal Mimarlık Akımı. See First National Style
Blueists, 109, 110, 111
Bodrum Mosque, 128, 130, 131, 132, 133
Bursa, 27, 30, 46, 48, 55, 63, 70, 73, 75, 80, 82, 138, 149, 156, 158
Byzantines, 5, 24, 31, 42, 70, 74, 75, 85, 97, 100, 102, 104, 108, 110, 112, 114, 117, 118, 120, 122, 124, 125, 127, 128, 129, 130, 131, 132, 133, 156, 194, 196, 197, 199

C

Cahide Aksel Tamer, 64, 127, 132, 147, 158
Carta del Restauro, 154, 157
Celâl Esad Arseven, 40, 66, 85, 86, 89, 137, 153, 157, 161
Cemil Topuzlu, 87
Cenabî Ahmed Pasha Mosque Complex, 180, 181
Charles Texier, 74
Church of the Holy Apostles, 124
Church of the Monastery of Myrelaion. *See* Bodrum Mosque, *See* Bodrum Mosque
Çinili Köşk. *See* Tiled Kiosk
Commission for the Preservation of Monuments, 86, 89, 111, 117, 130, 131, 195
Conservation Council of Monuments, 46, 91, 147, 149, 183
Cornelius Gurlitt, 31, 41, 156

D

Divriği Great Mosque and Hospital, 63, 136

E

Ebu'l Fazl Mahmud Efendi Madrasa, 87
École des Beaux Arts, 31, 35, 149, 168, 169, 170, 174, 177, 203
Edirne, 46, 56, 59, 107, 149, 156, 184
Ekrem Hakkı Ayverdi, 39, 52, 53, 59, 69, 70, 75, 103, 104, 114, 116, 170, 175, 184, 185, 196, 198, 201, 202
Ernst A. Egli, 152, 174
Eugène Emmanuel Viollet-le-Duc, 159, 160, 161, 162

F

Feridun Dirimtekin, 124
Fethiye Mosque, 89, 123
First National Style, 31, 34, 39, 83, 194
formalist art theory, 67
Fossati brothers, 156

G

Gayrimenkul Eski Eserler ve Anıtlar Yüksek Kurulu. *See* Supreme Council of Immovable Antiquities and Monuments

H

Hagia Sophia, 78, 117, 119, 122, 124, 127, 128, 129, 156
Halil Edhem Eldem, 86, 89, 94, 129
Halim Baki Kunter, 74, 124
Hamit Kemali Söylemezoğlu, 63, 66
Hasan Âli Yücel, 48, 109
Hikmet Turhan Dağlıoğlu, 180

I

International Congress of Byzantine Studies, 127, 132
İsmail Hakkı Uzunçarşılı, 188
İsmet İnönü, 45, 111
Istanbul Archaeological Museums, 86, 101, 112, 114, 116, 131
İstanbul Fetih Cemiyeti, 114
İznik, 95, 96, 100, 129

J

Jean Nicolas Louis Durand, 163
Joseph de Guignes, 93

K

Kemal Altan, 101, 102, 103, 116, 123, 129, 139, 196, 198, 200, 202
Konya, 42, 44, 51, 82, 137

L

Late Ottoman Empire, 17, 22, 30, 35, 43, 79, 165, 185, 193, 200
Léon Parvillée, 30, 156

M

M. Oluş Arık, 134
Macit Rüştü Kural, 32, 147
Mehmet Nihat Nigizberk, 37
Mesih Pasha Mosque. *See* Bodrum Mosque
Millî Mimari Semineri. See National Architecture Seminar
Modern Movement, 73, 167, 174, 203
Mosque of the Aghas, 184, 185
Muhafaza-i Asar-i Atika Encümeni, 89
Museum of Mehmed II, 116
Mustafa Kemal Atatürk, 1, 2, 5, 17, 20, 21, 44, 46, 47, 61, 79, 92, 93, 94, 106, 109, 111, 147, 180, 196, 198, 199, 204

N

National Architecture Seminar, 55, 71, 73, 102, 109, 152
Nicaea. *See* İznik

O

Office of Monuments, 48, 62, 149, 150
Oktay Aslanapa, 58
Osmanlı order, 27
Osmanlıcılık, 78
Ottoman conquest of Constantinople, 5, 18, 26, 111, 112, 113, 114, 118, 120, 122, 124, 127, 129, 138, 184, 199, 200

P

Pammakaristos Church. *See* Fethiye Mosque
Patriarch Konstatinias, 24, 194
Pietro Montani, 26, 30, 156

R

restitution, 133, 147, 177, 179, 184, 185
restoration, 10, 13, 22, 37, 40, 49, 61, 63, 64, 66, 86, 90, 94, 96, 101, 103, 112, 116, 123, 127, 129, 132, 137, 143, 145, 147, 150, 152, 154, 155, 156, 157, 158, 159, 160, 161, 162, 175, 176, 177, 180, 181, 184, 185, 188
Rölöve Bürosu. See Surveying Bureau
Royal Institute of British Architects, 38

S

Sedad Hakkı Eldem, 60, 61, 70, 71, 72, 73, 107, 108, 109, 151, 152, 158, 170, 174, 196, 197, 201, 202
Sedat Çetintaş, 21, 39, 41, 42, 46, 61, 75, 95, 103, 105, 106, 107, 112, 113, 114, 118, 122, 147, 149, 150, 170, 183, 184, 187, 196, 198, 202
Şehzade Mosque, 61, 139
Seljuks, 3, 5, 46, 56, 68, 75, 82, 83, 85, 91, 93, 94, 107, 108, 110, 114, 120, 121, 125, 133, 134, 137, 145, 161, 183, 193, 194, 196, 197, 198, 199
Şemseddin Günaltay, 93
Sivas Şifaiye Hospital, 183, 187
Siyavuş Pasha Pavilion, 73, 102
Skarlatos Byzantios, 24, 194
Sokollu Mehmet Pasha Mosque, 41, 61, 147, 149
Sultan Abdülaziz, 26, 30, 81, 156, 192
Sultan Abdülhamid I, 89
Sultan Abdülhamid II, 22, 31, 81, 82, 156
Sultan Abdülmecid, 156
Sultan Han, 143
Sultan I. İzzeddin Keykâvus, 184
Supreme Council of Immovable Antiquities and Monuments, 66, 132, 153, 157, 202
Surveying Bureau, 46, 64, 105, 107, 147, 149, 150, 158, 170, 183, 202
surveying offices, 64, 150
Suut Kemal Yetkin, 55, 56, 67, 68, 137

T

Tahsin Öz, 42, 66, 113, 114, 122, 159
Tanzimat period, 22, 26, 78, 79, 81, 82
Tiled Kiosk, 112, 113, 115, 116, 118
Topkapı Palace Museum, 42, 78, 112, 113, 118, 127, 158, 184, 186
Tulumcu Hüsam Mosque, 103
Türk Dil Kurumu. See Turkish Language Society
Türk Dili Tetkik Cemiyeti, 47, *See* Society for Turkish Language Research
Türk Islam Sentezi. See Turkish Islamic Synthesis
Türk Tarih Kurumu. See Turkish Historical Society
Türk Tarih Tezi. See Turkish History Thesis
Türk Tarihi Tetkik Cemiyeti, 47, *See* Society for Turkish History Research
Turkish Historical Society, 47, 93, 95, 109, 183, 187
Turkish History Congress, 2, 47, 93
Turkish History Research, 47
Turkish History Thesis, 2, 4, 5, 16, 47, 91, 92, 96, 102, 109, 112, 114, 195, 198, 199
Turkish Language Society, 47, 109
Turkish War of Independence, 16, 37, 44

U

Usūl-i Mi'mārī-i Osmānī, 26, 27, 30, 31, 39, 83, 156, 165, 192, 193

V

Vakıf Han
First Vakıf Han, 89, 113
Fourth Vakıf Han, 89, 113
Third Vakıf Han, 83
Venice Charter, 157

Y

Yahya Kemal Beyatlı, 112
Yayla Kambur Mustafa Pasha Mosque, 126
Yeni Mosque, 30, 139, 141, 200
Young Turk Revolution, 22, 31, 82, 85
Young Turks, 22, 79, 82, 85, 193, 195
Yunus Nadi Abalıoğlu, 61
Yusuf Akyurt, 51

Z

Zeynep Sultan Mosque, 139
Ziya Gökalp, 91

www.ingramcontent.com/pod-product-compliance
Lightning Source LLC
Chambersburg PA
CBHW072101020426
42334CB00017B/1588
9781648895654